First published 2019

Published by Capital Transport Publishing Ltd
www.capitaltransport.com

Printed in the EU

Title page Guy Motors used this very attractive casting on their commercial vehicles. London Transport used it to great effect on the bonnet of the GSs, combining it with their own enamelled plate containing the fleetname with roundel and green background. The motif around the Indian's Head contained the wording "FEATHERS IN OUR CAP" which was Guy's own motto. In a few cases, and in the days when garage staff took pride in their fleet, they took the trouble to pick out the letters in red. The flap of which the casting was part lifted up to give access to the radiator cap for topping up the water. This picture is of GS 62 owned by Alan Charman. *Alan Charman*

Opposite GS 33 was transferred from Amersham to Tring on 1st February 1958, remaining there until called in for its second overhaul on 12th October 1961. It returned for a brief period at Amersham before going to Tring once more on 12th January 1962 where it became Tring's last operational GS. It has yet to be fitted with indicators so this picture predates the second overhaul as it waits at Beaconsfield Road in Tring for a journey through the town to the station. It had the distinction of running on the 336A on the very last day of GS operation, and was then sold for preservation. It was purchased by the London Bus Preservation Group in 1985 and later broken up for spares for GS 34. *A D Packer*

The jacket photo of GS 42 near Datchet in 1966 is by Capital Transport

Operation of the 336A route is described in Chapter 4. GS 42 is in Loudwater Village between journeys to Rickmansworth, and the driver has wisely parked the bus on the opposite side of the road to avoid the repairs on the house. This picture was taken during the final London Country period of operation, and GS 33 and 42 would run together on the very last day of Country area GS operation. *Fred Ivey*

Given the enduring popularity of London Transport's fleet of GSs, it is perhaps surprising that a book which looks at their development and operation has not been published before. We are grateful to Jim Whiting at Capital Transport for his support when we suggested the book to him two years ago.

We decided that the book should concentrate mostly on the daily operations of the GSs, and try to cover as much detail as possible about their allocation to the routes on which they worked. We have been very fortunate in having access to the archives and collections of a number of people who have willingly assisted our research and provided a great deal of information which we didn't have in our own archives or recollections. We were both fortunate to have travelled on many GSs from the early 1960s while there were still large numbers in service. Alan Charman has many personal memories of the GSs at Dunton Green where his father drove them for many years, and was at the garage on the last evening of operation when GS 62 – which he would later come to own – was the last bus in on 30th December 1966. His extensive collection of panel timetables from the 1950s have provided much interest.

One of the most valuable archives to which we had access was London Transport's fleet records which recorded the movement of every bus around the fleet on a daily basis. Maurice Doggett kindly supplied a copy of Eastern Coachworks official schedule listing the delivery dates of chassis from Guy Motors and of the completed buses to London Transport. We were able to match this with the daily records which recorded the delivery of new buses to Aldenham Works and their initial allocation. We wanted to include as many running number schedules and driver rosters as we could. As far as we are aware, these had never been published, but they provide an insight into the often complex interworking of buses and drivers between routes which was always a factor in the Country Bus area. Whilst we had some of these ourselves, others came from Laurie Akehurst and Paul Brophy.

We wanted to include as many pictures as possible which had not been seen before. Given the popularity of the GS and the enormous volume of photographs in circulation this was not easy. Hugh Taylor very kindly gave access to Peter Mitchell's collection and was able to provide dates and confirm locations for each picture. Thanks also to Simon Butler who searched through the Peter Mitchell archive in an effort to satisfy our "wish list" and who arranged for the original negatives to be scanned. Laurie Akehurst, and Colin Rivers provided some more. A small number of our own original photographs have also been used.

Geoff Heels kindly loaned his archive for GS 42 which contains a number of LT documents, and Tony Beard provided records of LT Board meetings where alterations to the GSs were discussed. Ken Blacker made available copies of correspondence on the sale of the Cubs and purchase of GSs, together with the LT internal report of the GS's performance in service in 1954. Richard Moseling, a regular visitor to our running days, used his access to the Acton archives to locate a number of traffic circulars and other papers, and in particular found a copy of the timetable for the 400 and 413B which we could not otherwise have unearthed. Bob Williamson kindly provided all of the destination blind records reproduced in the book and answered questions about others. The late Colin Curtis spent many hours giving us his views about the GS and an insight into their early operation, the notes of which were carefully retained. Laurie Akehurst and Mike Lloyd looked through the proofs and supplied very useful comments and corrections.

Finally a thank you to our wives who have lived with our hobby since we first met. Alan's wife, a resident of Pratts Bottom and a regular traveller on the 471 during the 1960s, was not surprised when GS 62 joined the family in 1994.

August 2019   Peter Aves and Alan Charman

GS 66 is turning right at Westwood cross roads on a 489A from Meopham back to Gravesend. It carries running number NF11 so is covering an RF duty which became a common occurrence in the last period of GS operation at Northfleet. Transferred there after its second overhaul in September 1962, it spent the next five years there before being downgraded as a staff bus at Plumstead, and then to Garston in 1969 as a trainer. One of the GSs transferred to London Country, but in withdrawn condition, it was sold in 1971.
David Christie

1   A Replacement for the Cubs

London Transport acquired some 70 operators and their routes in the years leading up to the Second World War. Many decided to sell their business, while others were purchased under the compulsory powers granted in the 1933 Transport Act. From all these acquisitions came several bus routes and a large number of second hand buses, the majority of which were single deckers from a myriad of different chassis and body manufacturers. Some were relatively new, while many others were approaching the end of their useful life and, coupled with the great variety of chassis and bodies, this led to difficulties with general maintenance from the complete lack of standardisation. To resolve these issues, London Transport made the decision to purchase a fleet of new small single deckers which could become the standard bus to operate the less frequent rural routes. Among the acquired buses was a Leyland Cub which sufficiently impressed London Transport to the extent it was decided that it would be the model on which to standardise the small bus fleet.

In 1935 therefore, London Transport ordered 74 Leyland Cubs to operate many of the minor rural bus routes in their Country bus area. They began to arrive in April 1935 and were all in service by September that year. Chiswick works was fully occupied in building bodies for other parts of the fleet, so that London Transport turned to Short Brothers at Rochester and Weymann to build the bodies. Although Short built a number of bus bodies in the 1930s, they were better known for building airframes and bodies for flying boats which could be launched direct from their own yard on the edge of the river Medway at Rochester. Even by the standards of the time, the new Cubs looked antiquated with their long bonnets, large mudguards and heavy front bumper. It is recorded that the original cost of each completed bus was £1064 (approximately £70,000 at today's prices), and that their intended service life at the time was six years. They were perhaps expensive given their relatively short anticipated life, but the War prevented any replacement. In the event they were to prove robust reliable buses, and many would give 18 years' service.

The generally poor condition of the fleet in the immediate post-war years required urgent replacement of large numbers of buses, a situation made worse by the increase in passenger numbers as life returned to normal and people used bus services for leisure, commuting and shopping. The Central area fleet was the immediate priority, and it was 1948 before the Country area received its first new RTs along with the batch of thirty 15T13s. The rest of the single deck fleet had to wait until 1951 before the RFs began to arrive, but there was no early plan to replace the Cubs. Some 30 of them were delicensed by 1945 and it was decided to offer these for sale. In August 1945, a representative of the Dutch government inspected them, but LT's requested price of £800 per bus was not acceptable. On 10th October, the Belgian Economic Commission inspected the Cubs, following which, negotiations led to an agreed price of £650 per bus. Of the buses for sale, nine were from a second batch delivered in 1936 which had been bodied by Weymann rather than Short, further buses from this second batch also having been repainted green and transferred to the Country area.

In 1949 a proposal was put forward to sell a further 37 Cubs, and a letter was written to the British Transport Commission (BTC) on 16th June confirming that London Transport were inviting tenders for their disposal. Such was London Transport's strict protection of their area that purchasers would be required to provide an indemnity that the Cubs could not be used for carrying passengers anywhere within the 1933 boundary. The letter also refers to a BTC policy at the time whereby *'second hand vehicles surplus to requirements should be either broken up for spares or sold as scrap without licence books – thus ensuring that the vehicles were not used against us by some competitor'*. The letter went on to state *'it seems a little anomalous that London Transport should be offering vehicles for sale which could be used anywhere outside the London area in competition with the Commission'*. This all seemed short-sighted. Nothing came of it, and the Cubs remained in service.

The enormous increase in demand at the end of the 1940s led to the introduction of new routes, many of which provided some villages with a bus service for the first time, and whilst not all of these were operated by the Cubs, these additional routes put pressure on their numbers. One man operation was then limited to buses with a maximum capacity of 20 and increasing passengers meant that the Cub's limited seating capacity was becoming inadequate on some journeys.

Dorking's small fleet of Leyland Cubs were replaced on the 433 and 449 on 1st December 1953. C 8 waits at the stop in South Street, Dorking on a journey from Chart Downs. The driver is probably waiting for time so as not to arrive early at the Bus Station, which was the next stop. *Norman Rayfield*

This drawing was produced as part of the proposal to re-body the Cubs. It is recorded as drawing number 2548 and dated 23rd September 1949. The drawing is virtually identical to the original Weymann drawings and that company would almost certainly have built any new bodies. Although the Cub chassis did not lend itself to any great variation in body layout it seems doubtful that any new bodies would have been so close in design to the originals, so perhaps some wholesale renovation of the existing bodies was intended. It all came to nothing when Leyland announced they would no longer supply spares for the Cubs.

London Transport therefore gave thought to how the Cubs might be replaced. They were mechanically reliable and economic in service, and in 1949 there was a tentative plan to re-body them as a short term solution while long term replacements could be considered.

The layout and appearance of the proposed bodies was remarkably similar to the original design, but the Cub chassis gave little opportunity for fundamental change, and seating capacity remained limited to 20. In 1950 however, Leyland announced that from 31st December 1951 they would no longer manufacture or supply spares for the Cubs so that this plan came to nothing. Given that by then they were 15 years old, and spares would begin to run out, it became necessary to find a suitable replacement, and at this point it is worth considering what was available at the time.

The Bedford OB had become well established in the early post war years. Production had begun in 1939 when the O type lorry was introduced in August that year, but only 73 were built before production ceased on the outbreak of War. The post-war version of the OB began in October 1945, Bedford building chassis at their factory in Dunstable, while Duple modified their small coach body to fit the OB chassis at Hendon. Whilst the majority of OBs had the famous Duple Vista body – purchased in large numbers by small operators all over the country – Beadle produced a very attractive 30 seat bus body, several being purchased by a number of the nationalised Tilling Group companies between 1947 and 1950. Their 30 seat capacity however precluded them from being one man operated and Bedford replaced the OB in 1950 with the larger SB model which was of no interest to London Transport.

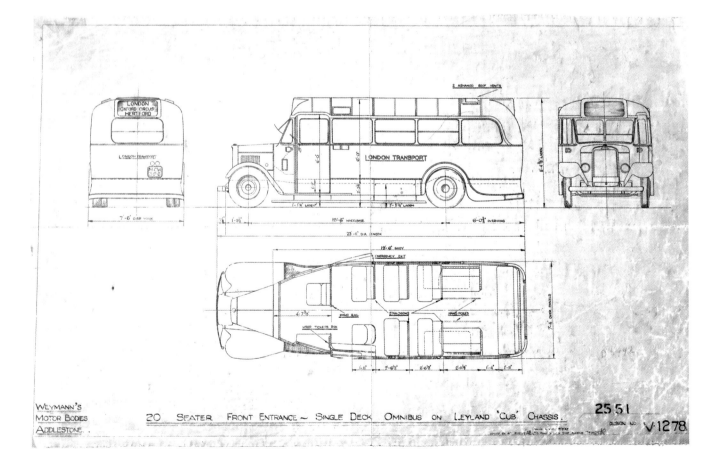

WEYMANN'S MOTOR BODIES ADDLESTONE.   20 SEATER FRONT ENTRANCE ~ SINGLE DECK OMNIBUS ON LEYLAND 'CUB' CHASSIS.   25·5·51   DESIGN NO. V·1278

One likely alternative might have been the small Dennis Falcon built in Guildford. They were produced in reasonable numbers and were fitted with Dennis built 20-seat bodies suitable for one man operation. Aldershot & District whose area bounded London Transport along its south west boundary were an ardent supporter of Dennis and purchased 15 of them in 1949/50 followed by 23 more in 1954/56 with 30 seat bodies, after legislation had changed to permit a higher seating capacity. At the time, the Falcon would therefore have been a perfectly practical choice to replace the Cubs, but there is no record of any interest by London Transport.

Other choices were quite limited. The Commer Commando, Leyland Comet and Albion Victor were all small chassis but were either not available with bus bodies at all, or only with seating for 30 or more. The 20-seat limit for omo buses was however becoming impractical for many operators, and there was pressure for the regulations to be relaxed to permit an increase to 30 or more. By 1950 it was anticipated that the limit would be increased, and London Transport obtained a relaxation from the BTC to increase the capacity of the buses which would replace the Cubs.

Guy Motors produced three potential models. The Wolf – originally produced in 1930 – ceased during the War, but from 1952 became available again with either a Perkins P4 diesel or Guy petrol engine. The Otter was introduced in 1950 as a forward control bus or truck chassis, the bus version being available with a 26-seat body. Finally, the Vixen had been introduced after the War, and was intended mainly as a truck chassis.

In August 1950, London Transport officially informed the BTC of the need to replace the Cubs since – following Leyland's announcement of the cessation of spares – the re-bodying plan and future 'special overhauls' were no longer feasible. London Transport therefore began discussions and negotiations with Guy and Ford which continued throughout 1951.

The choice of body builder however was somewhat forced upon London Transport. The 1947 Transport Act nationalised road and rail transport, and set up the British Transport Commission to exercise overall control. It formed a number of Transport Executives of which London Transport was one. Whilst the shareholdings in bus companies formerly owned by the railway groups were acquired, they did not form the majority holdings, and the two major bus operating groups – British Electric Traction (BET) and Tilling therefore remained outside State ownership. In 1948 however, Tilling Group – to the dismay of BET at the time – reached agreement for the sale of remaining shares to the BTC and thus became State owned. Tilling had intended to retain Bristol Motors and Eastern Coach Works (ECW) but it proved too complicated to separate them from the sale. The legislation provided that the State owned companies could purchase chassis and bodies only from Bristol and ECW, and that these two companies, apart from minor exceptions or to complete outstanding orders, could not sell their products outside this group.

The production at ECW had – like all other body builders – expanded rapidly in the immediate post war years. In four years from 1946 to 1949, they built just under 3300 bodies, a peak output of 1062 being reached in 1948. Whilst some of these numbers were as a result of the wartime backlog, there had been substantial orders from companies outside the Tilling Group. Such orders of course reduced rapidly after 1948, and production in 1950 was significantly below the previous year. Despite the strict limitations on supply within the BTC, London

Transport still had some way to go to complete their fleet replacement, significant long term commitments having been made to Park Royal, Weymann and Metro Cammell. Although the ECW order book remained buoyant, the peak of production had passed, and discussions therefore took place between the BTC and London Transport as to any orders it might place with ECW since, in a strict interpretation of the Transport Act, London Transport were limited to ordering from ECW.

The need to replace the small fleet of lowbridge buses could have been met by the ECW bodied Bristol LD Lodekka, but they were built to the newly approved width of eight feet and more importantly were only available with manual transmission, London Transport having long since settled on preselective transmission as standard. In a conversation the authors had some years ago with the late Colin Curtis he clearly recalled a meeting at which BTC proposed that London Transport would place an order with ECW. The agreement that came from these discussions was a commitment for 100 bodies, though it is not known how this round figure was arrived at. London Transport wished to renew its private hire fleet in time for the 1951 Festival of Britain in London, and so 15 of this total were ordered as coach bodies for the RFWs. The Routemaster was then only in the very early stages of development, but London Transport also made a commitment for a single body for one of the prototypes, thus leaving a further 84 bodies to fulfil the total of 100. Given the number of Cubs scheduled in 1950, and the intention to convert a small number of crew operated minor routes to omo, then, including engineering spares, a total of around 70-75 new buses would have been sufficient replacement, but it was the commitment to ECW of 100 bodies that resulted in the final total of 84 GSs, a number which has always been rightly regarded as too high.

Discussions with Ford led to the adoption of a complete prefabricated front end which was being supplied by Briggs Motor Pressings to Ford for its small 'Thames' truck chassis, and London Transport used this to build a complete mock-up of the front end of the new bus at Chiswick works. Having settled on a modified version of the Guy 'Vixen' chassis, detailed design work began on the bodies. Although ECW employed their standard construction methods, they had not built a small bonneted bus since the 1930s. They also had to design the body so that the Briggs front end assembly could be attached. London Transport's design input was immediately apparent in the completed bus, especially the rear end which was a smaller version of the RF. Internally, the finish was very much to London Transport's design, although ECW's standard sliding vent windows were a departure from the standard winding type.

Minute 1621 of London Transport's Executive Board meeting on 17th January 1952 record the approval of two Special Expenditure Requisitions, both dated 14th January 1952, authorising the purchase of 84 new GSs. Requisition 15/2374 totalled £116,130 for 84 bodies from ECW and Requisition 15/2375 totalled £83,975 for 84 chassis from Guy Motors. The cost of each completed bus was therefore £2,382, which at today's prices amounts to just under £70,000 each. This bears interesting comparison to the Leyland Cubs whose original cost in 1935 was almost the same as a new GS some 17 years later. The GS was larger and heavier than the Cub, but post war mass production had reduced manufacturing costs through higher volumes of output and greater efficiency. The orders to Guy Motors included the gearboxes and Perkins P6 engines, while that to ECW included the Briggs Motors front ends.

Prior to production by Eastern Coach Works, a mock-up of the complete front end was built in the Experimental Workshop at Chiswick under the direction of Colin Curtis. The Briggs moulding for the front wings and bonnet which they manufactured for Ford produced the distinctive and very attractive appearance, perhaps one of the GS's most endearing features. The distinctive Guy 'Indian's Head' casting sits on top of the bonnet with the 'London Transport' plate at the top of the grille. The ventilation grilles in the side panels are notable and were replaced on the production bodies by flutes. The ribbed plates on top of the wings are also missing and were added later. The kerb guide with the small red ball mounted on top of the stem is in place, but in practice was of little use in judging the nearside of the bus in a narrow lane. Eastern Coachworks staff visited Chiswick to inspect this, following which it was transported to their works at Lowestoft before bodywork production began. *London Transport Museum CME (Road Services)*

This official Eastern Coachworks picture of GS 1 is dated 6th October 1953 and shows off the appearance of the completed bus. It was perhaps the most attractive small bus of the period. Given London Transport's adherence to rigid policies it was rather surprising that it was fitted with 424 blinds for the photograph rather than one of the routes for which it was intended. *ECW Archive / Maurice Doggett collection*

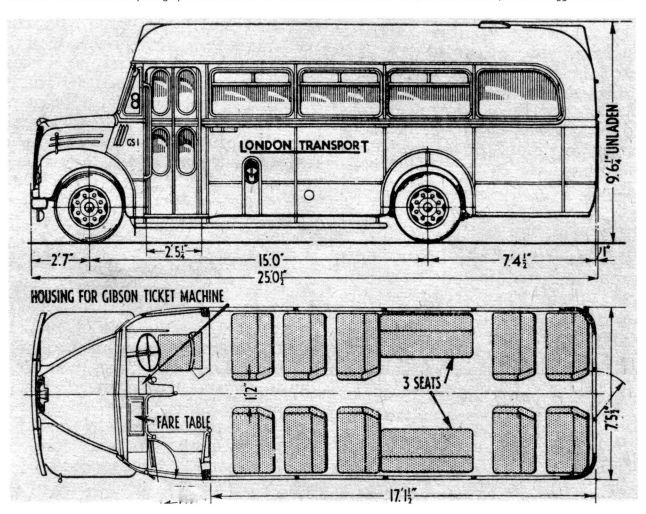

Chassis manufacture at Guy Motors' works in Wolverhampton commenced towards the end of that year. On 12th June 1953, Mr T.T. Shephard of the Chief Mechanical Engineer's (Road Services) office sent a memo to the Executive Board seeking authority to withdraw 64 Cubs due for replacement by the GSs. The memo stated *"the vehicles to be replaced have an expired life of 17-18 years against an assumed life of six years. The total book value is £142,682"*. The memo concluded by emphasising the diminishing lack of spare parts, stating that *"authority has been given for the breaking down of two Cub buses from which spares will be salvaged, and it may be necessary to break down further vehicles of this type before the new Guy buses are delivered"*. Although the condition of individual Cubs is not recorded, it was clear that although the GSs were in production and were all expected to be in stock before the year end, the problems associated with a lack of spares, exacerbated by the delay in delivery of the GSs that we will come to, was of some concern in efforts to keep sufficient buses on the road. Indeed, crew operated CRs were temporarily employed in some cases where Cubs were not fit for service.

London Transport's strict design criteria, in particular the requirement for access panels for maintenance, caused Guy Motors some difficulty given their unfamiliarity with these and the adaptations to the "standard" Vixen chassis. Originally, it had been anticipated that the first chassis would be available in August 1952, but it was January 1953 before Guy completed chassis numbers NVLLP 44208 / 44209 for GS 1 and 2. The chassis for GS 1 was delivered to ECW on 28th January 1953, whilst that for GS 2 was held at the Wolverhampton factory. In February, ECW visited the experimental workshop at Chiswick where London Transport had built the front end mock-up in order to agree final design details before they began work on building the first production body at Lowestoft. London Transport engineers also visited Guy's factory to inspect the chassis for GS 2. Having satisfied themselves with this chassis, it was sent to Lowestoft on 2nd April 1953 some nine weeks after that for GS 1. Guy then began the full production run for the remaining 82 chassis, those for GS 3, 4, 5 and 6 being delivered to Lowestoft on 29th and 30th April 1953. After a further two week gap, the remainder were delivered regularly until 6th November when chassis NVLLP 45066 for GS 84 went to Lowestoft.

Although 84 GSs were built, the gap between the Guy chassis serial numbers for GS 1 and 84 represents a total production of 858 chassis during the period between January and November 1953. This illustrates how busy Guy Motors were during that period and certainly must have been a factor in the completion of the first GS being some five months later than originally planned. This delay caused ECW some problems in re-programming their bodywork programme. The first complete bus – GS 2 – was eventually delivered to London Transport on 2nd October 1953, followed by GS 1 and 3 a week later. Deliveries then followed quickly, 74 buses being delivered before Christmas 1953, with the remaining ten completed when GS 84 was sent on 21st January 1954. In London Transport's 112 page maintenance book dated 27th October 1953, the new bus was referred to as "Guy Single Deck". The drawing dated November 1953 for the paint specification however referred to the bus as "Guy Special" and this is the first official reference we have found in print to the GS class code.

The table overleaf sets out the schedule of delivery dates for each bus together with its initial allocation.

DELIVERY SCHEDULE AND FIRST ALLOCATIONS

	REG NUMBER	ECW/LT BODY NUMBER		DATE CHASSIS TO ECW	DELIVERY DATE TO L.T.	DATE LICENSED FOR SERVICE	FIRST GARAGE	DATE ENTERED SERVICE	GARAGE	NOTES
1	MXX 301	6347	8166	28.1.53	8.10.53	14.10.53	CM	25.10.53	CM	
2	MXX 302	6348	8167	2.4.53	2.10.53	12.10.53	HN	1.11.53	HN	C13 withdrawn @ HN; C16 HN to TG -1.11.53
3	MXX 303	6349	8168	29.4.53	8.10.53	14.10.53	CM	25.10.53	CM	CM to HN 5.1.54, back to CM possibly 10.1.54
4	MXX 304	6352	8169	30.4.53	12.10.53	13.10.53	HG	unknown	CM	To DG 5.11.53; MA 23.11.53; then CM for service
5	MXX 305	6350	8170	29.4.53	12.10.53	14.10.53	LH	6.11.53	LH	
6	MXX 306	6351	8171	29.4.53	16.10.53	22.10.53	CM	25.10.53	CM	8 Cub withdrawn CM 26.10.53
7	MXX 307	6357	8172	22.5.53	23.10.53	26.10.53	CM	26.10.53	CM	To RG (U) 22.3.54
8	MXX 308	6358	8173	18.5.53	12.10.53	14.10.53	HN	1.11.53	HN	
9	MXX 309	6355	8174	20.5.53	12.10.53	16.10.53	CM	25.10.53	CM	
10	MXX 310	6360	8175	28.5.53	23.10.53	26.10.53	CM	26.10.53	CM	
11	MXX 311	6358	8176	22.5.53	20.11.53	22.10.53	CM	25.10.53	CM	
12	MXX 312	6361	8177	28.5.53	16.10.53	4.11.53	HG	9.11.53	HG	3 Cub withdrawn HG 9.11.53
13	MXX 313	6356	8178	20.5.53	16.10.53	21.10.53	CM	25.10.53	CM	
14	MXX 314	6354	8179	18.5.53	16.10.53	21.10.53	CM	25.10.53	CM	
15	MXX 315	6359	8180	22.5.53	20.11.53	22.11.53(U)	CM	1.2.54	CM	
16	MXX 316	6363	8181	12.6.53	23.10.53	4.11.53	HG	9.11.53	HG	
17	MXX 317	6362	8182	10.6.53	4.11.53	6.11.53	LH	6.11.53	LH	
18	MXX 318	6364	8183	12.6.53	23.10.53	4.11.53	HG	9.11.53	HG	
19	MXX 319	6365	8184	12.6.53	23.10.53	4.11.53	HG	9.11.53	HG	
20	MXX 320	6366	8185	18.6.53	4.11.53	4.11.53	SJ	15.11.53	SJ	
21	MXX 321	6369	8186	7.7.53	4.11.53	6.11.53	HG	9.11.53	HG	
22	MXX 322	6368	8187	20.6.53	30.10.53	4.11.53	HG	9.11.53	HG	
23	MXX 323	6367	8188	19.6.53	30.10.53	5.11.53	HG	9.11.53	HG	
24	MXX 324	6370	8189	7.7.53	11.11.53	16.11.53	DG	16.11.53	DG	
25	MXX 325	6371	8190	7.7.53	11.11.53	16.11.53	DG	16.11.53	DG	
26	MXX 326	6372	8191	14.7.53	6.11.53	11.11.53	SJ	15.11.53	SJ	2 Cub withdrawn SJ 16.11.53
27	MXX 327	6374	8192	15.7.53	11.11.53	16.11.53	DG	16.11.53	DG	3 Cub withdrawn DG 16.11.53
28	MXX 328	6379	8193	27.7.53	12.11.53	16.11.53	DG	16.11.53	DG	4 Cub transferred DG to MA 23.11.53
29	MXX 329	6376	8194	16.7.53	6.11.53	11.11.53	DG	16.11.53	DG	
30	MXX 330	6376	8195	16.7.53	12.11.53	26.11.53 (U)	GF	27.11.53	GF	5 Cub withdrawn GF 27.11.53
31	MXX 331	6380	8196	27.7.53	12.11.53	26.11.53 (U)	GF	27.11.53	GF	
32	MXX 332	6373	8197	14.7.53	6.11.53	12.11.53	DG	unknown	DG	Date in service not recorded – probably 16.11.53
33	MXX 333	6377	8198	27.7.53	13.11.53	26.11.53 (U)	GF	27.11.53	GF	
34	MXX 334	6407	8199	2.10.53	11.12.53	17.12.53	MA	unknown	MA	Date in service not recorded – probably 21.12.53
35	MXX 335	6378	8200	27.7.53	13.11.53	26.11.53 (U)	GF	27.11.53	GF	
36	MXX 336	6385	8201	25.7.53	17.11.53	26.11.53 (U)	DS	1.12.53	DS	4 Cub withdrawn DS 1.12.53
37	MXX 337	6383	8202	24.7.53	17.11.53	26.11.53 (U)	DS	1.12.53	DS	
38	MXX 338	6384	8203	25.7.53	17.11.53	27.11.53	EP	1.12.53	EP	
39	MXX 339	6381	8204	23.7.53	13.11.53	26.11.53 (U)	GF	27.11.53	GF	
40	MXX 340	6386	8205	28.7.53	25.11.53	27.11.53	EP	1.12.53	EP	
41	MXX 341	6389	8206	30.7.53	17.11.53	26.11.53 (U)	DS	1.12.53	DS	
42	MXX 342	6382	8207	24.7.53	13.11.53	27.11.53	DS	1.12.53	DS	
43	MXX 343	6387	8208	29.7.53	25.11.53	27.11.53	EP	1.12.53	EP	
44	MXX 344	6390	8209	30.7.53	25.11.53	27.11.53	EP	1.12.53	EP	4 Cub withdrawn EP 1.12.53 – to store RF
45	MXX 345	6388	8210	29.7.53	25.11.53	2.12.53	NF	9.12.53	NF	
46	MXX 346	6391	8211	8.9.73	25.11.53	2.12.53	NF	9.12.53	NF	
47	MXX 347	6392	8212	17.9.53	27.11.53	2.12.53	NF	9.12.53	NF	
48	MXX 348	6393	8213	18.9.53	25.11.53	2.12.53	NF	9.12.53	NF	
49	MXX 349	6394	8214	19.9.53	27.11.53	3.12.53	NF	9.12.53	NF	
50	MXX 350	6402	8215	25.9.53	9.12.53	17.12.53	MA	unknown	MA	Date in service not recorded – probably 21.12.53
51	MXX 351	6395	8216	21.9.53	27.11.53	3.12.53	NF	9.12.53	NF	
52	MXX 352	6403	8217	26.9.53	11.12.53	18.12.53	MA	21.12.53	MA	10 Cub withdrawn MA 21.12.53

53	MXX	353	6396	8218	22.9.53	27.11.53	3.12.53	NF	9.12.53	NF	
54	MXX	354	6399	8219	24.9.53	2.12.53	7.12.53	NF	9.12.53	NF	
55	MXX	355	6397	8220	23.9.53	9.12.53	16.12.53	MA	21.12.53	MA	
56	MXX	356	6401	8221	25.9.53	11.12.53	18.12.53	MA	21.12.53	MA	
57	MXX	357	6398	8222	23.9.53	2.12.53	7.12.53	NF	9.12.53	NF	9 Cub withdrawn NF 9.12.53. To store BW 14.4.54
58	MXX	358	6400	8223	24.9.53	9.12.53	11.12.53	EG	11.12.53	EG	
59	MXX	359	6404	8224	28.9.53	9.12.53	11.12.53	EG	11.12.53	EG	
60	MXX	360	6405	8225	29.9.53	9.12.53	16.12.53	MA	21.12.53	MA/TG	MA to TG 5.1.54, then back to MA
61	MXX	361	6406	8226	30.9.53	16.12.53	21.12.53	MA	21.12.53	MA	
62	MXX	362	6408	8227	2.10.53	16.12.53	21.12.53	MA	21.12.53	MA	
63	MXX	363	6410	8228	7.10.53	18.12.53	1..1..54	HN	unknown	HN	As spare bus – probable replacement for GS 3
64	MXX	364	6409	8229	2.10.53	11.12.53	17.12.53	MA	21.12.53	MA	
65	MXX	365	6411	8230	9.10.53	11.12.53	18.12.53	MA	21.12.53	MA	
66	MXX	366	6413	8231	9.10.53	11.12.53	18.12.53	MA	21.12.53	MA	
67	MXX	367	6412	8232	9.10.53	16.12.53	26.1.54 (U)	GR	19.5.54	GR	Licensed at GR 19.5.54
68	MXX	368	6413	8233	20.10.53	18.12.53	1.1.54	TG	unknown	TG	
69	MXX	369	6419	8234	23.10.53	21.12.53	24.2.54 (U)	GR	19.5.54	GR	Licensed at GR 19.5.54
70	MXX	370	6416	8235	23.10.53	18.12.53	1.1..54	TG	unknown	TG	3 Cub withdrawn TG 26.1.54
71	MXX	371	6415	8236	21.10.53	18.12.53	10.2.54 (U)	GR (U)	19.5.54	GR	Licensed at GR 19.5.54
72	MXX	372	6418	8237	23.10.53	21.12.53	10.2.54 (U)	GR (U)	8.4.54	EP/HG	Licensed to EP 8.4.54 then to HG 21.4.54
73	MXX	373	6419	8238	23.10.53	22.12.53	10.2.54 (U)	GR (U)	21.4.54	HG	To HG (U) 20.4.54 – licensed 21.4.54
74	MXX	374	6424	8239	30.10.53	12.1.54	10.2.54 (U)	GR (U)	21.4.54	HG	To HG (U) 20.4.54 – licensed 21.4.54
75	MXX	375	6420	8240	27.10.53	1.1.54	10.2.54 (U)	GR (U)	19.5.54	GR	Licensed at GR 19.5.54
76	MXX	376	6421	8241	27.10.53	1.1.54	10.2.54 (U)	GR (U)	19.5.54	GR	Licensed at GR 19.5.54
77	MXX	377	6423	8242	28.10.53	22.12.53	10.2.54 (U)	GR (U)	14.7.54	WR	To WR(U) 12.7.54 – licensed 14.7.54
78	MXX	378	6425	8243	30.10.53	1.1.54	10.2.54 (U)	GR (U)	14.7.54	WR	To WR(U) 12.7.54 – licensed 14.7.54
79	MXX	379	6422	8244	27.10.53	12.1.54	10.2.54 (U)	GR (U)	1.11.54	NF	To RG(U) 20.8.54. To NF 1.11.54 to replace GS 45
80	MXX	380	6427	8245	31.10.53	25.1.54	2.4.54 (U)	GR (U)	14.7.54	WR	To WR(U) 12.7.54 – licensed 14.7.54
81	MXX	381	6426	8246	30.10.53	14.1.54	10.2.54 (U)	GR (U)	21.12.54	CY	To RG (U) 20.8.54. To CY(U) 13.12.54
82	MXX	382	6428	8247	5.11.53	14.1.54	10.2.54 (U)	GR (U)	21.12.54	CY	To AM (U) 18.2.54: RG (U) 20.8.54: CY(U) 13.12.54
83	MXX	383	6429	8248	5.11.53	12.1.54	2.4.54 (U)	GR (U)	21.12.54	CY	To RG (U) 20.8.54. To CY(U) 13.12.54
84	MXX	384	6430	8249	6.11.53	25.1.54	10.2.54 (U)	GR (U)	1.1.56	LH	To RG(U) 20.8.54. Last GS to enter service

1. GS 34 was delivered to ECW out of sequence following an accident necessitating return to Guy Motors for repairs before final delivery.
2. GS 67, 69, and 71 – 84 inclusive were all transferred from Aldenham to Garston unlicensed until finally put into service.
3. Buses marked (U) denotes in store unlicensed

One of the first of a fleet of 84 special passenger chassis which are being supplied to London Transport by Guy Motors Ltd. The chassis are powered by Perkins P6 oil engines and will be fitted with 26-seater bodies designed for one-man operation on the Executive's country services. The bodies are being built by Eastern Coach Works.

This picture of the GS chassis appeared in an article in Modern Transport dated 24th October 1953.

GS 2 was delivered to Aldenham on 2nd October 1953 and was put through the standard tilt test before final licensing. It was allocated to Hitchin ten days later.

The completed bus was very attractive compared to similar small buses of the period, and perhaps this became one of the GSs most endearing features during their lifetime, contributing to their lasting popularity. Mechanically it was extremely robust with economic fuel consumption and was much more effective on steep climbs than the previous Cubs. The reversed gear change gate – first and second gear were on the right of the gate instead of the normal left – was unusual, but the crash gearbox was generally easy to use, although each bus drove slightly differently on the road. In later years, Colin Curtis still maintained that the GS was a far better bus than many small capacity models which followed.

An article in 'Modern Transport' dated 24th October 1953 described the GS as a 'novel one man bus for the London area', having a number of 'attractive maintenance features' and mentioned various removable panels for ease of access to the fuel pump, heater unit, battery, and brake fluid reservoir. The article stated that on the road the bus had 'attractive riding qualities' with good acceleration and a remarkably quiet performance from the P6 engine. Having driven them ourselves for many years, the noise in the driving seat is often quite loud, especially climbing hills, although it is much quieter towards the rear. It went on to report that fuel consumption of more than 20mpg was expected in service, but although consumption was quite good for a light small bus at the time, it proved to be somewhat higher than anticipated. In 1955, after a full year in service, London Transport produced a detailed report of actual consumption in daily service across all garages, a copy of which is reproduced in chapter seven.

As the GSs arrived, they replaced Cubs on the following routes:

329	Hertford – Knebworth – Nup End. (One crew operated bus remained until 21st April 1954)	433	Ranmore – Dorking – Coldharbour
		448	Guildford – Newlands Corner – Gomshall – Peaslake – Ewhurst
329A	Datchworth – Knebworth – Nup End – Hitchin (Tuesday and Saturday only)	448A	Guildford – Pewley Way
		449	Dorking – Chart Downs – Capel – Ockley – Ewhurst
333	Hertford – Bengeo – Chapmore End	450	Gravesend – Betsham – High Cross – Dartford
333B	Hertford – Bengeo – Ware Park Hospital	451	Gravesend – Betsham – Westwood – Longfield – Hartley Court
336A	Rickmansworth – Loudwater Village	452	Dartford – High Cross – Westwood – Longfield – West Kingsdown (Saturday and Sunday only)
348	Chesham Moor – Chesham – Bellingdon – Buckland Common or St Leonards	464	Holland – Oxted – Chart – Crockham Hill – Westerham
348A	Chesham Moor – Chesham – Pond Park Estate	465	Holland – Oxted – Chart – Crockham Hill – Edenbridge
373	Beaconsfield – Knotly Green – Penn	471	Orpington – Pratts Bottom – Knockholt Pound – Cudham – Orpington
381	Epping – Stewards Green – Toothill		
383	Hitchin – Willian – Weston	478	Swanley – West Kingsdown – Wrotham
387	Tring – Tring Station – Aldbury	479	Farningham – Sutton At Hone – Darenth – Dartford
393	Harlow – Nettleswell – Tylers Cross – Broxbourne – Hoddesdon	481	Epsom – Wells Estate
397	Chesham – Cholesbury – Wigginton – Tring	490	Singlewell – Gravesend – Southfleet – New Barn – Longfield – Hartley Court
398	Amersham – Coleshill – Beaconsfield	490A	Northumberland Bottom – Gravesend – Southfleet – New Barn – Longfield – Hartley Ct
398A	Amersham – Coleshill – Winchmore Hill	492	Gravesend – Betsham – Westwood – Longfield – West Kingsdown (Monday to Friday only)

Some of the above were those started between 1948 and 1953 and are referred to in later chapters where details of individual routes are covered. GSs 1, 2, 3 and 4 were initially allocated as training buses following which Hitchin and Chelsham put the first ones into service during October 1953. Conversion of all routes was completed quite quickly, buses being despatched direct from Aldenham after being inspected and licensed for service. The C class cubs were all withdrawn in a similar short period, the last in normal service being withdrawn from Tring on 26th January 1954. Once these conversions were completed, a significant number of GSs remained without work, although as referred to earlier it was intended to convert some minor crew operated routes to GS later in 1954. After completion of the initial allocations, a number of GSs remained at Aldenham, and following delivery of the final seven buses during the second half of January, all the spare buses were transferred unlicensed for storage at Garston until needed for service. GS 67 was the first on 22nd January, followed by 13 more in February, GSs 80 and 83 being the last on 2nd April. The table on page 14 shows the transfer date for each bus, and the initial allocation for service to all garages.

The displaced Cubs were delicensed and most soon moved to be stored at various garages – many initially to Garston. A number remained at their last operational garages for some time; thus on 16th March, ten from Chelsham and Dorking were moved to Reigate and five from Hertford to Wood Green. Having made space for the spare GSs at Garston, nine Cubs were moved from there to Poplar on 18th March, and Northfleet's were all moved to Bow during April.

As had always been the intention, the conversion of a few minor rural routes from crew to omo was completed in 1954, conversion taking place in three stages on the following dates.

<u>21st April 1954</u>

329   Hertford – Knebworth – Nup End (replacing remaining crew operated bus)

331   Hertford – Standon – Buntingford (Tuesday and Sunday only; single positioning journeys for 386)

386   Buntingford – Cromer – Walkern – Stevenage – Hitchin (Tuesday only)
Buntingford – Standon – Wellpond Green – Hadham Ford – Bishops Stortford (Thursday only)
Bishops Stortford – Buntingford – Hitchin (Sunday only). The Saturday service on 386/386A remained crew operated.

386A   Hertford – Much Hadham – Wellpond Green – Standon – Buntingford (Thursday and Sunday only, 386A was used only for positioning journeys)

389   Hertford – Stanstead Abbots – Eastwick – Gilston – Sawbridgeworth

<u>19th May 1954</u>

309   Rickmansworth – Woodcock Hill – Harefield

361   Rickmansworth – Heronsgate – Chorleywood

<u>14th July 1954</u>

442   Slough – Stoke Poges – Farnham Royal – extended to Burnham Beeches for summer season

445   Windsor – Eton – Datchet – Datchet Common

With the completion of these conversions, the total numbers of GSs rostered are shown in the table opposite and can be compared with those prior to the introduction of the GSs.

The article in *Modern Transport* referred to in the text included this illustration. It shows the ease with which the front windscreens could be removed, and the Gibson ticket machine in position next to the driver. Bottom right shows the fold out crate for the battery, and bottom left are the pipes which provided demisting to the windscreens and were located behind the panel which held the fare chart.

GARAGE	ROUTE	MAXIMUM REQUIRED FOR SERVICE				
		15.10.52	6.5.53	7.10.53	19.5.54	6.10.54
AMERSHAM	348; 348A; 397	5	5	6	6	6
	398; 398A; 373	4	4	4	4	4
	Schools Dup	1	1	with 348	with 348	with 348
CHELSHAM	464; 465; 485	7	7	8	8	8
	Schools Dup	1	1	with main roster		
DORKING	433	1	1	1	1	1
	433 Dup		1	1	1	1
	449	2	2	2	2	2
EAST GRINSTEAD	494	1	1	1	1	1
	Special Dup	1		1	1	1
DUNTON GREEN	471	5	5	5	5	5
	Special Dup	1				
EPPING	381	1	1	1	1	1
	393	2	2	2	2	2
	393 Dup	1	1	1	1	1
GARSTON	309	crew	crew	crew	1	1
	336A	1	1	1	1	1
	361	crew	crew	crew	1	1
GUILDFORD	448; 448A	4	4	4	4	4
HERTFORD	329; 329A; 333) 333B; 386) 386A; 388)	7	7	7	9	9
	329	part crew	part crew	part crew	with 333	with 333
	389	crew	crew	crew	1	1
HITCHIN	383	1	1	1	1	1
	Special Dup	1	1	1	1	1
	Contract	1	crew	0	1	1
LEATHERHEAD	481	1	1	1	1	1
	Dup	1	1	1	1	1
NORTHFLEET	450	1	2	2	1	1
	451,490; 490A	5	5	5	5	5
	492	with 451	with 451	with 451	with 451	with 451
	452	crew	crew	crew	1	1
	Special Dup	2	1	1	1	1
SWANLEY	478	1	1	1	1	1
	479	1	1	1	1	1
TRING	387	1	1	1	1	1
WINDSOR	442	crew	crew	crew	crew	1
	445	crew	crew	crew	crew	2
TOTALS		61	59	60	66	69

Allocations up to 7th October 1953 are all Cubs. Allocations for 1954 are all GS.

Many duplicates were operated only on Market Days (eg Hertford) or Saturdays. The duplicate at Dorking was required only on Sunday. Buses allocated as 'Special Duplicates' were often used to duplicate specific journeys, or 'to instructions'.

The only sign of a London Transport non-standard detail in these two pictures is the sliding vent windows. LT's influence on the interior is obvious with the hardwood floor slats, standard seat frames and handrails and beading above the windows. The fare chart case is visible below the front nearside windscreen and the cranked gear lever is visible with the shelf above, which house the bracket for the Gibson ticket machine. The driver's interior rear view mirror is mounted on the centre pillar above the windscreens.

Not all buses were required every day. The maximum number of GSs required for service on 16th October 1954 was 64 Monday, Wednesday and Friday, 65 Tuesday and Thursday, 63 Saturday, and 40 Sunday. The reason that the above total of 69 is greater is that some garages required an additional bus on certain days of the week where other garages rostered fewer buses that day. Hertford for example rostered a maximum of eight during the week but 10 on Saturday, whereas Amersham rostered 10 during the week, but only eight Saturday. The minimum allocation of buses to garages therefore has to account for this – hence the overall total of buses being higher than that required on any one day.

Not all of the routes in the table were restricted to operation by Cubs or GSs. Whilst GSs were approved for routes which traversed particularly narrow roads, there were several others which did not physically require them but were allocated because passengers numbers were lower. There were several anomalies in that a number of routes approved for RF (but which often carried greater numbers of passengers) also traversed some sections of equally narrow roads.

By the end of 1954 when the conversion programme was complete, only the following routes were restricted to 'Class A' – small single deck GS: 329A; 333; 336A; 348; 348A; 381; 388; 393; 397; 398A; 433 (Dorking – Coldharbour only); 448; 448A; 471; 479; 481. Double deck operation was permitted on the 471 between Knockholt Pound and Orpington via Pratts Bottom only. The Dorking to Ranmore section of the 433 was approved for 'Class B' (30ft 0in x 7ft 6in) because one journey each morning was rostered from the 425 schedule. Over time, all these restrictions were gradually eased as described in the chapters which follow.

That the total of 84 GSs immediately proved to be too many has been referred to in many books. It will be seen from the initial allocations that even with engineering spares, several were surplus to requirements. During the ensuing years, the whole GS class would become the most under-employed buses in the Country area fleet and, because of the less frequent timetables of the routes they operated, those that were in service on a daily basis covered much less mileage. The peak years of passenger numbers had also passed, and from the early 1950s began to reduce steadily. Increasing car ownership had the most impact on reducing the number of leisure journeys by bus, and within a few short years, Sunday timetables on many GS routes were greatly cut back in response to falling traffic. Cuts in evening services followed, and the once frequent need for duplication of heavily used journeys became less and less of a necessity. In less than five years, three of the GS routes would be abandoned completely, while the timetables of many others continued to be cut back. Timetable cuts across all the single deck routes began to reduce the efficiency in scheduling RFs, resulting in a number of spare buses. The GSs were of course non-standard within London Transport's rigid operational fleet policy, and replacement by RFs became increasingly possible. The wholesale replacement and reallocation of GSs in October 1962 covered in chapter six marked the beginning of an increasing decline in GS operations. By the end of 1968, Garston and Northfleet would be the only remaining garages running GSs. Northfleet's just failed to last long enough into the London Country era, the last being replaced in November 1969, leaving Garston's single bus for the 336A as the last one.

2   South East Operations

NORTHFLEET

GS 46 was one of Northfleet's original allocation, and remained there for its entire service life until withdrawn in February 1967. The 450 traversed some narrow roads, and this picture may have been taken in January or February 1963 during the heavy snow falls that winter. GS 46 had been fitted with heaters the previous year and were probably very welcome on days such as this.

INITIAL ALLOCATION   GS 45, 36, 47, 48 allocated 2nd December 1953
GS 49, 51, 53 allocated 3rd December 1953
GS 54, 57 allocated 7th December 1953
All entered service on 9th December 1953

ROUTES OPERATED   As described in text on page 24

Northfleet Garage was opened on 7th July 1937 and served the very urban community of Gravesend and Dartford plus the rural communities to the south of the A2 centred on Longfield. The routes 450, 451, 490, 490A and 492 were operated by the Cubs while the 452, 489 and 489A were crew operated by AEC T class buses. There was a major revision of services in the Longfield area from November 1947 which resulted in the routes detailed below, the 492 being added as a new route from 18th May 1949. The 451 had been reduced to a peak hour operation,

the 490 and 490A becoming the main route to Hartley Court while the crew operated 489 had an extension to Meopham covering the amended 423, and was numbered 489A. By October 1953 with a steady increase in housing, it was becoming necessary to duplicate some of the early morning and afternoon school services which led to the peak vehicle requirement being increased to nine Cubs, two of which were shown in the allocation book as scheduled duplicates. A further three 10T10s were also added for the 489/489A. The nine Cubs allocated to the 450 451, 490, 490A and 492 were all delicensed and withdrawn from service on Wednesday 9th December 1953, except two (C 93 and 94) which were retained until 1st January 1954, probably as a back-up in case the new vehicles failed in some way. The Cubs were replaced by eight of the new GS class on the same day. The reason for the change on a Wednesday was that at the time, it was the beginning of the rota week. The weekend 452 had been run by a crew operated 10T10 and was converted to GS operation from the following weekend on Saturday 12th December. It is worth mentioning that the 489, 489A had new RFs allocated shortly before the GSs in November 1953, but they were swiftly diverted for the increase in the peak vehicle requirement for the 725 Green Line route, the 10T10s remaining until withdrawn in July 1954 as some of the last in Country area service.

On 4th April 1959, GS 57 is between High Cross and Betsham on a journey to Gravesend and perfectly illustrates the narrow lanes on this route. The regular two-hourly headway on the 450 allowed the allocation of one bus to operate the service all day with the exception of a morning journey to Greenhithe which returned to Gravesend as a 480. The bus was part of Northfleet's original allocation and remained there until the end of 1962. After a brief spell at Crawley, it spent four years at Garston before finally returning to Northfleet.
Peter Mitchell

The GSs took over the following routes:-

- 450 Gravesend Clock Tower – Betsham – High Cross – Bean – Dartford Garage. Daily
- 451 Gravesend Clock Tower – Betsham – Westwood – Longfield – Hartley Court. Monday to Friday peak journeys and Saturday morning.
- 452 West Kingsdown – Longfield – Westwood – High Cross – Bean – Dartford Garage. Saturday and Sunday
- 490 Singlewell – Gravesend – Southfleet – New Barn – Longfield – Hartley Court. Daily
- 490A Northumberland Bottom – Gravesend – Southfleet – New Barn – Longfield – Hartley Court. Daily
- 492 Gravesend – Betsham – Westwood – Longfield – West Kingsdown. Monday, Tuesday, Thursday and Friday
- 480A Rosherville – Denton. Works service – Monday to Friday single lunchtime return journey.

GSs also operated occasional journeys on the 489 from Gravesend to Longfield and Ash during peak hours, and in later years on 489A to Meopham.

The timetables of the GS routes remained stable during 1954 but with the increase in overall seating capacity the opportunity was taken during 1955 to rationalise some of the peak hour duplicated services and remove the extensions from Gravesend to Singlewell and Northumberland Bottom of the 490 and 490A due to low passenger numbers. The most noticeable reduction in duplicated services was the removal of the duplicate to the 8.01am 450 from Dartford. From the timetable revision of October 1955 the peak GS requirement was therefore reduced from eight to seven buses although the garage allocation remained at nine vehicles. In total, 16 journeys were removed and two duties saved.

The Driver Rota for the 12 months from October 1956 until October 1957 details the running numbers for each bus, and these are shown on the attached schedule. There were 11 duties Monday to Friday, 11 on Saturday and five on Sunday, being covered by a pool of 14 drivers working the recently introduced eleven day fortnight, which meant a total of 88 hours work across two weeks. It provided a total of three rest days per fortnight which was an increase of one day from the previous agreement that had been in force since 1947. Noticeable are the Saturday duties, where an increase in the 490 service to cater for higher numbers of shoppers replaced the weekday school and commuter services. This was to remain a feature of the 490 schedules right up to the end of GS operation. From October 1957, the rota was combined with the 489 when this was converted to one man operation. By combining the two rotas it was possible to reduce the number of spreadvover duties, while at the same time an estimated saving of £1,850 per annum (approximately £33,000 at today's prices) was achieved by the elimination of conductors.

Parcels and Newspapers were regularly delivered by Country Buses with Agents being appointed in most towns.

LONDON TRANSPORT
COUNTRY BUSES

PARCEL
6d

Sa 0817

THIS STAMP TO BE
AFFIXED TO THE ARTICLE

Bell Punch Company, London.

LONDON TRANSPORT
COUNTRY BUSES

PARCEL 6d STAMP

CONDITIONS.

The London Transport Executive, who are not "common carriers" accept for carriage the unaccompanied parcel in respect of which this counterfoil is issued, subject to the following conditions :—

(1) The Executive shall not be liable for the loss or detention of or any damage to the said parcel or its contents, which is accepted for carriage at the owner's risk.

(2) If the said parcel is not claimed within one month of its being handed to the Executive it shall be deemed and shall be disposed of as Lost Property as defined in and set forth in the regulations issued by the Minister of Transport under the provisions of section 119 of the Transport Act, 1947.

(3) If the said parcel is not collected from the Conductor it will be left with the Agent nearest its destination. The Executive does not accept any responsibility for advising the consignee of the parcel's arrival.

THIS PORTION TO BE
RETAINED BY CONSIGNOR. No. Sa 0817

Bell Punch Company, Limited, London.

From the October 1955 timetables for the 450, 451, 490 and 492 started from Gravesend Clock Tower using a stand in Peacock Street. Buses then called at the London Transport waiting room in Gravesend centre, before running via Pelham Road and Perry Street to cross the A2 trunk road at the Perryhill Flyover, which today is a major interchange as the A2 has grown into a road of almost motorway standard. A minimum fare was imposed from Gravesend to Pelham Street to encourage local passengers to use the double deck routes 495 and 496 and was intended to retain the limited seating capacity of the GSs for passengers travelling out to the villages. From Perryhill a narrower road led a short distance to Southfleet Station which actually closed to passengers in August 1953 before the GS arrived. The station however continued to be shown as an intermediate point on the 450 blind for many years to inform passengers that the bus did not serve Southfleet village some distance from the actual station where 450 separated from the 489, 489A and 490. The 490 turned from the main road into Southfleet village where it continued down a single track lane to New Barn. The 450, 451 and 492 continued beyond Southfleet station towards Betsham before a further separation where the 451 and 492 turned left opposite the 'Colyers Arms' while the 450 continued along a narrow lane to High Cross where it turned right at the cross roads to Bean and Dartford. It ran to a two hourly headway throughout the day on weekdays and on Sunday afternoon and evening. This required one bus allocated to this service with running number NF57 from the 1957 duties. There were two early morning journeys on the 450 run by NF51 with a return journey to Greenhithe, and NF57 and ran a morning journey to Horns Cross which returned to Gravesend as a 480 – only a short 20 minute run, but an example of a GS working on a main trunk route. NF57 then worked the 8.01am from Gravesend Clock Tower to Dartford, duplicated in the days of the Cubs and up to 1955 by the GS.

In November 1969 GS 36 was one of last GS vehicles operating from Northfleet and here it is waiting in Gravesend to operate a peak hours journey on the 451 to Hartley Court. It was one of the vehicles transferred to London Country, where 36 spent two years as a manual gearbox trainer. The bus has now joined the ranks of the preserved vehicles. *Alan Charman collection*

NORTHFLEET GS SCHEDULES – 16TH OCTOBER 1956

MONDAY TO FRIDAY

ROUTE NUMBER	TIME DEPART	FROM	TO
NF 51			
450	7.58am	Northfleet Gar.	Greenhithe
450	8.35am	Greenhithe	Gravesend C.T.
LIGHT	9.11am	Gravesend C.T.	Northfleet Gar.
NF 52			
LIGHT	5.51am	Northfleet Gar.	Gravesend C.T.
490	6.00am	Gravesend C.T.	Fawkham Station
490	6.42am	Fawkham Station	Gravesend C.T.
490	7.21am	Gravesend C.T.	Hartley Court
490	8.12am	Hartley Court	Gravesend C.T.
490	9.38am	Gravesend C.T.	Hartley Court
490	10.32am	Hartley Court	Gravesend C.T.
LIGHT	11.14am	Gravesend C.T.	Northfleet Gar.
LIGHT	3.24pm	Northfleet Gar.	Gravesend C.T.
490	3.33pm	Gravesend C.T.	Hartley Court
490	4.22pm	Hartley Court	Gravesend C.T.
490	5.38pm	Gravesend C.T.	Hartley Court
451	6.28pm	Hartley Court	Northfleet Gar.
NF 53			
LIGHT	5.58am	Northfleet Gar.	Gravesend C.T.
489	6.07am	Gravesend C.T.	Fawkham Station
489	6.43am	Fawkham Station	Gravesend C.T.
490	7.18am	Gravesend C.T.	Hartley Court
490	8.10am	Hartley Court	Gravesend C.T.
LIGHT	8.55am	Gravesend C.T.	Northfleet Gar.
480A	12.55pm	Northfleet Gar.	Rosherville
480A	1.13pm	Rosherville	Denton
480A	1.45pm	Denton	Rosherville
480A	1.55pm	Rosherville	Northfleet Gar.
LIGHT	2.21pm	Northfleet Gar.	Gravesend C.T.
490	2.33pm	Gravesend C.T.	Hartley Court
490	3.23pm	Hartley Court	Gravesend C.T.
490	4.10pm	Gravesend C.T.	Hartley Court
490	5.06pm	Hartley Court	Fawkham Station
490	5.30pm	Fawkham Station	New Barn
490	5.42pm	New Barn	Fawkham Station
490	6.08pm	Fawkham Station	New Barn
490	6.20pm	New Barn	Longfield Rlwy Tav.
490	6.38pm	Longfield Rlwy Tav.	Hartley Court
490	7.05pm	Hartley Court	Gravesend C.T.
LIGHT	7.46pm	Gravesend C.T.	Northfleet Gar.
LIGHT	8.36pm	Northfleet Gar.	Gravesend C.T.
490	8.45pm	Gravesend C.T.	Hartley Court
490	9.52pm	Hartley Court	Gravesend C.T.
490	10.37pm	Gravesend C.T.	Hartley Court
490	11.22pm	Hartley Court	Northfleet Gar.
BF 54			
LIGHT	6.28am	Northfleet Gar.	Gravesend C.T.
451	6.37am	Gravesend C.T.	Hartley Court
451	7.20am	Hartley Court	Longfield Rlwy Tav.
451	7.35am	Longfield Rlwy Tav.	Hartley Court
451	7.50am	Hartley Court	Gravesend C.T.

ROUTE NUMBER	TIME DEPART	FROM	TO	NOTES
490	8.33am	Gravesend C.T.	Hartley Court	
490	9.55am	Hartley Court	Gravesend C.T.	
LIGHT	10.37am	Gravesend C.T.	Northfleet Gar.	
LIGHT	11.30am	Northfleet Gar.	Gravesend C.T.	
490	11.39am	Gravesend C.T.	Hartley Court	
490	12.32pm	Hartley Court	Gravesend C.T.	
490	1.17pm	Gravesend C.T.	Hartley Court	
490	2.02pm	Hartley Court	Gravesend C.T.	
LIGHT	2.43pm	Gravesend C.T.	Northfleet Gar.	
LIGHT	4.01pm	Northfleet Gar.	Gravesend C.T.	
*490	4.10pm	Gravesend C.T.	Hartley Court	
490	4.55pm	Hartley Court	Longfield Rlwy Tav.	
490	5.12pm	Longfield Rlwy Tav.	Hartley Court	
490	5.30pm	Hartley Court	Gravesend C.T.	
490	6.35pm	Gravesend C.T.	Hartley Court	
490	7.30pm	Hartley Court	Longfield Rlwy Tav.	
490	7.45pm	Longfield Rlwy Tav.	Hartley Court	
490	8.02pm	Hartley Court	Gravesend C.T.	
LIGHT	8.43pm	Gravesend C.T.	Northfleet Gar.	
NF 55 LIGHT	7.25am	Northfleet Gar.	Gravesend C.T.	
451	7.35am	Gravesend C.T.	Hartley Court	
451	8.23am	Hartley Court	Gravesend C.T.	
LIGHT	9.00am	Gravesend C.T.	Northfleet Gar.	
LIGHT	2.35pm	Northfleet Gar.	Gravesend C.T.	Not Wednesday
492	2.44pm	Gravesend C.T.	West Kingsdown	Not Wednesday
492	3.35pm	West Kingsdown	Longfield Rlwy Tav.	Not Wednesday
LIGHT	3.22pm	Northfleet Gar.	Gravesend C.T.	Wednesday only
451	3.32pm	Gravesend C.T.	Longfield Rlwy Tav.	Wednesday only
490	4.03pm	Longfield Rlwy Tav.	Gravesend C.T.	
489A	4.38pm	Gravesend C.T.	Longfield Hill	
489A	5.19pm	Longfield Hill	Longfield Rlwy Tav.	
490	5.38pm	Longfield Rlwy Tav.	Hartley Court	
490	5.54pm	Hartley Court	Longfield Rlwy Tav.	
489	6.10pm	Longfield Rlwy Tav.	Ash White Swan	
489	6.29pm	Ash White Swan	Longfield Rlwy Tav.	
490	6.46pm	Longfield Rlwy Tav.	Gravesend C.T.	
LIGHT	7.18pm	Gravesend C.T.	Northfleet Gar.	
NF 56 LIGHT	7.40am	Northfleet Gar.	Gravesend C.T.	
490	7.49am	Gravesend C.T.	Fawkham Station	
490	8.23am	Fawkham Station	Longfield Hill	
490	8.35am	Longfield Hill	Gravesend C.T.	
LIGHT	9.07pm	Gravesend C.T.	Northfleet Gar.	Wednesday only
492	9.21am	Gravesend C.T.	West Kingsdown	Not Wednesday
492	10.12am	West Kingsdown	Gravesend C.T.	Not Wednesday
LIGHT	11.00am	Gravesend C.T.	Northfleet Gar.	Not Wednesday
LIGHT	12.04pm	Northfleet Gar.	Gravesend C.T.	Not Wednesday
492	12.13pm	Gravesend C.T.	West Kingsdown	Not Wednesday
492	1.04pm	West Kingsdown	Gravesend C.T.	Not Wednesday
LIGHT	1.52pm	Northfleet Gar.	Gravesend C.T.	Not Wednesday
LIGHT	2.36pm	Northfleet Gar.	Gravesend C.T.	Wednesday only

	490	2.36pm	Overcliffe Church	Hartley Court		450	4.26pm	Gravesend C.T.	Dartford Garage
	490	3.25pm	Hartley Court	Gravesend C.T.		450	5.19pm	Dartford Garage	Gravesend C.T.
	490	4.28pm	Gravesend C.T.	Fawkham Station		450	6.26pm	Gravesend C.T.	Dartford Garage
	490	5.06pm	Fawkham Station	Gravesend C.T.		450	7.19pm	Dartford Garage	Gravesend C.T.
	490	5.45pm	Gravesend C.T.	Hartley Court		450	8.26pm	Gravesend C.T.	Dartford Garage
	490	6.30pm	Hartley Court	Gravesend C.T.		450	9.19pm	Dartford Garage	Gravesend C.T.
	LIGHT	7.12pm	Gravesend C.T.	Northfleet Gar.		LIGHT	10.09pm	Gravesend C.T.	Northfleet Gar.
NF 57	LIGHT	6.37am	Northfleet Gar.	Gravesend C.T.					
	450	6.48am	Gravesend C.T.	Horns Cross Bull					
	480	7.30am	Horns Cross Bull	Gravesend C.T.		Dup to 480 Jny			
	450	8.01am	Gravesend C.T.	Dartford Garage					
	450	8.58am	Dartford Garage	Gravesend C.T.					
	450	10.26am	Gravesend C.T.	Dartford Garage					
	450	11.19am	Dartford Garage	Gravesend C.T.					
	450	12.26pm	Gravesend C.T.	Dartford Garage					
	450	1.19pm	Dartford Garage	Gravesend C.T.					
	450	2.26pm	Gravesend C.T.	Dartford Garage					
	450	3.19pm	Dartford Garage	Gravesend C.T.					

1. Route 492 operated Monday, Tuesday, Thursday and Friday
2. Where buses ran light to and from Northfleet Garage for a shorter break this was to enable driver changes.
3. NF 51 worked only the morning 450 return journey to Greenhithe. 4. Could be rostered with NF 53 as duplicate to 480A lunchtime Roshcrville works journey to instructions as required.
5. *DUP to NF 53

GS 36 was allocated to Northfleet from May 1967 and is seen here turning towards Betsham having set out from Dartford via Bean Village on Route 450. In 1967 the Northfleet GS and RF blinds were combined into one set, primarily to extend the flexibility of working for the GS over the 489/489A roads. The 450 panels were also remade to exclude Southfleet Stn. Many GS blinds remained in upper case lettering throughout their service lives, but from 1961 where new panels were made the opportunity was taken to use lower case lettering. *Colin Rivers collection*

On 9th May 1964, GS 47 has left the terminus at Hartley Court on a 490 to Gravesend. It was delicensed and stored at Northfleet in February 1967 and was later converted to an Ambulance. *Peter Mitchell*

Facing page: The year is 1963 and GS 53 is making its way out of Gravesend towards Ash while standing in for the regular RF as NF9. GS 53 was the longest serving GS at Northfleet, arriving in November 1953 and finally being delicensed in May 1967. The bus had two overhauls in June 1957 and February 1963, when it also had a heater fitted.

The 450 (and 452 at weekends) would have met the London Trolleybus 696 route as they traversed Dartford Market Place. NF51 only had this one early morning duty and became a candidate for removal in the 1958 cuts. Today the 450 road from Bean village to Horns Cross is almost unrecognisable as first it passes over the HS1 Channel Tunnel railway line route on its way to Stratford and St Pancras and then past the Bluewater Shopping Complex – certainly not the rural tranquillity of the 1950s. From Betsham the 451, which by 1957 had become a peak hour service, followed the very narrow Westwood Lane to The Wheatsheaf pub at Westwood cross roads where it joined the 452, 489 and 489A down to Fawkham Station. This was renamed Longfield Station from 12th June 1961 and brought about a complete revision of the GS blinds, the new version being illustrated. On Saturday morning there were two short journeys on the 451 from Gravesend to Betsham, the returns matching the timings of the Monday to Friday 492 journeys from Kingsdown, thereby maintaining the hourly service from Betsham into Gravesend.

The 492 followed the same road as the 451 to Longfield cross roads after which it ran along the valley through the small hamlet of Fawkham. The route turned at Scratchers Lane and followed the lane around the Brands Hatch racing circuit before arriving at West Kingsdown where buses turned across the dual carriageway of the A20 opposite 'The Portobello Inn' before running back to Gravesend. Three journeys operated each day except Wednesday which was early closing day in Gravesend, and were primarily aimed at shoppers from West Kingsdown and Fawkham. At West Kingsdown, connections could be made with the 703 Green Line and local GS service 478 to Swanley described in the next section for Swanley's routes. The 492 afternoon return from West Kingsdown terminated at Fawkham station to run a journey on the 490 from to Gravesend. In order that

this 490 journey could be operated every day, a positioning journey was run on Wednesday afternoon via the 451 to Fawkham station. Passenger loads on the 492 were minimal, and it did not survive the cuts that were made in October 1958, thus reducing the service along the valley from Longfield to operate only at weekends on the 452. This ran from West Kingsdown to Dartford Garage following the same roads as the 492 as far as Westwood Cross Roads where it turned left to join the 450 at High Cross. It then followed the 450 road to Dartford, the timetables being arranged to provide a regular hourly headway from High Cross into Dartford. The running number for the 452 was NF49 at weekends and the last bus of the day returned to Gravesend from Dartford as a 450. Crew operated 10T10s were replaced by GSs when they arrived at Northfleet and remained until May 1959 when an RF replaced the GS. Although not part of this book, the 452 continued despite ever decreasing passengers until 1972, when it was finally withdrawn following removal of local authority support.

To return to the 490 route, having reached Fawkham station, it climbed up to Hartley to turn left by the War Memorial along church road before turning at the triangle beside the entrance to Hartley Court, a terminus which in previous years this had been referred to as Hartley Hill. In the 1957 duties, the major part of the 490 was operated by three GS with running numbers NF53, 54, and 55. In peak hours all three buses operated short journeys to New Barn, Hartley Court and Longfield Hill for commuters and school traffic to and from Fawkham station. NF56 also worked a 490 along the 489A road to Longfield Hill at 8.23am filling in a two hour gap in the 489A timetable. The 4.10pm 490 from Gravesend was duplicated all the way to Hartley Court, one bus then returning to Gravesend, the other to Fawkham station to work some of the short journeys referred to above. Between 4.00pm and 6.00pm, five GSs were required to cover the timetable.

GS 36 again, but this time at the Green Man terminus on Longfield Hill The GS covered an almost two hour gap in the 489A schedules by working short journeys which assisted with peak hour loadings. *Colin Rivers collection*

The 489 and 489A were operated with RFs, but a GS on NF53 ran an early morning 489 duplicate to Fawkham station and back while the RF on NF52 returned as a 490. The bus on NF55 which ran the 492 was used in the evening peak and ran short journeys on the 489 from Fawkham station to Ash. The 490 operated short journeys on Saturdays between Fawkham station and Gravesend in order to maintain an hourly service. From 1963 the Saturday service tended to have a the greater number of GSs allocated, only four being rostered on weekdays due to the use of the larger RF, but on Saturdays as many as six remained rostered as the shopping service into Gravesend remained intense.

An unusual working inherited from the Leyland Cub was a short lunchtime journey on the 480A works service from Rosherville to Denton where the bus waited 30 minutes for workers' lunch break before returning to Rosherville. NF53 worked this journey during the spreadover break between morning and afternoon service on the 490.

GSs were sometimes used as Green Line 725 Reliefs through to West Croydon. Two photos exist of GS 36 showing a 725 blind but they appear to have been posed, as no passengers are on board and they are both taken at an ordinary bus stop. One appeared on the cover of the Winter 1968/69 issue of Country Bus News. Laurie Akehurst tells us of a sighting at Elephant & Castle of a GS (and an RFW) working on the 701/2 in the bad winter of 1962/63, and GS owner Roy Gould of a GS operating a 715 Green Line journey into London from Guildford in January 1963. Also, when Cudham Lane was blocked by snow during that same winter, preventing operation of the 471, Dunton Green used two GSs to work a shuttle service from the garage to Sevenoaks bus station. One of these then worked at least twice to Westerham with 705 blinds. The crash gearbox and clutch of the GS gave more control in icy conditions than the pre-select and fluid flywheel of RF and RT.

Northfleet's initial allocation remained unchanged until October 1958, the only exception being with GS 45 which was replaced on 1st November 1954 after it suffered a serious front end accident and was sent into Chiswick for repair. The opportunity was taken to change the differential on GS 45 and after leaving Chiswick, it spent time at various southern area garages as described later in chapter seven. It returned to Northfleet on 11th May 1955 but returned to Chiswick on 1st June, eventually being returned for a long period to Dorking. GS 75 was transferred from Garston on 1st November to replace GS 45. On 12th October 1955 GS 47 was transferred to Chelsham.

GS 54 departing from Gravesend on its way to Fawkham Station operating an early morning duplicate Service. Fawkham was renamed Longfield Stn in 1961 which resulted in a remake of the NF blind. GS 54 was converted by new age travellers in the early 90s and was noted as recently as 2015 on the South Downs at Brighton. *Mick Webber*

GS 57 was part of Northfleet's original allocation and stands at the terminus at Singlewell sometime in 1955. As the estates to the south of Gravesend expanded, the route network was extended and in 1956 this section of the 490 was replaced, the route being cut back to the town centre. *Alan Charman collection*

GS 36 at Longfield Hill once again, this time working the full route through to Meopham. It was not unusual in the later years of GS operation to find the normal RF replaced by a GS. In 1967 the GS and RF blinds were combined. GS 36 together with GS 55 were the last two operational vehicles at NF. *Dick Dapre*

The view of GS 54 was taken in 1954. The bus is without grab handles below the front screen windows and has an earlier style of one man operation notice affixed to the front nearside. The 452 was converted from crew 10T10 operation on the first Saturday of GS operation, operating weekends only from Kingsdown to Dartford. *Peter Aves collection*

GS 57 running as NF 55 from Northfleet Garage to Gravesend before taking up the afternoon duty on the 492 to West Kingsdown, then back to Fawkham Station to operate school and peak duties. *Peter Mitchell*

The first overhaul cycle took vehicles away for several weeks between February and October 1957. GS 49 was the first to go on 12th February, returning on 15th April two weeks after GS 51 departed and returning on 15th May. This released GS 46 for overhaul, returning on 21st June. GS 48 and 54 followed, both returning in August. During this overhaul cycle, GS 28 came in from Garston 11th February, and GS 26, which was transferred around a number of garages as a float bus, was drafted to Northfleet on 19th June. Both remained until withdrawn on 1st October. GS 28 was used occasionally in the first few months of 1958 and later transferred to Garston on 20th August 1958.

The first reduction in allocation came in 1959 when GS 51 and GS 26 were both transferred to Chelsham on 1st August, GS 79 having returned from overhaul on 1st April and relicensed one month later. The allocation then remained stable until February 1961 when GS 49 went into store at Romford, reducing the number to six operational vehicles. 1962 was of course a significant year for the GS. Not only was the second overhaul cycle underway but October saw the reduction of

over 20 GSs at Chelsham, Amersham, Tring and Epping as described in chapter six. GS 53 went for its second overhaul on 4th June 1962, GS 58 being allocated later from overhaul on 9th August. GS 53 returned and was relicensed on 1st September, releasing GS 48 and 53 to go to Works. These in turn were replaced by GS 47 from East Grinstead, and GS 65 and 66 were transferred to Northfleet as part of the fleetwide re-allocations. On 24th October GS 7, 8, 11, and 81 arrived for temporary storage after their withdrawal from Chelsham and were joined by Northfleet's GS 79, which was withdrawn on 1st November.

In 1963, 1964 and 1965 the allocation remained stable with GS 46, 47, 53, 58 and 66 while for 1966 the only change was GS 47 being delicensed and stored in February. 1967 saw the regular allocation become due for overhaul and expiry of Certificates of Fitness. GS 46 and 53 had spent their whole working life at Northfleet when they were delicensed, GS 46 being replaced by GS 10 in February 1967. On 13th May 1967, GS 53, 58 and 66 were all delicensed. They were replaced by GS 36 and 54 from Grays following the withdrawal of the 399 there, and by GS 57 from Garston. GS 53 and 58 remained stored at Northfleet until sold the following year. GS 66 went to Plumstead as a staff bus and is referred to in chapter seven.

From the summer 1967 schedules, Northfleet required only two GS Monday to Friday and three Saturday and in the last two years of operation, GS 28, 54, 55 and 57 spent a few months at Northfleet, as engineering spares, GS 55 being the last to be drafted in from Grays on 8th September 1969, and licensed for service. The last formal day of GS operation at Northfleet was 4th October 1969, the last two operational buses – GS 36 and 55 – being delicensed and withdrawn that day. GS 54 had been in store there and was sold to Midland Poultry on 4th November, the last GS to go from Northfleet.

C Class and GS MAX VEHICLE REQUIREMENT

	MONDAY TO FRIDAY				SATURDAY	SUNDAY	
	450	451, 490, 492	DUP	Total			Notes
May 52	1	5	2	8	5	3	Ex 452
May 53	2	5	1	8	5	3	
May 54	2	5	1	8	6	3	Incl. 452
May 55	2	5	1	8	7	3	
May 56	2	5	0	7	6	3	
Oct 57	2	5	0	7	6	3	
Dec 58	1	4	0	5	6	3	NF 54 OMO RF
Oct 59	1	4	0	5	5	2	452 OMO RF NF 54
Jun 62	1	3	0	4	5	2	NF 50 & NF 54
Oct 62	1	3	0	4	6	1	NF 50 CREW RF
Oct 63	1	3	0	4	5	0	
Nov 64	1	3	0	4	5	0	
Jul 66	0	3	0	3	4	0	
Dec 66	0	3	0	3	3	0	
Jul 67	0	2	0	2	3	0	
Jun 68	0	1	0	1	2	0	MF: NF 52; SAT: NF 54,55
Nov 68	0	1	0	1	1	0	MF: NF 53; SAT: NF 52

October 1969 allocation book on Saturday 6 x RF , 450 , 490 , 452

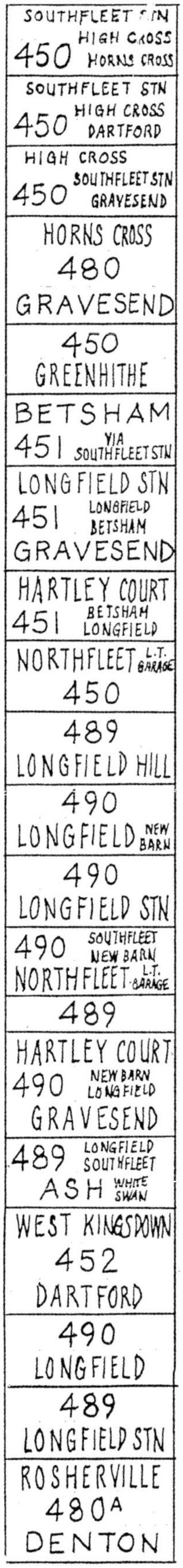

In 1961 Fawkham Station was renamed Longfield, resulting in the first major change to the GS blind set. The 490A and 492 were removed but reference to Southfleet Station, although closed in 1953, was retained. Panels for the 489A did not appear until the mid-1960s when GSs regularly substituted for RFs. *R J Williamson*

Sidebar – destination blind panels:

450 SOUTHFLEET STN HIGH CROSS HORNS CROSS

450 SOUTHFLEET STN HIGH CROSS DARTFORD

450 HIGH CROSS SOUTHFLEET STN GRAVESEND

480 HORNS CROSS

450 GRAVESEND

GREENHITHE

451 BETSHAM VIA SOUTHFLEET STN

451 LONGFIELD STN LONGFIELD BETSHAM GRAVESEND

451 HARTLEY COURT BETSHAM LONGFIELD

450 NORTHFLEET L.T. GARAGE

489

490 LONGFIELD HILL

490 LONGFIELD NEW BARN

490 LONGFIELD STN

490 SOUTHFLEET NEW BARN NORTHFLEET L.T. GARAGE

489

490 HARTLEY COURT NEW BARN LONGFIELD

489 GRAVESEND LONGFIELD SOUTHFLEET

ASH WHITE SWAN

452 WEST KINGSDOWN

452 DARTFORD

490 LONGFIELD

489 LONGFIELD STN

480A ROSHERVILLE

DENTON

SWANLEY

INITIAL ALLOCATION:
GS 20 allocated 4th November 1953
GS 26 allocated 11th November 1953
Both buses entered service on 14th November 1953

ROUTES OPERATED
478 Swanley Station – Kingsdown – Wrotham
Operated from 14th November 1953 to 16th October 1956
479 Farningham – Horton Kirby – Darenth – Dartford
Operated from 14th November 1953 to 28th October 1958

PEAK VEHICLE REQUIREMENT – Two buses

Swanley was a small garage dating from the 1920s, the SJ garage code standing for Swanley Junction. It catered for the three double deck routes that connected the Dartford area to Sevenoaks, Orpington and Longfield, and was situated on the A20 trunk road from London to the Kent Coast via Maidstone. From the 1930s it also operated Green Line route B that served Wrotham Village via Farningham and Kingsdown. When Green Line operations ceased on 2nd September 1939 with the outbreak of war a section of the A20 from Farningham to Wrotham was left without any bus service so that on 25th September 1939 the 478 was introduced using one Cub and the occasional STL. Before the new GSs arrived, Swanley's allocation of small single deckers was two Cubs. GS 20 arrived for driver training on 4th November 1953, GS 26 arriving a week later on 11th. The daily records show that both buses entered service on Saturday 14th and both Cubs were delicensed and withdrawn from service on Monday 16th November. From this date, the two GSs operated most of route 478 and the whole timetable of the 479.

The original 478 route ran from Swanley Station into London Road (A20) past the garage and down the hill into Farningham Village and the Darenth Valley. The route then followed the long climb up past Brands Hatch racing circuit, a section of road locally known as 'Death Hill' due to frequent motor cycle accidents. Two miles further on at West Kingsdown, a major passenger point on the journey, connections could be made with the 492 to Gravesend during the week and the 452 to Dartford at weekends. Three miles further the village of Wrotham was reached where the route terminated and is probably the only point on the route that has changed very little between 1953 and the present time. The 478 ran to a very irregular timetable, the majority of which was run by a GS, occasional journeys being crew operated with an STL and subsequently RT. One morning journey to Wrotham was worked by the GS scheduled to take up service later on the 479, the early morning journeys being run before the Green Line timetable commenced at 6.51 am from Wrotham to provide a morning service to Swanley Station.

The GS allocated to SJ22 on the 478 was rostered from 5.25am to 7.51am after which it was not required again until 12.36pm. It then ran the afternoon service, returning to the garage late in the evening at 10.02pm. The GS allocated to SJ20 left the garage at 5.49am to run one of the early journeys to Wrotham referred to above. It returned to the garage at 7.01am, and left again at 7.11am to work on the 479 for the remainder of the day. The 479 terminated at Farningham, the only journeys to and from Swanley garage being the first out and last back, plus another in the afternoon to change drivers. During the day, the 479 timetable was arranged to provide the driver with breaks at Dartford garage, the first mid-morning, the second late afternoon.

During the morning, the 478 timetable was operated with a crew operated double decker on SJ21, and rostered again along with the GS in the afternoon between 3.43pm and 7.33pm when additional journeys were run to Kingsdown with a small number on to Wrotham. It is most likely that this spreadover duty was worked by one crew.

The 478 received a short extension in 1953 to the newly built council estate at St Marys, approximately half a mile north of Swanley Station. The May 1954 timetable had the maximum GS service but from the winter schedules in October that year, the Sunday service on 478 was withdrawn.

The long gap each morning during which the bus on SJ20 was not required allowed routine maintenance to be carried out on Swanley's GSs. In the event of anything more extensive being required, then a spare bus was readily available from Northfleet.

The 478 was always an irregular service, mostly covering the peak hours and school traffic with many journeys turning at West Kingsdown, With the winter schedules from 16th October 1956 the GS was replaced by a crew operated RT and the 478 amalgamated with the 477/ 423 schedule on a reduced headway. This change reduced Swanley's allocation to one bus for the 479. Eventually by the mid-1960s, the 478 route number was dispensed with and the 423 was extended to Wrotham Square.

GS 26 at Farningham Village on its way to Wrotham, probably in 1955. The GS was removed from the 478 schedule in 1956 being replaced by RTs from the 423 schedule. GS 26 spent its first four years at Swanley but after overhaul became an overhaul float vehicle, spending time at eight garages before its second overhaul in October 1961. It finally settled at Guildford until the 448 was withdrawn by LT and then the bus was moved to DG for six months, being sold by LT in January 1968. GS 26 was one of the first GSs to be preserved and is still a regular at rallies. *Mick Webber*

To DARTFORD **Route 479**

Weekdays

P.M. times are in heavy figures

Swanley *London Transport Garage*	712						**335**					
FARNINGHAM *The Bull*	719	829	939	1126	1236	**146**	**342**	**5 0**	**615**	**810**	**930**
Horton Kirby *Westminster Mills*	726	836	946	1133	1243	**153**	**349**	**5 7**	**622**	**817**	**937**
Sutton-at-Hone *Ship*	732	842	952	1139	1249	**159**	**355**	**513**	**628**	**823**	**943**
Darenth *Chequers*	738	848	958	1145	1235	**2 5**	**4 1**	**519**	**634**	**829**	**949**
Dartford *Market Street*	746	856	10 6	1153	1 53	**213**	**4 9**	**527**	**642**	**837**	**957**
Dartford *Westgate Road*	748	858	10 8	1155	**1 5**	**215**	**411**	**529**	**644**	**839**	**959**
DARTFORD *London Transport Garage*	749	859	10 9	1156	**1 6**	**216**	**412**	**530**	**645**	**840**	**10 0**

Sunday

Swanley *London Transport Garage*	311				
FARNINGHAM *The Bull*	318	445	**610**	**810**	**930**
Horton Kirby *Westminster Mills*	325	452	**617**	**817**	**937**
Sutton-at-Hone *Ship*	331	458	**623**	**823**	**943**
Darenth *Chequers*	337	5 4	**629**	**829**	**949**
Dartford *Market Street*	345	512	**637**	**837**	**957**
Dartford *Westgate Road*	347	514	**639**	**839**	**959**
DARTFORD *London Transport Garage*	348	515	**640**	**840**	**10 0**

To FARNINGHAM **Route 479**
and SWANLEY

Weekdays

P.M. times are in heavy figures

DARTFORD *London Transport Garage*	754	9 4	1051	12 1	**1 11**	**221**	**425**	**538**	**727**	**845**	**10 5**
Dartford *Westgate Road*	755	9 5	1052	12 2	**1 12**	**222**	**426**	**539**	**728**	**846**	**10 6**
Dartford *Overy Liberty*	757	9 7	1054	12 4	**1 14**	**224**	**428**	**541**	**730**	**848**	**10 8**
Darenth *Chequers*	8 5	915	11 2	1212	**1 22**	**232**	**436**	**549**	**738**	**856**	**1016**
Sutton-at-Hone *Ship*	811	921	11 8	1218	**1 28**	**238**	**442**	**555**	**744**	**9 2**	**1022**
Horton Kirby *Westminster Mills*	817	927	1114	1224	**1 34**	**244**	**448**	**6 1**	**750**	**9 8**	**1028**
FARNINGHAM *The Bull*	824	934	1121	1231	**1 41**	**251**	**455**	**6 8**	**757**	**915**	**1035**
Swanley *London Transport Garage*	....	....	....	....	....	**258**	....	....	....	....	**1042**

Sunday

DARTFORD *London Transport Garage*	410	530	**725**	**845**	**10 5**
Dartford *Westgate Road*	411	531	**726**	**846**	**10 6**
Dartford *Overy Liberty*	413	533	**728**	**848**	**10 8**
Darenth *Chequers*	421	541	**736**	**856**	**1016**
Sutton-at-Hone *Ship*	427	547	**742**	**9 2**	**1022**
Horton Kirby *Westminster Mills*	433	552	**748**	**9 8**	**1028**
FARNINGHAM *The Bull*	440	6 0	**755**	**915**	**1035**
Swanley *London Transport Garage*	....	....	....	....	**1042**

NOTE: While every effort will bejmade toJkeep to the timetable, London Transport does not undertake that its buses will be operated in accordance with them, or at all. London Transport will not be responsible for any loss, damage or inconvenience caused by reason of any operating failure or be consequence of any inaccuracies in the timetables.

LONDON TRANSPORT, 55 BROADWAY, S.W.1. ABBey 1234. 18.4.56

The 479 had been operated by a Cub to an approximately hourly service. The route ran through the villages of the Darenth Valley through Horton Kirby and South Darenth, the only route to use Darenth Lane into Dartford where it terminated at the garage together with the 450 and 452 operated from Northfleet garage. The GS replaced the Cub on the same headway. Like a number of the minor rural routes introduced in the early post-war period, it was initially a busy route but with growth of private car ownership passenger numbers began to drop away sharply. By 1958 loadings on the 479 had dropped below a sustainable level, and it became a casualty of the 1958 post strike cuts, being withdrawn completely on 28th October of that year. Today it is impossible to travel the full length of the 479 due to the re-building of the A2 and the Darenth interchange at the junction of the M2 and M25 over what was a section of Darenth Lane. In 2004, Country Bus Rallies operated GS 2 and 62 over the route as far as Darenth village where the old road is now a dead end and finishes before the M25.

GS 20 and 26 were included in the 1956 overhaul programme and GS 20 was the first to go on Friday 22nd June 1956, being replaced on Monday 25th by GS 13 fresh from its first overhaul. GS 20 was returned to Dunton Green after overhaul. GS 26 went for overhaul on 19th October immediately following the replacement of the GS on the 478 and went to Epping on its return to service. GS 13 was thereafter Swanley's only GS left to maintain the 479 until GS 32 was eventually transferred from Dorking on 1st November 1957 as a spare. GS 13 operated the 479 until the last day and was noted as withdrawn on 1st November 1958. It remained at Swanley until relicensed and transferred to Leatherhead on 31st January 1959 as a float bus. Swanley was therefore the first garage to lose its GS allocation, and they would never return.

GS 13 was sent to Swanley after overhaul in June 1956, and on 28th July 1958 it is travelling through Horton Kirby towards Farningham with the paper mill chimneys in the background. The 479 was to be a casualty of the 1958 service reductions after the long strike, GS 13 was to be a long term survivor and was one of the few GS to have three overhauls finally finishing service in April 1973 after four years as the Abbey Wood staff bus, today it is owned by Peter Cartwright and is a regular at running days.
Peter Mitchell

DUNTON GREEN

INITIAL ALLOCATION
GS 4 5th November 1953 – 23rd November 1953 (trainer).
GS 29 11th November 1953
GS 32 12th November 1953
GS 24, 25, 27, 28, 16th November 1953
All were licensed for service 16th November 1953

ROUTES OPERATED
471 Orpington – Green Street Green – Cudham – Knockholt Pound
Pratts Bottom – Green Street Green – Orpington Circular route in both
    directions
Operated from 16th November 1953 – 30th December 1966
479 Orpington – Leaves Green – Biggin Hill (Saturdays only)
Operated from 16th February 1963 – 15th June 1963
413B Chipstead – Riverhead – Sevenoaks Station (Monday to Friday peaks only)
Operated from 18th January 1961 – 25th April 1961

GS 23 is standing at the offloading point outside Orpington station after operating the full circular route via Pratts Bottom and Cudham. A long term resident at Dunton Green, the bus arrived in October 1956 after its first and remaining until withdrawn from service in December 1964. This shot probably dates from 1961 soon after the second and final overhaul. *Alan Charman collection*

Located on the main A21 Dunton Green garage was not on the direct route of any GS route. Buses for the 471 covered a nine minute run to and from Knockholt Pound to take up the line of the route. The 471 was longstanding route with origins as far back as the Penfold & Brody operation and became part of the reorganised routes from 1935. It was operated by the C Class, the November 1953 allocation consisting of five.

Dunton Green received GS 4 as its first GS on 5th November 1953, being sent as a type trainer and Alan Charman's father recalls driving the bus from Sevenoaks to Ide Hill and around the Pratts Bottom and Cudham loop of the 471. Three cubs were withdrawn on 16th November, the GSs all being licensed for service the same day. There had been a tentative plan to use GSs on at least part of the 413/413A timetable, but the route remained crew operated with RFs since loadings on a number of journeys would have exceeded the capacity of GSs. The final two Cubs were withdrawn on 1st December 1953 a two week period being maintained as a safety measure against possible problems with the new vehicles. The GSs then settled down to 13 years continuous work on the 471. Passenger loads into Orpington were consistently good, and since the section of the route between Knockholt Pound and Green Street Green via Cudham was not approved for RF operation, an intense service was run, mostly to a 30 minute headway in each direction round the circular route for much of the daytime. For much of the period of GS operation, Dunton Green did not have an operational spare vehicle such was the reliability of the GSs.

Ultimately three routes would be operated although the 479 and 413B did so for only a few months in each case.

The 471 routeing could be described as like a large frying pan, with the 'handle' being the section between Green Street Green and Orpington and the pan representing the circle through Cudham, Knockholt and Pratts Bottom. Today almost the whole route is contained within Greater London, but in 1953 it was very rural. From Orpington station where buses took their stand time parked in station approach, the 471 was the only bus route that worked from the station towards the local hospital and the significant housing developments along the Sevenoaks Road towards Green Street Green.

This led to the intense peak hour service to and from the station which required the peak vehicle run-out of five buses plus one RT from the Fort Halstead works services allocation. Four GSs returned to the garage after the morning run out, not being required until the afternoon when all four returned to service, a timetable which required a number of spreadover duties as can be seen from the operational driver roster.

Because of the remoteness from the garage, Green Street Green was the main crew changeover point, and a small café 'The Larches' was used by crews from the 51A, 471, and 854. Drivers for the 471, and later crews for the 854, travelled to and from Dunton Green on the 402 or, with special clearance, the 704. From 1959 the rosters of the 471 were amalgamated with the 404, 413 and 413A following the conversion of those routes to omo. This led to a number of joint duties where a driver woud work on both GS and RF on the same duty. At the same time, a change of ticket machine was made from the Gibson to Ultimate, and where a GS duty was combined with omo RF, the ticket machine used was an Ultimate. This was a major cost saving exercise as the number of drivers allocated to both routes was reduced from 22 to 20 and the number of expensive spreadover duties was halved.

Another early sixties view, this time of GS 16 calling at the stop for Orpington Hospital. The 471 was the only route that operated from Orpington Station to the Hospital, which resulted in additional short workings on Sundays and very often using an RT as well. GS 16 ended its life as a playbus and was eventually dismantled to provide spares for preserved GS 42. *Alan Cross*

A very good rear shot of well loaded GS 16, this time at the Glentrammon Road stop in Green Street Green, today the location of the Metrobus garage. The timing clock is visible that was used by the Central area routes 51 and 51A, as this was the point where the routes finally parted – the 51 to Farnborough Village and the 51A a short run to the Rose and Crown at Green Street Green. GS 16 would work from Dunton Green after its second overhaul in August 1960 until finally withdrawn in November 1964. *Mick Webber*

From Green Street Green, the route turns right at the roundabout with the A21 and follows Cudham Lane, which was always the busier of the two directions with houses for the first three miles followed by a short section of narrow road before reaching the village of Cudham. Until 1956, a school journey terminated at Cudham Church for children from the village who used the Primary School at Green Street Green. Falling numbers however removed the necessity for this trip which was run as a duplicate journey. Beyond Cudham, the normal circular continued for another two miles to Scotts Lodge, the road being narrow in places between high hedges. Here, the 471 turned sharp left at the top of the ridge towards Knockholt Pound. Scotts Lodge was a convenient turning point for an early morning service that worked back down through Cudham to provide the morning school bus to Green Street Green and additional capacity on the run into Orpington Station. This journey was well used and continued to operate until 1966. The route from Scotts Lodge ran through another rural section into Knockholt, with the Church, the Crown Inn, School and Village Hall, all of which supplied good passenger levels during the GS period. The Crown was the starting point for the afternoon peak hour bus on DG29, and was primarily for the children from Knockholt School going back towards Knockholt Pound where newly built housing had been erected immediately after the War. DG29 went to Kelvin Parade at Orpington rather than the station, a small parade of shops to the north of the station that was used by the 431, 471 and 477, mostly as a means of avoiding congestion on the station stand when it was full. The 471 bus from Kelvin Parade provided an empty bus at the stops in Station Road and Orpington War Memorial for passengers requiring Sevenoaks Road, Orpington Hospital and Green Street Green, since some buses coming down from the station might have limited space. In the evening peak there were up to seven additional short journeys between the Station and Green Street Green, three of which were operated by an RT as can be seen from the running number schedules included below.

Knockholt Pound is where the 471 met the 431 route, which was crew operated with RTs and worked from Orpington Station through Chelsfield and Halstead to Sevenoaks, passing Dunton Green garage. Knockholt Pound was a hive of activity around 8.00am with RTs on the 431 mixing with RTs on the Fort Halstead Works journeys and GSs on the 471. After these few brief moments each morning, it went back to the typical quiet rural village. Garage journeys on the 471 were unusual worked in service, the timetable allowing nine minutes down and ten up due to the long steep ascent of Star Hill from Dunton Green to Knockholt Pound. The timetable of the 431 however allowed nine minutes for both the ascent and descent of Star Hill. Even with accurately adjusted fuel injectors, the ascent with a good load of passengers on an RT could sometimes require first gear, so that the anomaly seems somewhat perverse.

At Knockholt Pound, the bus might take on several passengers at busier times before setting off down Rushmore Hill to Pratts Bottom. The 471 was the most direct route to Orpington, the 431 taking a little longer via Halstead and Chelsfield. After two miles the village of Pratts Bottom was reached where a few children used the 471 to reach the school there, although most of the children were local and in the 1950s and 1960s walked to school. The well-known independent Margo's Coaches of Bexleyheath operated a separate school bus to Orpington Secondary Modern that ran from Knockholt Pound through Pratts Bottom to Charterhouse Road and in the 1960s used one of their many former London Transport roof box bodied RTs. At Pratts Bottom, the route joined the main A21 to Green Street

Green. There was only one request stop on this two mile section, which was rarely used, and the GSs maintained a good speed along the main road and might catch up a little time if running late. Many passengers would be waiting at the stop at Green Street Green, Queens Head, served by the 402, 471 and 704. The 471 was the only route from Pratts Bottom into Orpington, the 402 and 704 continuing on the A21 to Bromley. From the Queens Head stop there would be steady and constant traffic back into Orpington Station where the bus would terminate before the next journey round the circle.

The journey time round the circle was 53 minutes, and when the main timetable ran with a 30 minutes headway in both directions, a bus left Orpington Station every 15 minutes on alternate clockwise and anti-clockwise journeys providing a frequent and convenient service on the route. This required four buses with the fifth operating at school and peak times. Only during mid-morning Monday to Friday – when four out of five buses returned to the garage after the peak period – was one bus required running alternate journeys every two hours. The only adjustment to the schedules during 1950s was the steady increase in the Orpington to Green Street Green short journeys, and the removal of the Cudham Church journey from the school duty that was covered by DG29. The Saturday timetable did not have the peak hour shorts but ran the 30-minute service in both directions around the circuit from lunchtime until mid-evening. The Sunday service during the 1950s ran to a similar timetable with four buses, but as Sunday passengers fell away from the mid-1950s the timetable progressively dropped first to an hourly service using two buses and with the winter 1960 schedules to just one working round the circle alternately.

Approaching Scotts Lodge from Knockholt, GS 52 is at the top of the North Downs Ridge and will now turn right and run down the long stretch of Cudham Lane towards Green Street Green and Orpington. Scotts Lodge was a turning point for a peak hour trip to provide an additional vehicle from Cudham to Orpington Station. GS 52 was allocated to DG from April 1963 for four months as a staff bus before becoming part of the operational fleet until its last day of operation in December 1966. *Mick Webber*

The Orpington Hospital traffic however remained on Sundays since it was an important day for hospital visitors and, as the main 471 timetable reduced, an RT was rostered for three short journeys to and from Green Street Green, the bus working to and from Sevenoaks as a 431A. The crew rosters for 22nd May 1959 show this duty as DG9. The duty commenced at 1.23pm at Dunton Green to run as a 471 into Sevenoaks before the 1.47pm 431A to Orpington. The journey into Sevenoaks is actually noted as running as a 471 despite the fact that this was never on the route, and it is difficult to believe that the crew wound up the 471 route number before changing to 431A at Sevenoaks. At Orpington, the three short journeys to Green Street Green were run before returning on the 3.47pm 431A to Sevenoaks. Here the crew came off for their break before taking over DG1 at 5.25pm on the 402. The crew which had worked on DG15 and CM1 on the 403 having come off at Sevenoaks then took DG9 back to Dunton Green to complete their shift.

DUNTON GREEN GS SCHEDULES – MAY 1959
MONDAY TO FRIDAY

TIME
DEPART

RUNNING NUMBER DG 8

471	6.55am	DUNTON GREEN Garage – ORPINGTON Stn via Cudham
471	7.49am	ORPINGTON Stn – ORPINGTON Stn via Pratts Bottom
471	8.51am	ORPINGTON Stn – ORPINGTON Stn via Pratts Bottom
471	9.56am	ORPINGTON Stn – ORPINGTON Stn via Pratts Bottom
471	10.56am	ORPINGTON Stn – ORPINGTON Stn via Cudham

DRIVER CHANGE AT GREEN STREET GREEN 11.05AM

471	11.56am	ORPINGTON Stn – ORPINGTON Stn via Pratts Bottom
471	12.56pm	ORPINGTON Stn – ORPINGTON Stn via Cudham

DRIVER CHANGE AT KNOCKHOLT POUND 1.28PM

471	1.56pm	ORPINGTON Stn – ORPINGTON Stn via Pratts Bottom
471	2.56pm	ORPINGTON Stn – ORPINGTON Stn via Pratts Bottom

DRIVER CHANGE AT GREEN STREET GREEN 3.39PM

471	3.56pm	ORPINGTON Stn – ORPINGTON Stn via Pratts Bottom

DRIVER CHANGE AT GREEN STREET GREEN 4.41PM

471	4.56pm	ORPINGTON Stn – ORPINGTON Stn via Pratts Bottom
471	5.59pm	ORPINGTON Stn – ORPINGTON Stn via Pratts Bottom

DRIVER CHANGE AT GREEN STREET GREEN 6.43PM

471	6.57pm	ORPINGTON Stn – ORPINGTON Stn via Pratts Bottom

TIME
DEPART

471	8.11pm	ORPINGTON Stn – ORPINGTON Stn via Pratts Bottom
471	9.31pm	ORPINGTON Stn – ORPINGTON Stn via Pratts Bottom
471	10.31pm	ORPINGTON Stn – DUNTON GREEN Garage via Cudham

RUNNING NUMBER DG 9

471	7.09am	DUNTON GREEN Garage – ORPINGTON via Pratts Bottom
471	7.59am	ORPINGTON Stn – ORPINGTON Stn via Cudham
471	9.11am	ORPINGTON Stn – DUNTON GREEN Garage via Cudham

SPREADOVER 9.52AM – 2.35PM

471	2.35pm	DUNTON GREEN Garage – ORPINGTON via Pratts Bottom
471	3.11pm	ORPINGTON Stn – ORPINGTON Stn via Cudham
471	4.14pm	ORPINGTON Stn – ORPINGTON Stn via Cudham

DRIVER CHANGE AT GREEN STREET GREEN 4.23PM

471	5.12pm	ORPINGTON Stn – ORPINGTON Stn via Cudham
471	6.11pm	ORPINGTON Stn – ORPINGTON Stn via Cudham
471	7.15pm	ORPINGTON Stn – DUNTON GREEN Garage via Cudham

RUNNING NUMBER DG 10

471	7.33am	DUNTON GREEN Garage – ORPINGTON via Pratts Bottom

471	8.21am	ORPINGTON Stn – ORPINGTON Stn via Pratts Bottom
471	9.26am	ORPINGTON – DUNTON GREEN Garage via Pratts Bottom

SPREADOVER 9.56AM – 2.37PM

471	2.37pm	DUNTON GREEN Garage – ORPINGTON Stn via Cudham
471	3.26pm	ORPINGTON Stn – ORPINGTON Stn via Pratts Bottom
471	4.26pm	ORPINGTON Stn – ORPINGTON Stn via Pratts Bottom
471	5.26pm	ORPINGTON Stn – ORPINGTON Stn via Pratts Bottom

DRIVER CHANGE AT GREEN STREET GREEN 5.35PM

471	6.35pm	ORPINGTON Stn – ORPINGTON Stn via Pratts Bottom
471	7.33pm	ORPINGTON – DUNTON GREEN Garage via Pratts Bottom

RUNNING NUMBER DG 11

471	7.39am	DUNTON GREEN Gar – ORPINGTON Stn via Cudham
471	8.36am	ORPINGTON Stn – ORPINGTON Stn via Cudham
471	9.41am	ORPINGTON Stn – DUNTON GREEN Gar via Cudham

DRIVER WORKS PM PART OF DUTY ON 404 / 413

471	12.56pm	DUNTON GREEN Gar – ORPINGTON Stn via Cudham
471	1.43pm	ORPINGTON Stn – ORPINGTON Stn via Cudham
471	2.41pm	ORPINGTON Stn – ORPINGTON Stn via Cudham
471	3.41pm	ORPINGTON Stn – ORPINGTON Stn via Cudham
471	4.41pm	ORPINGTON Stn – ORPINGTON Stn via Cudham

DRIVER CHANGE AT GREEN STREET GREEN 4.50PM

471	5.43pm	ORPINGTON Stn – ORPINGTON Kelvin Parade via Cudham
471	6.43pm	ORPINGTON Kelvin Parade – ORPINGTON Stn via Cudham
471	7.49pm	ORPINGTON Stn – ORPINGTON Stn via Cudham
471	8.59pm	ORPINGTON Stn – ORPINGTON Stn via Cudham
471	9.59pm	ORPINGTON Stn – ORPINGTON Stn via Cudham

RUNNING NUMBER DG 29

471	6.26am	DUNTON GRN Gar – ORPINGTON Stn via Cudham
471	7.37am	ORPINGTON Station– SCOTTS LODGE
471	8.07am	SCOTTS LODGE – ORPINGTON Station
471	8.37am	ORPINGTON Stn – DUNTON GREEN Garage via Cudham

SPREADOVER 9.07AM – 3.22PM

471	3.22pm Sch	DUNTON GREEN Garage– KNOCKHOLT Crown
471	3.41pm Sch	KNOCKHOLT Crown– ORPINGTON Kelvin Parade
471	4.23pm Sch	ORPINGTON Kelvin Parade – GREEN STREET GREEN
471	4.44pm Sch	GREEN STREET GREEN – ORPINGTON Station
471	4.19pm NSch	DUNTON GREEN Garage – KNOCKHOLT Crown
471	4.29pm NSch	KNOCKHOLT Crown– ORPINGTON Station
471	4.55pm	ORPINGTON Station – GREEN STREET GREEN
471	5.09pm	GREEN STREET GREEN – ORPINGTON Station
471	5.25pm	ORPINGTON Station – GREEN STREET GREEN
471	5.39pm	GREEN STREET GREEN – ORPINGTON Station
471	5.55pm	ORPINGTON Station – GREEN STREET GREEN
471	6.09pm	GREEN STREET GREEN – ORPINGTON Station
471	6.25pm	ORPINGTON Stn – DUNTON GREEN Garage via Cudham

RUNNING NUMBER DG 23*

431B	5.08pm	FORT HALSTEAD – ORPINGTON Station
471	5.42pm	ORPINGTON Station – GREEN STREET GREEN
471	5.54pm	GREEN STREET GREEN – ORPINGTON Station
471	6.11pm	ORPINGTON Station – GREEN STREET GREEN
471	6.23pm	GREEN STREET GREEN – ORPINGTON Station
471	6.43pm	ORPINGTON Station – GREEN STREET GREEN
471	6.55pm	GREEN STREET GREEN – ORPINGTON Station
431A	7.14pm	ORPINGTON Station – DUNTON GREEN Garage

Sch Schooldays Only NSch Not Schooldays

*DG 23 run by RT from 402 / Fort Halstead allocation

The 30 minute Saturday headway was altered to start after lunch in 1964, and in the winter schedules of 1965 was reduced to hourly in each direction all day. Other than this, almost no change was made to the timetable, even the two hourly Sunday service being maintained despite many rural routes having lost the Sunday service by then. No further changes were made until the final day of GS operation on Saturday 30th December 1966, RFs replacing GSs the following day. The last bus home that night was GS 62 working Duty DG10 at 11.00pm on a wet and windy night. Alan Charman went to Dunton Green to witness the last vehicle back and has had the pleasure to own GS 62. Each year it is driven round the 471 route, and both the Authors have been fortunate to drive it round the route a number of times in the past.

There were two unusual workings for the GS. One involved the bus on DG29 which was covered by a spreadover duty returning each morning to Dunton Green just after 9.00am. Every Friday, this bus was used to transport the week's takings to the bank in Sevenoaks, an additional 1 hour 15 minutes being allowed for the driver in the duty rota. Alan Charman recalls being with his father on a Friday when he was driving DG29 and the Garage Inspector wrote out a paper ticket for him to travel into Sevenoaks on a 431 or 402 as he was not allowed to travel on the GS with the cash. The thought of carrying a large amount of cash to pay into the bank in such a way would never be entertained today! The other working involved DG8 which was second bus out of the garage in the morning at 6.30 am and stayed out all day, not returning until 10.30pm at night. The 471 was a hilly route requiring a proportion of second and third gear running, and a full tank of fuel was required for the day's work. Occasionally the bus would actually run out of fuel on the run down Star Hill going back to the garage at night, so it was arranged that DG8 should exchange running plates with DG11 after it came into service during the afternoon and the buses met at Knockholt Pound. This sometimes involved an exchange of passengers but gave DG8 sufficient fuel for the rest of the day as DG11 was back in the garage by 7.30pm having covered less mileage. This arrangement lasted a few years until the duties were re-arranged to avoid such a long day for DG8.

In addition to the 471, Dunton Green operated two other routes, although both for only very short periods.

The 413B was introduced between Chipstead and Sevenoaks Station on 18th January 1961. The end to end running time was only nine minutes and was started in advance of the closure of the Dunton Green to Westerham branch railway line. The route was provided at the request of the Transport Users' Consultative Committee. The bus worked from The Square at Chipstead village to Riverhead and to Sevenoaks station where buses reversed into a side road of Hitchen Hatch Lane which was opposite the station. The timetable below shows the very limited timetable in the morning and evening peak on Monday to Friday only, running via Bessells Green to Chipstead in the morning, then direct back to Riverhead and the station. The routeing was reversed in the evening and the duty had running number DG32.

SEVENOAKS STATION – CHIPSTEAD												London Transport 413B
For Complete Service between Sevenoaks and Riverhead (direct) see pages 48 to 52												
MONDAY to FRIDAY ONLY											(TT.667)	
SEVENOAKS STATION	D	8 26	9 5	9 32	...	4 40	5 22	5 49	6 25	6 57	...	...
Riverhead St. Marys Church	7 30	8 30	9 9	9 36	...	4 44	5 26	5 53	6 29	7 1	...	...
Bessels Green Kings Head	7 32	8 32	9 11	G	...						...	...
CHIPSTEAD The Square	7 35	8 35	9 14	...	...	4 48	5 30	5 57	6 33	7 5	...	...
CHIPSTEAD The Square	7 40	8 2	8 40	9 19	...	...	4 53	5 35	6 2	6 38	7 10	...
Bessels Green Kings Head	...	...	...	...	...	D	4 56	5 38	6 5	6 41	7 13	...
Riverhead St. Marys Church	7 44	8 6	8 44	9 23	...	4 31	4 58	5 40	6 7	6 43	7 15	...
SEVENOAKS STATION	7 48	8 10	8 48	9 27	...	4 35	5 2	5 44	6 11	6 47	G	...

D–departs Dunton Green LT Garage 4 mins. earlier. G–Arrives Dunton Green LT Garage 4 mins. later.

The existing routes from Chipstead, 413, 413A and 454 all ran to Sevenoaks via Bat and Ball and the 413B was perhaps a welcome addition providing a direct service to Sevenoaks Station. The route however was a complete failure, not lasting beyond three months, the last day of operation being 25th April 1961. For this short period in 1961 it meant that the GS allocation required an extra bus. GS 30 had been transferred in November 1959, and on 15th February 1961 GS 38 arrived from overhaul. However on 1st March GS 30 was delicensed, and went for overhaul on 2nd May after the 413B had been withdrawn.

The second short lived route was the 479, introduced on 16th February 1963 to run between Biggin Hill and Orpington, its sole purpose to provide a facility for shoppers and hospital visitors into Orpington. Much has been written elsewhere

Early January 1963 and after a night of extensive snowfall two GSs were unable to complete their journey down Cudham Lane. They were 50 yards apart and it took three days to free them. *Alan Charman collection*

Parked in Sevenoaks Bus Station, GS 28 is covering the Friday morning duty from Dunton Green Garage to Sevenoaks in order to take coinage to and from the Bank. Ninety minutes was added to the Duty for DG29 on Friday only to cover this trip. GS 28 was part of the initial allocation to DG and this shot is probably from 1955, as the front screen grab handles have yet to be added. Another long term survivor, GS 28 was to become a staff bus in 1969, remaining with LT until finally withdrawn at Reigate in February 1973. *Alan Charman collection*

about this route, including London Transport's reluctance to operate it. It was principally that because the route was within the LPTA and 'Special Area', London Transport did not want any 'competition' from another operator. A bus service linking Biggin Hill to Orpington was first discussed by the Parish Council as far back as 1948 and continual pressure for a service was eventually to bear fruit, London Transport agreeing to operate a trial service. From Biggin Hill, the 410 and Green Line 705 maintained a frequent service into Bromley, Sevenoaks also being reached on the 705, but Orpington with its large hospital that catered for the community at Biggin Hill was a 90 minute trip, and with growing shopping facilities at Orpington, it had become increasingly very difficult for London Transport to continually ignore the requests for a service.

A three month trial service operated on Saturday only using a GS and was initially planned to commence before the 1962 Christmas period starting in November. The running number was DG32. GS 76 had been relicensed and sent to Guildford on 21st September 1962 as part of the many reallocations in the 1962 changes, having been in store at Romford. It was transferred to Dunton Geen on 17th October 1962 in preparation for the start of the 479 but suffered a major failure and was immediately delicensed. It would spend the next 18 months parked behind the vehicle wash in Dunton Green garage until finally sold in May 1964 having seen no further use. GS 19 was then transferred to Dunton Green from Windsor and the start of the 479 was delayed until February 1963. Those readers 'of a certain age' will remember the winter of 1962/1963 when heavy snow fell during Christmas week and would remain on the ground until early March. Such conditions were not the most auspicious time to start the trial of a shoppers' service, and conditions were so bad on the lanes of the 471 high on the North Downs that two GSs on the route were stuck in four and five feet deep drifts near Stag Lane in Cudham. It took three days before they could be dug out and released!

GS 22 in early May 1963 at Leaves Green on its way to Biggin Hill. This was the duplicate bus for the 479's first day of operation in February 1963 and was driven on both occasions by Alan Charman's father. There was always a good load of 12-15 people on each of the four journeys but this was deemed inadequate by LT and the service was withdrawn. GS 22 spent its first three years at Hertford, and after first overhaul was sent to DG until finally withdrawn in December 1964.
Alan Charman

February 16th 1963 – the first day of the 479 – was cold and damp when GS 16 inaugurated the service with GS 22 driven by Alan Charman's father as duplicate. Two London Transport officials in full uniform together with parish councillors travelled on the buses on that first run. The route ran via the main road past Biggin Hill airfield which by then was not operational but still in use for aircrew selection, and on into Leaves Green with its substantial population before turning right into Downe Road where the 479 shared about half a mile with the 146 from Bromley. It turned left into the very rural Shire Lane, along which for two or three miles the bus ran without a stop until arriving at the junction with A21 at Farnborough hill. The route crossed the main road, and down to Glentrammon Road at Green Street Green where the 479 met the 471 and could make connections with the 51, 51A, 402 and 705. The 479 then followed the 471 into Orpington Station. Four journeys were run in each direction, the bus starting and finishing at Biggin Hill which required a long run out of service to and from Dunton Green In addition to the first day, Alan Charman made three further trips, and the bus was usually well loaded especially the first service in the morning. London Transport however deemed it a failure and the route ran for the last time on Saturday 15th June 1963 being taken over by Orpington Rural Transport the following week.

It can be legitimately asked why it failed. As a shoppers' service, it missed out Orpington High Street, whereas double running to the loop at Chislehurst Road would have added only eight minutes overall. The main request was for a service to Orpington Hospital but where visiting times were very much geared to Sundays in 1963, and it would not have been difficult to roster two round trips to Biggin Hill from the 471 allocation on Sunday afternoon. The delay in starting the service until after Christmas 1962 did not help loadings, and the weather during the route's operation was probably the worst time for a trial service geared towards shoppers.

GS 19 entering Dunton Green garage after working the final 479 journey. The bus worked out of service from Biggin Hill to the garage, hence the Private blind. GS 19 was transferred in to DG to cover the 479 following the failure of GS 76, which on the date of this photograph was parked behind the wash facility inside the garage with a defective engine. On the main road and also about to enter the Garage is GS 52, which in June 1963 was working as a staff bus ferrying conductors to and from Dartford garage. *Alan Cross*

For most of the period 1954-1966 there were six GSs allocated, five for service and one spare. This was reduced to five during most of 1962 and 1963 when many GSs were taken out of service.

The schedule changes of 30th December 1966 saw changes at many garages. At Dunton Green, the 431, 431A and some Fort Halstead works journeys which had been run from the 431 allocation were converted from crew RT to omo RF. The night of 30th December was therefore one of great activity. Dunton Green's GS allocation had remained unchanged throughout 1966, and GS 10, 52, 55, 56, 59, and 62 were all delicensed that evening, as well as RT 3220 and RT 3901 having completed their day on the 431 for the last time. To replace the GSs and convert the 431, seven RFs were transferred in. RF 242 and 251 came from Harlow, RF 243 from Hertford, RF 187 and 210 from Reigate, and RF 117 from Northfleet. These were all former Green Line coaches among many that had by then been converted to omo bus status. The movement records show the RFs coming from the garages as noted, but in fact, they were all assembled at Grays that morning, and in the late afternoon of 30th December, Grays ferry drivers drove all seven RFs to Dunton Green. They then waited until the GSs came in after service. As soon as they arrived, the blinds were removed, and driven straight away to Grays for storage. Alan Charman recalls being there that evening and seeing GS 62 come in last just after 11.00pm having worked DG10 back in for the last time. Its blinds were removed and it was quickly driven away. A spare Grays driver had travelled to Dunton Green on one of the RFs, leaving two spare drivers to take the RTs also withdrawn that night back to Grays for storage. Three of Dunton Green's other RTs were transferred for further service; RT 1097 and 1616 to Dartford, and RT 2741 to East Grinstead.

Of the six GSs displaced, GS 10 saw a short period at Northfleet for a few months in 1967 and GS 52 and 55 would become two of Hertford's last in November 1968. GS 55 was reprieved again to spend a last few weeks at Northfleet in September 1969 before their final replacement on the 451 and 490. GS 56 and 59 remained in store and were sold towards the end of 1969. GS 62, along with GS 10 would outlast the others being used for periods as staff buses until both were sold in October 1973. Both buses are referred to in chapter seven in the section describing staff buses.

A cold wet day on Saturday 30th December 1966 finds GS 62 working as DG 10 at the first stop in Cudham Lane opposite the Rose and Crown in Green Street Green. This was the final day of GS working on the 471 and GS 62 was to be the final bus into the garage at 11pm that night. Blinds were removed and a ferry driver was on hand to take the bus to Grays garage for storage. I was not to know that 28 years later I would become the owner of GS 62. *Alan Charman*

EAST GRINSTEAD

INITIAL ALLOCATION
GS 58 and 59 allocated 11th December 1953
Entered service 16th December 1953

ROUTES OPERATED
494 East Grinstead – Lingfield – Crowhurst – Tandridge – Oxted
Operated from 16th December 1953 – 5th May 1964.

PEAK VEHICLE REQUIREMENT   One bus

Another former East Surrey garage, East Grinstead dated from the 1920s and served the trunk route 409 to Croydon, and the 424 route to Reigate. It also provided some short journeys on the 434, the main service being provided by Crawley garage. Single deck routes stretched as far as Edenbridge, Crawley and Horsham, and a Green Line service began in 1931. With the formation of the L.P.T.B., East Grinstead became a border town, services from Southdown, Maidstone and District and the Independent East Grinstead Motor services.

The 494 was started on 7th January 1948 after a period of lobbying by residents in Crowhurst and Tandridge who at the time had no bus service to either Oxted or East Grinstead. One Cub was allocated to the route which ran six journeys each weekday, and five on Sundays. One morning arrival into Oxted at 11.31am did not leave to return to East Grinstead until 12.09pm to allow a short period for basic shopping.

Maintenance on the Cub fleet was becoming more difficult, and in 1951, a rear engine CR class was allocated. CR 14 ran the 494 until shortly before the GSs arrived, being finally delicensed on 1st November 1953 and replaced on the same day by C 25 which had only recently come out of service at Chelsham. CR 14 was sent to Reigate for storage on 9th Nov 1953. GS 58 and 59 arrived on Friday 11th December 1953, and after a short period of driver training they entered service from Wednesday 16th December 1953. The garage's last cub, C 25, was finally delicensed and withdrawn on 1st January 1954 and was then sent to Reigate for storage.

The 494 started from King Street Bus Station, driver's meal reliefs being taken only at East Grinstead garage, a few minutes' drive away. After picking up at the stops in the High Street, the route ran along the Lingfield road through Baldwins Hill and Felcourt before reaching Lingfield. This section paralleled the 428 route which in the 1950s ran to a 30-minute headway for much of the day. After Lingfield, the 494 ran out into the Surrey countryside, through Crowhurst village before making the sharp right turn at the T junction by the Brickmakers Arms and passing under the narrow bridge of the Redhill to Tonbridge railway line. At Tandridge, the route climbed steeply up through the village before joining the A25 and running down through Old Oxted (today's by-pass being non-existent in 1954) into Oxted Station where the route terminated by the west side entrance working in anti-clockwise and taking stand time opposite the station. Here the 494 would often meet with a 464 whilst on relief using the same stand. Only one bus was required to work the service but due to the timetable running seven days each week it was necessary to have a second vehicle allocated for engineering purposes.

In August 1954, the bus worked from 7.42am to 3.09pm and 3.25pm to 10.37pm. On Sundays, the morning working was 10.36am to 3.09pm, the afternoon working being the same as during the week. It was common practice on the majority of routes in the 1950s that after a later start on Sunday mornings, the timetable for the remainder of the day was almost identical to that on weekdays.

GS 58 was the first bus to go for overhaul on 24th April 1957, to be replaced by GS 26 from Amersham. After overhaul, GS 58 was sent back to Reigate for two months before being relicensed and returned to East Grinstead on 1st August. GS 59 went for overhaul on 1st May 1957, and returned on 14th June. It was replaced by GS 32 which arrived on 1st May also from Amersham, and noted in the daily records officially as 'float bus', GS 26 being the bus formally allocated for the 494. GS 58 remained at East Grinstead for a lengthy period before being sent for its second overhaul on 14th May 1962 and was replaced by GS 47 which was fresh from overhaul but had spent two weeks at Harrow Weald as temporary staff transport. GS 58 returned to Reigate on 12th July before transfer to Northfleet on 9th August.

GS 59 went for second overhaul on 14th June 1962, GS 39 coming in from Amersham the same day as replacement. It returned on 5th September and was sent to Northfleet on 21st September for five days as temporary replacement for GS 57. It returned on 26th September, GS 47 replacing it in turn at Northfleet. GS 39 stayed as the spare bus until going to Dorking in February 1963 after which GS 59 remained the only bus allocated. Such was their reliability however, that failure was rare, and the 494 was by then approved for RF anyway so that there was no need for a spare GS. Apart from two overhauls and the five days at Northfleet, GS 59 would remain at East Grinstead until the 494 was converted to RF on 6th May 1964, and was delicensed on the completion of its final day on the route. It had the distinction of having spent the longest period at one garage, GS 53 at Northfleet being the bus that achieved the longest period of all. It remained in store at East Grinstead for three months before being relicensed and transferred to Dunton Green on 1st August.

King Street bus station in East Grinstead finds GS 59 working the 494 as EG14. Apart from time out for overhauls, GS 59 was to remain at this garage until the 494 was converted to RF in May 1964. After three months unlicensed at EG, the bus transferred to Dunton Green until withdrawn in August 1964 and sent to Grays for storage.

CHELSHAM

INITIAL ALLOCATION
GS 1 and 3 allocated 14th October 1953
GS 9 allocated 16th October 1953
GS 13 and 14 allocated 21st October 1953
GS 6, 11 and 15 allocated 22nd October 1953
GS 7 and 10 allocated 26th October 1953
All entered service on 26th October 1953

ROUTES OPERATED
464, 465, 485, 26th October 1953 – 23rd October 1962
453 (school and odd journeys only)
400 New Addington – Warlingham Park Hospital (Sundays only)
Operated from 22nd June 1958 – 26th October 1958

PEAK VEHICLE REQUIREMENT   Eight buses

October 1953 and GS 1 is parked in the yard at Chelsham garage beside one of the withdrawn Cubs. It is always possible that the GS entered service before 26th October as all three buses in this picture look to have been in service. GS 1 was to spend its entire life at CM being withdrawn in October 1962 and sold on to Tillingbourne in March 1963 for use in the Guildford area.
Michael Dryhurst

   Chelsham garage was based on the ridge to the east of Warlingham and approximately five miles from the centre of the GS operated routes at Oxted. The GSs took over from Leyland Cubs on 26th October 1953, Chelsham's entire allocation consisting of C 4, 24, 25, 32, 59, 61, 82 and 90, all being delicensed on that day. They were replaced by GS 1, 3, 6, 7, 9, 10, 11, 13, 14 and 15. The records indicate that although GS 15 arrived with the main allocation, it was not licensed for service until 1st February 1954. The allocation of 10 buses provided the additional vehicle to cover the possibility of engineering issues with the new buses. The Cubs were replaced on a one for one basis using the existing 1953 timetable which meant that a number of early morning and school journeys were duplicated. It was not until 1955 that the opportunity was taken to rationalise some of the peak hour journeys although the number of vehicles remained at eight.

GS 6 has arrived at Westerham as 464 from Holland and Oxted using the lazy blind display for the full 464 route. A blind change and the bus is ready to leave on the 485 to Edenbridge where a further change of route to the 465 will send it back to Holland as a 465. Two hours 30 minutes was needed for the full round trip, a good example of the flexibility of the Country area schedules, where buses changed routes on a regular basis. GS 6 was a CM bus from 1953 until October 1962, taking time out for two overhauls, a few months at Dorking and then being downgraded to trainer at WR and GR until sold in July 1963 to Tillingbourne.
Michael Wickham collection

464/465 ran Holland, Broadbridge Green, Old Oxted, Oxted High St, then via Gresham Road to Limpsfield Village to the A25 before turning towards Edenbridge through Limpsfield Chart and Crockham Hill, where the two routes diverged. The 464 turned left up a climb towards Hosey Common before dropping down into Westerham. The 465 descended through Crockham Hill village towards Edenbridge, reversing at the south end of the High Street into Hever Road opposite the 'Star Inn'. In later years, the reverse at Hever Road was replaced by a short run along Hever Road to turn on the forecourt of Maidstone and District's small garage.

485 (Edenbridge to Westerham via Crockham Hill) was introduced 29th May 1946 as one of the first route enhancements after the end of World War Two.

The origins of a bus route to Oxted were founded in an East Surrey route 34 which ran as far as Hurst Green through Oxted from Edenbridge and was the precursor of the 434. The 465 came about as a replacement for the pre-war Green Line route F which had been withdrawn on 1st September 1939. When the Green Line route was reinstated in 1946 it was numbered 707 and terminated at Oxted; hence the introduction of the 465.

The three routes were combined to allow a cleverly designed timetable to operate with a maximum of efficiency. A 464 worked out from Holland to Westerham from where it became a 485 to Edenbridge running back to Holland as a 465. A second bus worked in the opposite direction. Each route ran to a regular two hourly headway, the timetable being designed to provide an hourly headway between Holland and Crockham Hill. On the legs to Westerham and Edenbridge there were alternate 30 and 90 minute gaps. In 1953, the round trip took two hours ten minutes. During the day additional buses worked short journeys from Holland to Chart, and from Holland a new estate at Chalkpit Wood only four minutes' journey time from Oxted and which was shown on the blind as 'Barrow Green Road'. Peak hour services primarily for local schools worked to Staffhurst Wood south of Hurst Green and Holland in order to serve Merle Common School. These were always operated as 465 inbound although services leaving Staffhurst Wood were very often blinded as 464 since they ran to Limpsfield or Oxted. Anecdotal evidence has suggested that the children were taught the number 465 during their lessons as so many of them originated from Hurst Green and caught one of the four buses that would head for Staffhurst Wood during the morning. Buses from Oxted and Staffhurst Wood would travel to the Primary School at Limpsfield Common, some buses from Staffhurst Wood via Holland Lane others via Pollards Oak which was a growing new estate built around Hurst Green railway station. Limpsfield Common School was located on the A25 facing Westerham, and to avoid the children having to cross a busy main road, the school journey buses set down outside the school. They then returned by crossing the carriageway to run via the small lane through Limpsfield Chart Golf Course known as Golf Links Road in order to return to Holland via Pollards Oak, or in the case of one journey, to Limpsfield Chart.

A well-loaded GS 10 on the roster as CM 21, which only worked one journey to Edenbridge as the 12.54pm from Holland arriving at Edenbridge at 1.40 pm, usually turning at the Maidstone and District garage in Hever Road. GS 10 was at CM until its first overhaul in June 1956, when it transferred to Hertford, finally ending its time as a staff bus at Plumstead and Reigate. Withdrawn at Chiswick in October 1973, it now resides in Belgium and has been seen painted white on wedding duty in Bruges during 2018. *J H Aston*

The classic Oxted scene from the early 1960s, with GS 1 working a peak hour service to Tatsfield and RLH 45 loading for Godstone, Redhill and Reigate. The Tatsfield destination was added to the blind schedule in October 1959 to cover amendments made to the routeing of 707 Green Line services. The RLH was required due to the low bridge at Oxted Station.
Alan Cross

The duty roster below is dated October 1955 and represents the first changes made after introduction of the GSs. Eight vehicles remain rostered but the second duplicated service in the morning has been removed from the early morning service to Holland. Originally four Cubs had provided 80 seats and these were now replaced by three GS offering 78 seats, thus providing one bus to strengthen schools journeys to Limpsfield. Following the long 1958 strike, there was the pressure to reduce costs, and this service was removed resulting in the first reduction in the peak vehicle requirement to seven. At the same time a service was introduced where one bus per hour when leaving Holland would double run through Pollards Oak, offering a direct service to Oxted. Further reductions took place in 1960 which reduced the peak vehicle requirement to six and the Green Line RF which ran a positioning journey as a 464 prior to taking up service on the 707 was diverted via Tatsfield as replacement. On Saturday the regular round trip service 464/485/465 remained with short journeys to Chart maintaining the 20 minute headway across the core route from Chart to Holland. The Sunday timetable was progressively reduced through the late 1950s but it was perhaps surprising how well the timetable was maintained with four buses working the round trip service up to 1960 and only being reduced in 1961 to three.

Operating from Holland to Chart Church is GS 8, the core service operated from Holland and Hurst Green through Oxted to Westerham and Edenbridge with swingers operated from Holland to Limpsfield Chart, Oxted Station and Barrow Green Road, which gave a 20-minute service between Oxted and Hurst Green. GS 8 is loading at Oxted beside the unusual concrete shelter. GS 8 arrived at Chelsham in May 1956 after first overhaul and remained until October 1962 when it went into store at Northfleet until sold in May 1963. *A D Packer*

Having been part of Chelsham's initial allocation, GS 11 went to Dorking at the end of 1954, returning to Chelsham on 27th April 1956 after its first overhaul. It remained there until October 1962 when it was delicensed and stored at Northfleet awaiting sale. The blind illustrates London Transport's rather idiosyncratic policy of not showing the final destination in larger letters where a route was indirect and an alternative service took a more direct route – in this case the 410 which went along the A25 between Limpsfield Common and Westerham. GS 11 has stopped in Limpsfield village on a journey from Westerham.

The schedule below shows the RF peak vehicle requirement in 1963 when their larger capacity was used to reduce the frequency.

PEAK VEHICLE REQUIREMENT

	Monday to Friday	Saturday	Sunday	
1952	7	6	5	
1953	8	6	5	
1954	8	6	5	
1955-7	8	6	5	
1958	7	7	4	
			1	400 Sunday
	1			453 CM 44
1959-60	8	6	4	453 CM 44
1961-62	7	5	3	
1963 (RF)	5	4	3	453 Duplicate removed

In 1958 there were new routes allocated for GS operation.

The 453 from Warlingham Green to Caterham via Whyteleafe was a crew operated route but it became necessary to introduce a duplicate to the normal service to cater for schools traffic into Whyteleafe. This was run with a GS allocated running number CM44. Initially the duplicate bus worked to Caterham-on-the-Hill but in 1961 cut back to turn at Whyteleafe Salmons Lane. By turning at Whyteleafe it was possible to make two journeys and this can be seen in the attached annual run out schedule. The 453 duplicate did not continue after 24th October and was withdrawn with the end of GS operation.

21st October 1961 and GS 1 is coming up the Hill to its terminal point at Westerham where it will change the blind to a 464 and work back to either Holland or the Limpsfield Schools service via Pollards Oak , GS 1 would be purchased by Tillingbourne Valley in 1963 for use in the Guildford area before becoming a regular at the Country Bus Rallies running days.
Peter Mitchell

The 400 was introduced to provide a link between the large new estates at New Addington and Warlingham Hospital, to run on Sunday afternoon only as a non-stop service for hospital visitors. It ran via Fickleshole Road and had originally been intended to start in May 1958, during the period of the strike. Its start was therefore delayed and the first Sunday of operation was 22nd June. It was a complete failure and never attracted sufficient passengers to a route which provided such a limited facility of just one return journey. It ran for the last time on Sunday 26th October.

With a maximum run-out of eight buses, Chelsham had ten from the beginning. On 22nd March 1954, GS 15 was delicensed and sent to Reigate until 1st June when it was relicensed and returned. The reason for this is not known unless GS 15 suffered some minor problem. Other than that Chelsham's allocation remained unchanged until 13th April 1955 when GS 45 was allocated for two weeks before going to Dunton Green. The trials with the revised differential on the southern area hilly routes are described in chapter seven. On 10th October 1955 GS 1 was delicensed and remained out of use until it was sent for its first overhaul on 23rd February 1956, but there is no record as to why it remained delicensed for such a lengthy period. It was replaced by GS 37 from Dorking, but only for two weeks before it was sent to Reigate, GS 47 transferring to Chelsham from Northfleet. On 15th March GS 4 arrived fresh from overhaul having been at Amersham beforehand, and would remain at Chelsham for the rest of its service life.

The 400 was introduced as a Sunday afternoon service between New Addington estate and Warlingham Park Hospital. Originally planned to start on 18th May 1958, it was delayed due to the six week strike, finally starting on 22nd June. The service consisted of just one return journey arriving at the hospital at 2.00pm, returning at 4.10pm at the end of visiting times. It was a complete failure and was withdrawn after operation on Sunday 26th October. GS 38 arrived at Chelsham on 25th October 1956 after its first overhaul and was delicensed on 1st January 1960, later spending four years at Dunton Green. *Ron Wellings*

```
------L----CM-----
        ⌐530¬
·403·
WESTERHAM
CHELSHAM
—464—
OXTED STN
464  VIA
     OLD OXTED
HOLLAND
—464—
LIMPSFIELD SCHOOLS
464  VIA
     OLD OXTED
OXTED BARROW GREEN
          ROAD
464    AND
      HOLLAND
OXTED BARROW GREEN &
        ROAD
464 HOLLAND
VIA POLLARDS OAK
OXTED STN &
464 HOLLAND
VIA POLLARDS OAK
465 OXTED CHART
    POLLARDS OAK
HOLLAND
465 OXTED CHART
    CROCKHAM HILL
EDENBRIDGE
485  VIA
    CROCKHAM HILL
WESTERHAM
CHART CHURCH
464  OXTED
     LIMPSFIELD
OXTED
LIMPSFIELD
464 CROCKHAM HILL
    WESTERHAM
CROCKHAM HILL
LIMPSFIELD
464 OXTED
    HOLLAND
CROCKHAM HILL
OXTED
464 POLLARDS OAK
    LIMPSFIELD SCHOOLS
465 OXTED
    POLLARDS OAK
STAFFHURST WOOD
465 OXTED
    HOLLAND
LIMPSFIELD SCHOOLS
```

GS 3 was the first of Chelsham's original allocation to be called in for overhaul, having gone to Works on 1st January 1956. During the following five months, all of the original allocation went for overhaul, the sequence being GS 3, 1, 11, 6, 7, 9, 14, 15, 13, and GS 10, the last on 17th May. Following overhaul, GS 1, 3, 6, 7, 10 and 11 returned to Chelsham, GS 9, 14 and 15 went to Hertford and GS 13 to Swanley. GS 8 arrived on 4th May after overhaul from Hitchin. On 16th January 1957, GS 40 arrived from overhaul to release GS 47 which had acted as permanent cover during 1955. It returned from overhaul on 21st March, allowing GS 40 to go to Epping where it had been from new. There were no other changes until GS 4 was delicensed for two months in June and July 1958, following which it spent short periods in and out of service until delicensed on 1st May 1959, remaining out of use until going for second overhaul in August. Chelsham's buses were called in for second overhaul in the second half of 1959, GS 26 and 51 being received as cover. GS 9 went to Hertford in 1959, GS 81 coming in as replacement.

There were few further changes, until the complete replacement of Chelsham's GS fleet in October 1962. Its allocation had been the largest after Amersham. GS 1, 3, 6, and 7 spent their whole service life with London Transport based there, and apart from vehicles being drafted in to cover the overhaul cycle, it had had the most stable allocation of any garage. There was only one difficult engineering issue which related to Chelsham being the coldest garage within London Transport. In the early months in service during the winter of 1953–1954, the Perkins Engines turned the cold oil into a substance resembling black treacle and during the morning run down to Oxted with oil pumps failing to circulate the thick cold oil, a number of engines seized. This was an early issue for many garages, but was most pronounced at Chelsham, and was overcome with a change of oil type and a light warming within the garage to prevent the vehicles from the extreme cold.

The end came on 23rd October 1962 when the GSs were replaced the following day by the RFs that had been made available from Green Line services after introduction of the RMCs. In preparation for the changeover, RF 308, newly converted from Green Line coach to omo bus, arrived at Chelsham on 1st October 1962 as a driver trainer. Although Chelsham operated RFs on their Green Line routes, the rosters for the GS duties were separate, and although some of the GS drivers might occasionally drive an RF to cover for a regular driver, or on a duplicate, most drivers probably remained unfamiliar with the RF. The replacement RFs had been stored around various garages, and on the day of the changeover, Chelsham had received RF 309 from Reigate, 310 from Dunton Green, 311 from East Grinstead, and 313 from Staines which, with RF 308 provided five RFs for the new schedules. GS 1, 3, and 4 went to Reigate, GS 7,8,11 and 81 to Northfleet. GS 6 was the only one to be transferred for further service at Dorking, but was delicensed in February 1963 to spend two months as a training bus before withdrawal. None of Chelsham's GSs saw further service and were all sold in 1963, the only exception being GS 81, which languished in store at Northfleet for two years before sale on 16th October 1964 to a Mr C J Mayhew at Bromley. The last day of Chelsham's GSs was almost exactly nine years to the day since their first day in service, and the loud whine of a GS climbing Crockham Hill and Titsey Hill would not be heard again.

This blind schedule is dated March 1958 and would have been prepared prior to the introduction of the services through Pollards Oak. Later inserts were provided for the short lived 400, 453 school duplicate journeys and the diversion of the 464 through Tatsfield. Of interest are the Staffhurst Wood inbound journeys blinded only as 465, and the use of lazy blind sections for the 464 to and from Holland and Westerham. *R J Williamson*

GS 1 again when the A 25 ran through Old Oxted before the by pass was built. The blind panel shows it to be a short working to Oxted Station that has worked the double run through the Pollards Oak Estate which was introduced in 1958. *Peter Aves collection*

GS 7 is laying over in the side road outside of Chelsham Garage having worked CM 43 on its morning school duty, GS 7 would be sold to Southern Motorways in 1963 and would eventually be broken up for spares primarily to restore and maintain GS 2. *Colin Rivers collection*

CHELSHAM GS SCHEDULES – 16TH OCTOBER 1955

MONDAY TO FRIDAY

ROUTE NUMBER	TIME DEPART	FROM	TO
RUNNING NUMBER CM 18			
464	7.41am	CHELSHAM GARAGE	HOLLAND
464	8.21am	HOLLAND	CHART
464	8.49am	CHART	STAFFHURST WOOD
464	9.25am	STAFFHURST WOOD	CHART
464	10.10am	CHART	HOLLAND
464	10.40am	HOLLAND	OXTED STN East
MEAL RELIEF BREAK OXTED			
464	11.36am	OXTED STN East	HOLLAND
464	11.54am	HOLLAND	WESTERHAM
485	12.45am	WESTERHAM	EDENBRIDGE
465	1.21pm	EDENBRIDGE	HOLLAND
464	2.09pm	HOLLAND	BARROW GREEN RD
464	2.32pm	BARROW GREEN RD	HOLLAND
465	2.55pm	HOLLAND	EDENBRIDGE
485	3.45pm	EDENBRIDGE	WESTERHAM
464	4.20pm	WESTERHAM	HOLLAND
464	5.09pm	HOLLAND	OXTED STN East
464	5.36pm	OXTED STN East	HOLLAND
464	5.58pm	HOLLAND	WESTERHAM
485	6.50pm	WESTERHAM	EDENBRIDGE
465	7.21pm	EDENBRIDGE	HOLLAND
464	8.24pm	HOLLAND	CHART
464	9.10am	CHART	HOLLAND
464	9.39pm	HOLLAND	CHELSHAM GARAGE
RUNNING NUMBER CM 19			
464	7.23am	CHELSHAM GARAGE	HOLLAND
464	8.10am	HOLLAND	CHART
464	8.39am	CHART	STAFFHURST WOOD
LIGHT	9.13am	STAFFHURST WOOD	HOLLAND
464	9.39am	HOLLAND	OXTED Police Stn
464	10.06am	OXTED Police Stn	HOLLAND
464	10.24am	HOLLAND	CHART
464	11.10am	CHART	HOLLAND
464	11.39am	HOLLAND	BARROW GREEN RD
464	12.02pm	BARROW GREEN RD	HOLLAND
464	12.24pm	HOLLAND	CHART
464	1.10pm	CHART	HOLLAND
464	1.39pm	HOLLAND	CHELSHAM GARAGE
464	3.01pm	CHELSHAM GARAGE	STAFFHURST WOOD
464	3.45pm	STAFFHURST WOOD	CHART
464	4.25pm	CHART	HOLLAND
465	4.54pm	HOLLAND	EDENBRIDGE
485	5.45pm	EDENBRIDGE	WESTERHAM
464	6.20pm	WESTERHAM	HOLLAND
464	7.24pm	HOLLAND	CHART
464	8.10pm	CHART	HOLLAND
465	8.54pm	HOLLAND	EDENBRIDGE
485	9.45pm	EDENBRIDGE	WESTERHAM
464	10.30pm	WESTERHAM	CHELSHAM GARAGE

ROUTE NUMBER	TIME DEPART	FROM	TO
RUNNING NUMBER CM 20			
464	8.11am	CHELSHAM GARAGE	LIMPSFIELD COM.
LIGHT	8.54am	LIMPSFIELD COM.	OXTED Police Stn
465	9.08am	OXTED Police Stn	EDENBRIDGE
485	9.45am	EDENBRIDGE	WESTERHAM
464	10.30am	WESTERHAM	HOLLAND
464	11.09am	HOLLAND	OXTED Police Stn
464	11.55am	OXTED Police Stn	CHELSHAM GARAGE
464	2.55pm	CHELSHAM GARAGE	LIMPSFIELD COM.
465	3.31pm	LIMPSFIELD COM.	STAFFHURST WOOD
464	3,49pm	STAFFHURST WOOD	WESTERHAM
465	4.45pm	WESTERHAM	EDENBRIDGE
485	5.21pm	EDENBRIDGE	HOLLAND
464	6.09pm	HOLLAND	BARROW GREEN RD
464	6.32pm	BARROW GREEN RD	HOLLAND
465	6.54pm	HOLLAND	EDENBRIDGE
485	7.45pm	EDENBRIDGE	WESTERHAM
464	8.20pm	WESTERHAM	HOLLAND
464	9.29pm	HOLLAND	CHART
464	9.58pm	CHART	CHELSHAM GARAGE
RUNNING NUMBER CM 21			
464	8.20am	CHELSHAM GAR – Pollards Oak – LIMPSFIELD COMMON	
464	9.05am	LIMPSFIELD COMMON – Holland – OXTED Police Stn	
464	9.29am	OXTED Police Stn	HOLLAND
464	9.54am	HOLLAND	WESTERHAM
485	10.50am	WESTERHAM	EDENBRIDGE
465	11.21am	EDENBRIDGE	HOLLAND
464	12.09pm	HOLLAND	OXTED Police Stn
464	12.36pm	OXTED Police Stn	HOLLAND
465	12.54pm	HOLLAND	EDENBRIDGE
485	1.45pm	EDENBRIDGE	WESTERHAM
464	2.20pm	WESTERHAM	HOLLAND
464	3.09pm	HOLLAND	OXTED Police Stn
465	3.31pm	OXTED Police Stn	STAFFHURST WOOD
465	3.54pm	STAFFHURST WOOD	LIMPSFIELD COM.
465	4.11pm	LIMPSFIELD COM – Holland – OXTED Police Stn	
464	4.31pm W	OXTED Police Stn	CHELSHAM GARAGE
464	5.05pm NW	OXTED Police Stn	CHART
464	5.20pm NW	CHART	CHELSHAM GARAGE
RUNNING NUMBER CM 42			
464	6.37am	CHELSHAM GARAGE	CHART
464	7.06am	CHART	HOLLAND
465	7.43am	HOLLAND	EDENBRIDGE
465	8.33am Sch	EDENBRIDGE	STAFFHURST WOOD
465	9.26am Sch	STAFFHURST WOOD	CHELSHAM GARAGE
464	8.33am NSch	EDENBRIDGE	HOLLAND

Route	Time	From	To
464	9.31am NSch	HOLLAND	CHELSHAM GARAGE
Light	10.42am	CHELSHAM GARAGE	OXTED Police Stn
464	11.06am	OXTED Police Stn	HOLLAND
464	11.24am	HOLLAND	CHART
464	11.24am	HOLLAND	CHART
464	12.10pm	CHART	HOLLAND
464	12.39pm	HOLLAND	OXTED Police Stn
464	1.06pm	OXTED Police Stn	HOLLAND
464	1.24pm	HOLLAND	CHART
464	2.10pm	CHART	HOLLAND
464	2.39pm	HOLLAND	OXTED STN East
Light	3.11pm	OXTED STN East	CHELSHAM GARAGE
Light	3.42pm	CHELSHAM GARAGE	OXTED Police Stn
464	4.06pm	OXTED Police Stn	HOLLAND
464	4.24pm	HOLLAND	CHART
464	5.10pm	CHART	HOLLAND
464	5.39pm	HOLLAND	OXTED STN East
464	6.06pm	OXTED STN East	HOLLAND
464	6.29pm	HOLLAND	CHART
464	7.10pm	CHART	HOLLAND
464	7.54pm	HOLLAND	WESTERHAM
485	8.45pm	WESTERHAM	EDENBRIDGE
465	9.21pm	EDENBRIDGE	HOLLAND
464	10.09pm	HOLLAND	CHELSHAM GARAGE

RUNNING NUMBER CM 43

Route	Time	From	To
403	6.59am	CHELSHAM GARAGE	WESTERHAM
464	7.19am	WESTERHAM	OXTED STN east
464	7.58am	OXTED STN east	HOLLAND
464	8.18am	HOLLAND	OXTED Police Stn
465	8.36am	OXTED Pol Stn – Holland – LIMPSFIELD COMMON	
465	9.01am	LIMPSFIELD COMMON	STAFFHURST WOOD
		VIA POLLARDS OAK AND HOLLAND	
464	9.18am	STAFFHURST WOOD	CHELSHAM GARAGE
464	2.43pm	CHELSHAM GARAGE	HOLLAND

Route	Time	From	To
464	3.31pm	HOLLAND	CHART
464	4.10pm	CHART	HOLLAND
464	4.39pm	HOLLAND	OXTED STN East
464	5.06pm	OXTED STN East	HOLLAND
464	5.29pm	HOLLAND	CHART
464	6.10pm	CHART	HOLLAND
464	6.53pm	HOLLAND	CHELSHAM GARAGE

RUNNING NUMBER CM 44

Route	Time	From	To
Light	7.14am	CHELSHAM GARAGE	OXTED STN East
464	7.39am	OXTED STN East – Holland – WESTERHAM	
464	8.14am	WESTERHAM – Oxted – Holland – LIMPSFIELD COM.	
464	9.10am	LIMPSFIELD COM.	CHART
464	9.29am	CHART	HOLLAND
464	10.09am	HOLLAND	BARROW GREEN RD
464	10.32am	BARROW GREEN RD	HOLLAND
464	10.54am	HOLLAND	EDENBRIDGE
464	11.45am	EDENBRIDGE	WESTERHAM
464	12.20pm	WESTERHAM	HOLLAND
464	1.09pm	HOLLAND	OXTED STN East

MEAL RELIEF OXTED

Route	Time	From	To
464	2.06pm	OXTED STN East	HOLLAND
464	2.24pm	HOLLAND	CHART
464	3.10pm	CHART	HOLLAND
464	3.39pm	HOLLAND	BARROW GREEN RD
464	4.02pm	BARROW GREEN RD	OXTED STN East
464	4.10pm	OXTED STN East	CHELSHAM GARAGE

RUNNING NUMBER CM 45

Route	Time	From	To
Light	1.13pm	CHELSHAM GARAGE	OXTED Police Stn
464	1.36pm	OXTED Police Stn	HOLLAND
464	1.54pm	HOLLAND	WESTERHAM
485	2.45pm	WESTERHAM	EDENBRIDGE
465	3.21pm	EDENBRIDGE	LIMPSFIELD COM.
464	4.33pm	LIMPSFIELD COM.	CHELSHAM GARAGE

W: Wednesday Only   NW:- Not Wednesday
Sch:- Schooldays only   NSch:- Not Schooldays
CM 21 finished earlier on Wednesday as that was early closing day in Oxted

On 18th April 1960, GS 3 has arrived at Edenbridge from Westerham as a 485 and the driver has changed the blind for the return 465 to Holland. Buses on the 485 were timed to connect with a 434, and RF 613 has pulled up behind on its way to Crawley. The GS will reverse off the main road into Hever Road to turn, a manoeuvre which later became hazardous so that buses ran a short distance along Hever Road to turn on the forecourt of Maidstone and District's small garage. Apart from a few days at Hitchin in January 1954, GS 3 spent its entire life at Chelsham garage.
Peter Mitchell

3   South West Operations

On Saturday 8th June 1963, GS 54 has arrived at Crawley having worked the 11.02am journey from Horsham and will work the next 12.15pm back to Horsham. The Southdown Guy Arab behind is blinded for a duplicate journey on service 79, a short town service to Gossops Green which had been started on 10th December 1959 and was part of an agreement with London Transport whereby both operators ran across the 1933 boundary which ran through the town. GS 54 was the only GS fitted with 'Loadmeter' equipment which recorded the number of passengers on each journey, and the results obtained on the 852 may have been a deciding factor in the drastic reduction of the timetable in November 1964. *Peter Aves*

CRAWLEY

ORIGINAL ALLOCATION
GS 81, 82, AND 83 – Transferred from store at Reigate on 13th December 1954
- ROUTE 852/852A Commenced 22nd December 1955
- ROUTE 434 'Special Duplicates' operated from 22nd December 1960 until 3rd February 1965
- 852A Morning positioning journey to Faygate (Withdrawn 21st March 1956 and route number ceased)
- 852 Withdrawn completely on 3rd October 1965

Peak vehicle Requirement   2 GS 21.12.54 to 17.5.54.
                                            1 GS 18.5.54 to 3.2.60
                                            2 GS 3.12.60 to 3.2.65
                                            1 GS 3.2.65 to 3.10.65

GS operation at Crawley came about only as a result of the sudden and unexpected collapse of the Hants and Sussex company three days before Christmas 1954. Were it not for this, Crawley might never have operated GSs since it ran no minor rural routes. The single deck routes they did operate were the circular 426 through Ifield and Horley and the 434/473 from Horsham to East Grinstead and Edenbridge, both being busy routes running to generally hourly headways requiring crew operation with some duplication.

Hants and Sussex had operated four routes into Horsham. Following their collapse London Transport took over three of them at short notice, Aldershot & District absorbing the fourth into their route to Haslemere which shared some parts of the former Hants and Sussex route. The former 32/32A were Horsham town services to Roffey Corner running every 20 minutes, with one journey per hour via Littlehaven, and were absorbed into the 434 timetable. Route 33 had run between Three Bridges, Crawley and Horsham via Lambs Green and Faygate village, and route 34 from Horsham to Ewhurst via Oakwood Hill and Wallis Wood, Hants & Sussex having acquired this latter from another local operator in 1946. London Transport combined the 33 and 34 into one route, numbered 852, the timetable requiring two buses all day. Only five months before their collapse, Hants and Sussex had begun route 33A as a town service in Crawley from the town to Langley Green. As Crawley was outside the Special Area, London Transport had no absolute right to operate in Crawley and Hants and Sussex's existing presence had led to that company being granted a licence for the Langley Green route. London Transport also took over this route, absorbing it into the 476 rather than becoming part of the new 852.

The Hants and Sussex 33 timetable had included one morning journey running on to Three Bridges and another in the afternoon peak during the week. These also ran on Saturdays with two further early evening journeys presumably to provide more connections with trains on the main London to Brighton line. At weekends, a final late evening journey left Crawley at 10.15pm to Three Bridges with a note stating that the bus would *wait for cinema patrons*. Between Horsham and Crawley, there were six journeys Monday to Friday, eight Saturday and two on Sunday – one late morning and another late evening. Not all these journeys worked through however; on some departures from Horsham, passengers were required to change buses at Roffey Corner and two or three journeys a day terminated at the Royal Oak in Ifield where a connection could be made into Crawley on London Transport's 426. This somewhat disconnected facility was not ideal and London Transport replaced it with seven journeys a day between Crawley and Horsham. The Sunday service was discontinued, although an afternoon service was run on Bank Holiday Mondays until 1960. An eighth early morning journey ran from Faygate into Crawley and on to Three Bridges for which a bus ran direct to Faygate via the A264 as 852A, a working which was withdrawn after 21st March 1956.

The former 34 to Ewhurst operated through sparsely populated countryside, the hamlets of Wallis Wood and Oakwood Hill also being served by Brown Motor Services' route to Forest Green via Ockley. There were seven journeys on Wednesday, four on Thursday (Horsham early closing day) and six every other day. Given that Brown Motors ran between three and six journeys a day, then the capacity between Oakwood Hill, Wallis Wood and Horsham was – even given passenger levels at the time – greater than was necessary. The Sunday timetable had just five journeys – a factor which could not have helped their finances.

This lovely period picture shows Horsham Carfax as it was in 1954 as GS 81 departs for a journey to Ewhurst. As well as London Transport, The Carfax was the terminus for Southdown, Aldershot & District and the Independents which ran routes into Horsham. The Harrington centre entrance body on Southdown's Leyland Royal Tiger coach was one of a large number purchased by them throughout the 1950s and stands in front of one of Southdown's Leyland PDs waiting to leave on route 69 to Bognor Regis. Southdown's enquiry office and waiting room is in the background and the cars are all of the period – the Austin A35 on the left being almost new at the time. The 852 blinds continued the Hants and Sussex practice of including the 'Bulls Head' qualifying point which did not appear on the blinds for the 448 and 449 which terminated at the same stop in Ewhurst. *Peter Jones collection*

Although it had been necessary for another operator to step in at short notice to provide replacement services, London Transport were the subject of an immediate objection by Brown Motor Services of Forest Green to running between Horsham and Ewhurst. Whilst just inside the 1933 LPTA boundary, the route was equally some distance outside the *Special Area* within which London Transport had absolute rights to run any service without the need for a licence. Five years earlier, they had introduced the 383 from Hitchin to Weston, also outside the *Special Area*, contending that additional powers granted to them under the 1947 Transport Act permitted them to introduce such routes. Even though London Transport eventually won an acrimonious dispute permitting the continuation of the 383, they were widely criticised for their apparently high handed dismissive attitude towards local independent operators. Brown Motors argued that London Transport could not operate the route without a formal licence application through the Traffic Courts.

Having been moved from Garston to Reigate in August 1954, GS 81, 82, and 83 were licensed for service and transferred to Crawley on 13th December. This date is interesting. The collapse of Hants and Sussex on 22nd December resulted in London Transport immediately taking over at short notice. However, since Crawley had not operated GSs previously, and some driver training would have been necessary, the fact that three GSs were transferred to Crawley nine days earlier suggests that London Transport had prior notice of the need to take over. It is known that Hants and Sussex's standards of maintenance had declined, with some journeys cancelled when no serviceable bus was available. The Traffic Commissioner had issued warnings to the company, so it is not impossible to surmise that the Commissioners had informally advised London Transport of their likely collapse in advance so that suitable preparations could be made.

Although the former Sunday service was discontinued, the 852 timetable ran six journeys a day to Ewhurst, the only exception being a Thursday afternoon journey which terminated in Horsham on early closing day. The 7.03am and 9.18am from Horsham to Ewhurst each morning must have carried almost nobody as would the 6.35pm and 8.05pm return in the evening. This was uneconomic to operate and with an end to end running time of more than 90 minutes from Crawley, the two buses were covering considerable mileage for little return. Perhaps as a result of the adverse criticism received over the operation of the 383, combined with the entirely justifiable objection from Brown Motor Services, London Transport cut the route back to Horsham after 17th May 1955. Brown Motors took over the following day extending the route from Ewhurst to Forest Green, running four journeys a day with a fifth in the evening on Wednesday and Saturday. Although Brown Motors withdrew the original route from Forest Green via Ockley and Wallis Wood in March 1961, the Ewhurst route would continue almost unchanged until the company sold out to North Downs Rural Transport in November 1970.

Between Crawley through Ifield to the point where the 852 turned at Ifield Wood towards Lambs Green, it followed the same road as the 426 which ran to a two-hourly service increasing to hourly on Saturday afternoon. In addition, town services to Ifield expanded quickly during the 1950s providing a frequent service from Crawley. There were almost no houses along the road through Ifield Wood, and Lambs Green was a small village offering few passengers. Less than two miles further on the route joined the main road at Faygate and ran alongside the 30-minute headway on the 434/473, which was replaced by the 405 in 1957. Ifield

Wood and Lambs Green were therefore the only places served solely by the 852, so that its potential passenger numbers were always limited. Once the Ewhurst section had been abandoned, the seven journeys a day between Crawley and Horsham remained unchanged for the next nine years until the 1964 winter schedules when the timetable was cut to just four journeys. After the first two journeys, the bus ran back into Crawley garage at 11.30am and was not required again until just after 2.00pm to run the two afternoon journeys, arriving back at Crawley bus station at 5.22pm.

The remaining four journeys lasted only a further year before the route was withdrawn completely on 3rd October 1965 when that year's winter schedules were introduced. It had almost certainly lost money for several years before and was one of the first minor rural routes to be abandoned.

852 to HORSHAM via Faygate Station

This service is operated with Pay As You Enter buses.
Please have your fare ready as you get on.

Weekdays

	MF 6 am	§745 am	am	pm	pm	pm	pm	pm					
Three Bridges Station	6												
Crawley Bus Station	655	§751	1012	1215	2 3	347	612	757					
Ifield Royal Oak	7 5	8 1	1022	1225	213	357	622	8 7					
Ifield Wood Letter Box	A	8 4	1015	1228	216	4 0	625	810					
Lambs Green		814	1035	1238	226	410	635	820					
Faygate Station		820	1041	1244	232	416	641	826					
Roffey Corner		827	1048	1251	239	423	648	833					
Horsham Station		833	1054	1257	245	429	654	839					
Horsham Corfax		836	1057	1 0	248	432	657	842					

ROUTE
852 to CRAWLEY and THREE BRIDGES via Faygate Station

This service is operated with Pay As You Enter buses.
Please have your fare ready as you get on.

Weekdays

	am	am	am	pm	pm	pm	pm	pm					
Horsham Corfax		841	11 2	1 5	253	437	7 7	847					
Horsham Station		844	11 5	1 8	256	440	710	850					
Roffey Corner		850	1111	114	3 2	446	716	856					
Faygate Station		857	1118	121	3 9	453	723	9 3					
Lambs Green	MF	9 3	1124	127	315	459	729	9 9					
Ifield Wood Letter Box	9	913	1134	137	325	5 9	739	919					
Ifield Royal Oak	714	916	1137	140	328	512	742	922					
Crawley Bus Station	724	926	1147	150	338	522	752	932					
Three Bridges Station	730							6					

A—To Ifield Bonnets Lane 2 minutes later. B—From Ifield Bonnets Lane 2 minutes earlier.
F—From Crawley LT Garage on Saturday. 6—To or from Crawley LT Garage. § or MF—Monday to Friday only.

NOTE—This timetable does not necessarily apply on Bank Holidays. While every effort will be made to keep to the timetables, London Transport does not undertake that its buses will be operated in accordance with them, or at all. London Transport will not be responsible for any loss, damage or inconvenience caused by reason of any operating failure or in consequence of any inaccuracies in the timetables.

LONDON TRANSPORT, 55 BROADWAY, LONDON, S.W.1.   ABBey 1234   22.5.63

263 649Z 300 (85)   L1003   11501 Bournehall Press Ltd., Bushey, Watford

The timetable for May 1963 shows the service which had remained unaltered since 1956. The winter timetables of 4th November 1964 cut the 852 to four journeys, a reduction which was surely overdue since the previous timetable had quickly become a generous over provision. At the same time the single morning journey to Three Bridges station was withdrawn. (Peter Aves collection)

schedules were introduced. It had almost certainly lost money for several years before and was one of the first minor rural routes to be abandoned.

Two buses were required for the 852, running numbers being CY23 and 24. Following the withdrawal of the Ewhurst section, the remaining bus carried the number CY24 until the end of operation. Of these first three GSs, only GS 81 remained at Crawley for any length of time. It was delicensed in January 1959 before being overhauled and sent to Chelsham where it remained until replaced with RFs in October 1962. After the Ewhurst operation ceased, GS 82 and 83 were transferred to Dorking on 18th May 1954. GS 81 remained Crawley's only official allocation until 16th January 1959 when GS 12 arrived as its long term replacement. It had been at Leatherhead for two years and was temporarily delicensed and stored at Grays before transfer to Crawley. GS 12 was delicensed in October 1963 and stored at Dorking before becoming Leatherhead's training bus for a few months in 1964. On 9th September 1964, it was overhauled for the second time after which it returned to Crawley until the 852 was withdrawn. The day after GS 12 arrived, GS 81 was delicensed and sent to Reigate where it remained out of use until 4th March, when it was sent for its first – and what would prove to be – its only overhaul. On 1st December 1959, GS 16 arrived from Chelsham as a spare bus, but was delicensed at the end of January 1960, then to Reigate awaiting overhaul. It was replaced by GS 51 which led an extremely peripatetic life over the following years, being moved frequently as a spare float bus around several garages. It was delicensed at Crawley on 1st June 1960 where it remained out of use for four months. On 22nd September it went to Reigate, then on 1st November it was sent to New Cross garage as a trainer to replace T 785 which in turn went

Crawley's second GS allocated in December 1960 ran duplicate journeys on the busy section of the 434 between Crawley and Crawley Down. The journeys were never in the public timetable, and the bus carried the 'Extra' plate in the side holder as shown here. Having been overhauled in October 1964, it was allocated to Crawley where it remained until the end of GS operation when the 852 was withdrawn completely.

to Abbey Wood. Why such complex changes were made is unclear, and replacing a T type with a GS for training seems illogical at best! GS 51 was in turn replaced by GS 84 from Leatherhead, and remained until 24th October 1962 when it was delicensed and stored as one of those earmarked for sale. During 1962 and 1963, GS 20, 21, 35, 54, and 57 all spent short periods at Crawley, but apart from a short period in 1964 when GS 12 was sent to Harlow for the short lived 389 route, it remained at Crawley until the last day of operation.

On 3rd December 1960, an additional GS working was added to the Crawley schedules. Capacity between Crawley and Crawley Down on the 434 during peak time and main shopping hours was at times insufficient. Scheduled duplicates were therefore added to ease overcrowding, and a GS was allocated to these journeys. The 852 timetable at the time provided no spare capacity to run this, so a second GS was officially allocated for 'Special Duplicates'. These journeys, which never appeared in the public timetable, continued for many years. Indeed, London Country allocated a double decker at times in the early 1970s. After the winter 1964 schedules reduced the 852 timetable, there was also the lengthy gap already mentioned between 11.30am and 2.00pm and the finish at Crawley at 5.22pm. This allowed the bus to be used to run the duplicated 434 journeys. However, GS working of these duplicates was changed soon after with the allocation book amendments of 3rd February 1965 when the working was converted to omo RF.

After Crawley's operation on the 426, 434, and 473 were converted to omo, the crew duties for RF and GS were combined together, the roster for the 852 having been previously separate. The combined, crew duties for 25th May 1960 required 18 drivers, the 852 being covered each day by two drivers on duty 45 and 46 Monday to Friday, duty 47 and 48 Saturday. Of the total of 18 drivers, the 852 was covered by rosters 4, 5, 7, 8, 10, 15, and 16 as shown opposite.

CRAWLEY SINGLE DECK ROSTERS COVERING GS WORKING Commencing 25th MAY 1960
DRIVER DUTIES COVERING ROUTE 852

MONDAY TO FRIDAY	DUTY NUMBER	RUNNING NUMBER	START TIME	LOCATION	MEAL RELIEF	FINISH TIME	LOCATION	DUTY FINISH
	45	CY 24	6.39am	CY	9.27am		CK	
			10.19am	Bus station		1.49pm	CK	
		WALK	1.49pm	Bus station		2.00pm	CY	2.15pm
	46		1.38pm	CY				
		WALK	1.53PM	CY		2.04pm	CK	
		CY 24	2.04pm	Bus station	5.21pm		CK	
			6.13pm			9.33pm	CY	9.48pm
SATURDAY	47	CY 24	7.49am	CY	9.27am		CK	
			10.19am	Bus station		1.49pm	CK	
		WALK	1.49pm	Bus station		2.00pm	CY	2.15pm
	48		1.38pm	CY				
		WALK	1.53PM	CY		2.04PM	CK	
		CY 24	2.04pm	Bus station	5.21pm		CK	
			6.13pm			9.33pm	CY	9.48pm

Codes: CY:- Crawley garage; CK:- Crawley Bus Stn.

DRIVER ROSTERS (ONLY THOSE COVERING DUTIES ROUTE 852) TOTAL 18 DRIVERS

ROSTER POSITION	WEDNESDAY	THURSDAY	FRIDAY	SATURDAY	SUNDAY	MONDAY	TUESDAY
4	OFF	OFF	**46**	**48**	32	4	**45**
5	1	2	OFF	**47**	36	10	8
7	**46**	9	7	17	OFF	**46**	3
8	**45**	**45**	OFF	25	OFF	**45**	5
10	5	8	**45**	19	OFF	OFF	12
15	12	**46**	6	23	OFF	13	11
16	8	7	4	16	OFF	OFF	**46**

Duty numbers for the 852 are highlighted in bold. Saturday duty 22 not covered
in roster – worked by overtime

In practice, rather than walk, both drivers on the lunchtime changeover probably travelled by 405 or 476 to and from the garage (especially if the weather was bad). These duties were unchanged until the 852 timetable was reduced to only four journeys a day when a driver covered both GS and RF on the same day.

DORKING

ORIGINAL ALLOCATION GS 36, 37, 41, 42,

ROUTES OPERATED

433	1st December 1953 to 4th October 1968. Withdrawn Saturdays from 31st December 1966.
449	Dorking – Ewhurst 1st December 1953 to 29th October 1958 Dorking – Chart Downs 1st December 1953 to 25th May 1956 (weekdays) 12th October 1956 (Sunday) Part RT operation to Chart Downs from 21st March 1956

Although Dorking operated only two routes using small single deckers – one of which was withdrawn early – it rostered as many as four buses at weekends until the mid-1950s. GS 36, 37 and 41 were transferred unlicensed from Aldenham to Dorking on 26th November 1953, followed the next day by GS 42, which had been licensed for service before delivery. Dorking's Cubs were all withdrawn on 1st December on which day all four GSs entered service.

Ranmore Common was very popular for visitors, Leith Hill even more so, the 433 route needing duplication on fine Sundays and Bank Holidays to cater for the additional passengers. Before the War and until the early post war years, the 433 timetable was quite limited when compared to the improved service in response to the enormous post-war increase in demand for leisure trips to places like the Surrey Hills beauty spots. Until 1939, during the week there had been only two journeys in the afternoon to Coldharbour with another late evening, while

GS 42 was one of Dorking's initial allocation, and after serving at four other garages and time as a training bus, it returned to Dorking on 1st January 1967, and would be Dorking's last GS in service. It waits at Ranmore, one of the more remote termini, buses reversing into the narrow Dog Kennel Lane to wait at the stop. Despite being served by only six journeys a day and any passenger there being a rarity, there was a proper bus stop with timetable frame, e-plate and fare stage sign. A few weeks before the 433 was withdrawn in October 1968, Peter Aves travelled up to Ranmore on this bus on the 11.15am from Dorking and was the only passenger after two were dropped off in Randalls road before the long climb up to Ranmore Common. Nobody boarded on the return journey.
Dick Dapre

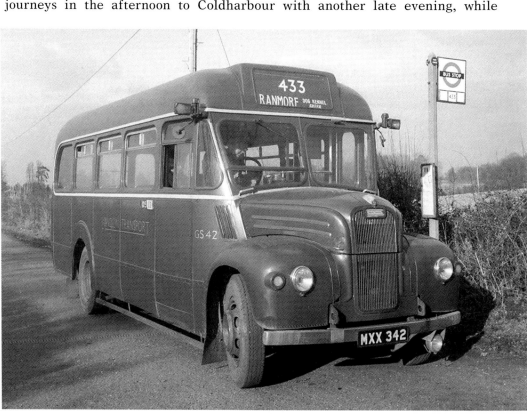

This panel timetable dated 14th May 1958 was the last issue printed before the 449 was withdrawn five months later between Ewhurst and Holmwood Common where the new terminus at Four Wents Pond was four minutes beyond the Plough at Blackbrook. The majority of the Chart Downs journeys were RT operated, but the remaining GS journeys can be identified from the 12 minute running time between Chart Downs and Dorking Bus Station as opposed to the 11 minutes allowed for those which were crew operated. It can also be seen therefore that the Sunday service remained GS operated. *Alan Charman collection*

ROUTE
449

to CHART DOWNS ESTATE
and Ewhurst
via Holmwood and Ockley

A 5/- ROVER TICKET will take you as far as you like on this and on nearly every other Country Bus route. Ask the conductor for details.
Part of this service is operated with Pay As You Enter buses. Please have your fare ready as you get on.

Monday to Friday

	a.m.	a.m.	a.m.	a.m.	a.m.	a.m.	a.m.	a.m.	a.m.	p.m.	p.m.	p.m.	p.m.	p.m.	p.m.	p.m.	p.m.
Goodwyns Farm Estate.......	..	739	822	..	9 6	..	..	..	..	1237	..	118	2 7	..			
Dorking *Bus Station*........	713	745	828	828	912	940	955	1037	1119	12 1	1243	1 0	124	213	3 2	346	351
Dorking *White Horse*..........	716	748	831	831	915	943	958	1040	1122	12 4	1246	1 3	127	216	3 5	349	354
Chart Downs *Estate*.........	725	756	839	840	923	952	10 6	1048	1130	1212	1254	112	135	224	313	357	4 3
Blackbrook *Plough*..............	..	..	..	..	..	956	..	..	..	..	..	116	..	..	..	..	..
Holmwood *Mill Lane*........	..	..	..	..	..	10 2	..	..	..	..	..	122	..	..	..	..	..
Capel *Crown*.......................	..	..	..	..	..	1012	..	..	..	..	..	132	..	..	..	..	..
Ockley *Station*....................	..	..	..	..	..	1016	..	..	..	..	..	136	..	..	..	..	..
Ockley *Kings Arms*...........	..	..	..	..	..	1020	..	..	..	..	..	140	..	..	..	..	..
Forest Green *P.O.*.............	..	..	..	..	..	1027	..	..	..	..	..	147	..	..	..	..	..
Ewhurst *Bulls Head*..........	..	..	..	..	..	1034	..	..	..	..	..	154	..	..	..	..	..

	p.m.	p.m.	p.m.	p.m.	p.m.	p.m.	p.m.	p.m.	p.m.							
Goodwyns Farm Estate.......	..	..	525	..	611	7 1	..	..	1016	..	..					
Dorking *Bus Station*........	428	459	531	533	617	7 7	837	942	1022	..	..					
Dorking *White Horse*..........	431	5 2	534	536	620	710	840	945	1025	..	..					
Chart Downs *Estate*.........	439	511	542	545	628	718	848	953	1033	..	..					
Blackbrook *Plough*..............	..	..	..	549	..	..	..	..	..							
Holmwood *Mill Lane*........	..	..	..	555	..	..	..	..	..							
Capel *Crown*.......................	..	..	..	6 5	..	..	..	..	..							
Ockley *Station*....................	..	..	..	6 9	..	..	..	..	..							
Ockley *Kings Arms*...........	..	..	..	613	..	..	..	..	..							
Forest Green *P.O.*.............	..	..	..	620	..	..	..	..	..							
Ewhurst *Bulls Head*..........	..	..	..	627	..	..	..	..	..							

Saturday

	a.m.	a.m.	a.m.	a.m.	a.m.	a.m.	a.m.	a.m.	a.m.	a.m.	p.m.	p.m.	p.m.	p.m.	p.m.	p.m.	p.m.
Holmwood *Holly & Laurel*......	..	..	..	..	..	..	..	..	..	1248	..	118	148	218	248	318	
Dorking *Bus Station*........	714	756	831	920	940	10 2	1044	1129	1145	12 9	1258	1 0	128	158	228	258	328
Dorking *White Horse*..........	717	759	834	923	943	10 5	1047	1132	1148	1212	1 1	1 3	131	2 1	231	3 1	331
Chart Downs *Estate*.........	725	8 7	842	931	952	1013	1055	1140	1157	1220	1 9	112	139	2 9	239	3 9	339
Blackbrook *Plough*..............	..	..	..	..	956	..	..	..	..	..	116	..	..	..	..	..
Holmwood *Mill Lane*........	..	..	..	..	10 2	..	..	..	..	..	122	..	..	..	..	..
Capel *Crown*.......................	..	..	..	..	1012	..	..	..	..	..	132	..	..	..	..	..
Ockley *Station*....................	..	..	..	..	1016	..	..	..	..	..	136	..	..	..	..	..
Ockley *Kings Arms*...........	..	..	..	..	1020	..	..	..	..	..	140	..	..	..	..	..
Forest Green *P.O.*.............	..	..	..	..	1027	..	..	..	..	..	147	..	..	..	..	..
Ewhurst *Bulls Head*..........	..	..	..	..	1034	..	..	..	..	..	154	..	..	..	..	..

	p.m.	p.m.	p.m.	p.m.	p.m.	p.m.	p.m.	p.m.	p.m.	p.m.	p.m.					
Holmwood *Holly & Laurel*......	348	418	448	518	..	548	..	..	..	..						
Goodwyns Farm Estate........	358	428	458	528	..	↓	..	..	..	1016						
Dorking *Bus Station*........	4 1	431	5 1	531	533	558	628	7 7	837	921	1022					
Dorking *White Horse*..........	4 9	439	5 9	539	536	6 1	631	710	840	924	1025					
Chart Downs *Estate*.........	..	..	..	..	545	6 9	639	718	848	932	1033					
Blackbrook *Plough*..............	..	..	..	..	549	..	..	..	..							
Holmwood *Mill Lane*........	..	..	..	..	555	..	..	..	..							
Capel *Crown*.......................	..	..	..	..	6 5	..	..	..	..							
Ockley *Station*....................	..	..	..	..	6 9	..	..	..	..							
Ockley *Kings Arms*...........	..	..	..	..	613	..	..	..	..							
Forest Green *P.O.*.............	..	..	..	..	620	..	..	..	..							
Ewhurst *Bulls Head*..........	..	..	..	..	627	..	..	..	..							

Sunday

	p.m.	p.m.	p.m.	p.m.	p.m.	p.m.	p.m.	p.m.	p.m.	p.m.	p.m.	p.m.			
Dorking *Bus Station*........	2 0	240	320	4 0	440	520	6 0	634	8 0	840	920	10 0	..	..	..
Dorking *White Horse*..........	2 3	243	323	4 3	443	523	6 3	637	8 3	843	923	10 3	..	..	..
Chart Downs *Estate*........	212	252	332	412	452	532	612	646	812	852	932	1012	..	..	..

NOTE: While every effort will be made to keep to the timetables, London Transport does not undertake that its buses will be operated in accordance with them, or at all. London Transport will not be responsible for any loss, damage or inconvenience caused by reason of any operating failure or in consequence of any inaccuracies in the timetables.

LONDON TRANSPORT, 55 BROADWAY, S.W.1.   ABBey 1234   14.5.58
258/213Z/300(100)   113

Leonard Ripley & Co. Ltd., London

Ranmore had only one morning and one mid-afternoon journey with two others which turned at Ranmore Common. The Saturday service to Coldharbour was much better with eight journeys, but there was no service from Ranmore Common into Dorking until after lunchtime. The first trip to Ranmore itself did not leave Dorking until 4.00pm and there was a return just before 10.00pm – probably timed to take people home after the cinema performance finished. Even before the war, the popularity of Coldharbour was such that on Sundays two buses operated a 30 minute headway from 10.00am all day until just before 10.00pm with only a few one hour gaps while one bus ran up to Ranmore. The timetable was cut back to just a very limited shopping service during the War, but much improved from 1947. By 1951, twelve journeys ran up to Coldharbour and six to Ranmore, a timetable which continued until the minor changes in 1958 as noted below.

Coldharbour, situated high on the South Downs necessitated a mostly steep 700 foot climb on the road from Dorking. To allow for this, the 15 minute running time from Coldharbour to Dorking bus station was increased by three minutes in the opposite direction up to Coldharbour to allow for the long slow ascent of Boar Hill. This remained in force until the more powerful GSs replaced the Cubs in December 1953 when the schedule allowed 15 minutes in each direction. The lane was narrow, with a number of places where a bus could not always pass another vehicle, and a restriction to operations by Cubs and later GSs remained in force until 1964 when RFs were approved – although never actually rostered. The climb up onto Ranmore Common was equally long, but not as steep. The road was also much wider, the restriction for smaller buses not being necessary.

The weekday timetable only ever required one bus which ran as DS11 for the entire life of the route. The sole exception was a Monday to Friday journey at 8.57am from the Star and Garter pub opposite Dorking North Station to Ranmore. This bus had left the bus station at 7.48am, to run the 7.55am Dorking North to Gomshall journey on the 425. On its return it then ran this single 433 trip to Ranmore, arriving back at the bus station at 9.33am. This was run by a crew operated TF allocated to DS2 which later in the day ran Dorking's share of the 412 route – the main service to Sutton and Holmbury St Mary being run by the bus outstationed there which was always DS1. Later this working was changed and the Ranmore journey incorporated in the 425 roster. This arrangement continued until the Winter 1958 schedules when the 433 Monday to Friday timetable was altered so that the one bus ran the whole timetable, but a minor change on Saturday required a second bus to work the 8.12am from the bus station to Ranmore and back using the spare RF on DS2 which remained for the additional 412 journeys later in the day.

The enhanced service on summer Sundays ran until 1955, after which the Coldharbour journeys were reduced to hourly in the morning, the second bus not starting until a 2.00pm departure from Dorking North Station. The second bus on Sundays ran as DS16, and was later used during the week on the 449 when the timetable was increased as noted below. From 1957, the Sunday timetable was reduced to operate the same service all year round, one bus running a limited service in the afternoon and evening although a duplicate bus would remain, operating *'to instructions'* as required, particularly in fine weather.

Sunday duplication for the 433 required an additional GS so that three buses were rostered. The running number used is not known, but the duplicate RF used on the 425 ran as DS201. Given London Transport's policy of sequential running numbers for single deck, double deck and Green Line routes, it is therefore likely that the duplicate GS for the 433 ran as DS202. Timing had to be carefully managed so that two buses were not required to pass each other between the end of Knoll Road a few minutes from the bus station and the top of Boar Hill, or indeed on the short single track lane into Coldharbour itself. Although no records remain, it is likely that the duplicate would have run before one of the timetabled journeys, picking up passengers from trains at Dorking North and from Green Lines at the bus station. The duplicate remained in the allocation books until October 1958 when the Sunday service was withdrawn completely each year for the winter.

The 433 summer Sunday service, was also operated on Bank Holiday Mondays with 11 journeys to Coldharbour and four to Ranmore. This ran every year until the last summer, 1968 – the year in which the route was finally abandoned – despite the normal summer Sunday service being withdrawn after 1966. The duplicate bus was also allocated until 1959 but not thereafter. On Good Friday each year, the enhanced service ran only until 1959 after which the normal Sunday service ran from early afternoon. This too was operated until Good Friday 1968. From 1960 to 1966, a scheduling oddity on Bank Holiday Mondays was the last bus down from Coldharbour at 9.56pm being extended to Chart Downs estate in place of the last 449 journey operated on other Sundays. An additional blind panel was made, and with the introduction of the summer time-tables from 7th June 1961, this journey ran every Sunday. The Sunday service was seasonal, so that this late journey did not run once the winter schedules came into force, and was not repeated for 1962.

The introduction of the 449 route on 1st March 1950 was principally intended to provide a service to the new housing estate at Chart Downs then being developed to the south of Dorking on land that had been part of Chart Park, which in turn had been part of the even larger Deepdene Estate. The significant rise in demand for post-war travel encouraged London Transport to run the 449 all the way to Ewhurst. Beyond Chart Downs, the route passed the few cottages and pub at Blackbrook, through woodland on Holmwood Common where at the remote cross roads by a pond, the route turned back to meet the main London to Worthing road. The route then ran in parallel with the 414 as far as Capel where it continued westwards through the villages of Ockley and Forest Green to Ewhurst. When begun, there were 15 journeys to Chart Downs, three of which continued over the full route to Ewhurst. On Sundays there were seven journeys to Chart Downs, and in the first summer of operation, the same three journeys worked through to Ewhurst. These were reduced to just two – one mid-afternoon and one in the evening – for summer 1952, and withdrawn at the end of the summer season in 1954, leaving only the three weekday Ewhurst journeys. The timetable required only one bus, which ran as DS18.

As more houses at Chart Downs were built and occupied, the 449 timetable was increased, and by 1955 there were 23 journeys, the first leaving Dorking bus station at 7.13am and the last at 10.18pm. During the week, the 8.43am from Chart Downs was duplicated and in the afternoon a number of journeys were timed to run six or seven minutes behind each other. On Saturdays, although the morning duplicate did not run, the 2.51pm into Dorking was duplicated (although timed at 2.53pm) after which there were two journeys an hour (although irregular) all afternoon. This enhanced timetable required two GSs, the second bus running as DS16, odd journeys also being worked from the 425 allocation. Further expansion of the estate led to the capacity of the GSs becoming inadequate so that on 21st March 1956 the majority of the service was converted to RT. Traffic south of Dorking to Holmwood was also increasing so at the same time part of the 449 was extended to South Holmwood during the week, and on Saturdays to the new Goodwyns Farm Estate just south of the town centre on the Horsham road. The three Ewhurst journeys remained, the GS allocated to DS18 continuing to run them in addition to some Chart Downs journeys – four Monday to Friday and two Saturday. A note in the timetable above these journeys stated that '*26 seat bus will run*' to distinguish them from those operated by the RT. After these changes, the GS left Dorking bus station at 8.28am as a duplicate to the RT. With rigid adherence to operating procedure and Union agreements, because it was a one-man bus the GS was allowed one minute more than the RT to get to Chart Downs despite the fact that it ran behind it and would have picked up no passengers. On the return, the crew operated RT was allowed the agreed three minute layover whereas the Union agreement for a one-man bus allowed five minutes.

GS 82 was transferred to Dorking from Crawley on 18th May 1955, and has worked one of the three journeys to Ewhurst on the 449. It waits by the Crown Inn before running back to Dorking. The Aldershot & District bus behind is on route 23 to Guildford and is one of the large number of Dennis Lance double deckers purchased by them in the early 1950s. *Steve Fennell collection*

The GS therefore left Chart Downs three minutes behind the RT, and because of the minute extra running time arrived back in Dorking four minutes behind the RT. In reality, it was far more likely that the GS driver ran up behind the RT to avoid bothering with any passengers and perhaps waited in South Street before arriving at the bus station on time to avoid the displeasure of the inspector! Although only one GS was required after 1958, the allocation for 1959 and 1960 notes a second GS Monday to Friday as DS16 'to instructions' which presumably ran duplicates to the scheduled GS when one bus had insufficient capacity. On Sundays, there were significantly fewer passengers and a service was run to a regular 40 minute headway by one GS as DS18 from early afternoon to late evening.

The demand for even a limited service into Dorking had been minimal even in 1950 when the 449 began, and although no figures are available for loadings, the route could hardly have covered its costs but must have been a pleasant interlude for the drivers. Many years ago, having asked a Dorking driver if he had driven that route, he recalled that since the timetable was very generous, there was time to stop by the woods near Forest Green in May each year and pick some bluebells to take home to his wife who especially liked them.

The significant cuts which came with the winter schedules on 29th October 1958 included the withdrawal of the Ewhurst journeys. Local independent operators ran services from Ockley into Horsham, and from Forest Green to both Horsham and Guildford, while Aldershot & District ran an hourly service from Ewhurst to Cranleigh and Guildford. The small hamlet of Blackbrook however retained a very limited service during the week with two journeys extended beyond Chart Downs through Blackbrook to turn at Four Wents crossroads by the pond on Holmwood Common. They ran in the afternoon four days a week with no service on Wednesday, being early closing day in Dorking. The GS was retained for these, also running a small number of the Chart Downs journeys including the morning duplicate referred to above. The GS worked the 1.00pm from Dorking to Four Wents each day where it waited at this isolated spot for no less than 40 minutes before departing at 2.00pm for the return journey. This alone seemed a completely unnecessary cost, but this arrangement continued unchanged into London Country days. The Sunday afternoon timetable remained unaltered. This limited GS operation continued until 25th May 1960 when the Four Wents journeys were incorporated into the 425 roster, the Sunday timetable retaining the GS until the winter schedules on 12th October.

The 433 saw few reductions from the 1958 cuts. Crew operation of the Saturday morning journey was converted to omo RF, and two Saturday journeys to Coldharbour were removed. With minor changes to the actual departure times, the 433 timetable became the same six days a week, and would remained unchanged until the Saturday service was withdrawn completely at the end of 1966 on 30th December. The seasonal Sunday service was finally withdrawn at the end of that year's summer timetable. Despite the continuing fall in traffic when increasing losses on rural routes such as this were being made, the Monday to Friday timetable had continued unchanged for ten years until the last day of operation on 4th October 1968 and illustrated London Transport's apparent lack of reaction to such situations, which was prevalent on many other routes.

Dorking's initial allocation was short lived. On 21st January 1955, GS 42 was transferred to Garston, GS 37 going to Chelsham later in the year on 14th October. GS 41 was delicensed on 1st June that year and stored at Reigate. It later went

This 433 summer timetable dated 16th May 1956 shows the hourly headway to Coldharbour on Sunday morning and half hourly headway in late afternoon. Later departures from Coldharbour at 7.10pm and 7.20pm, 8.14pm and 8.20pm, and finally at 9.20pm and 9.34pm reflect the numbers of passengers and the popularity of Leith Hill at the time.

to Epping where its use on the 381 involved probably the least mileage at any garage. The experiments with the rear differential on GS 45, partly in an effort to improve fuel consumption, and to test hill climbing on hilly routes are referred to in chapter seven. It arrived from Chiswick on 4th March 1955 and spent five weeks (apart from a brief return to Chiswick) on route 433 until moving on to Chelsham on 13th April. After spells at other southern garages with hilly routes, it returned to Chiswick where it remained delicensed until 1st February 1956. It was returned to service at Dorking and remained there (other than two overhauls) until February 1963. After withdrawal of the Ewhurst section on the 852, GS 82 and 83 were surplus to requirements at Crawley, and transferred to Dorking on 18th May 1955. Between 1955 and 1958, Dorking's allocation changed frequently, GS 16, 29, 32, being allocated. GS 41 was one of the first to be withdrawn. During the 15 years, during which Dorking operated GSs, a total of 14 different buses were allocated. GS 39 spent four years at Dorking until the withdrawal of the Saturday service on 30th December 1966. It was delicensed on 2nd January 1967 and transferred to Reigate. GS 42 arrived on 31st December 1966 having been removed from the 445 at Windsor. It was perhaps appropriate that GS 42 was the last one to arrive having been part of the first allocation. It was delicensed on 9th October 1968 and remained out of use at Dorking until transfer to Garston in July 1969.

Without any spare bus, in the event of breakdown or servicing, a spare RF would be used, the restriction to Coldharbour on the use of GSs having been lifted in 1964, although the exact date of this is not recorded. The use of an RF was rare given the narrow steep hill to Coldharbour but in 1967 I travelled up to Coldharbour on RF 540. The reverse at Coldharbour was quite difficult given the additional length of the RF, and today would probably be impossible given the number of cars parked there, especially at weekends.

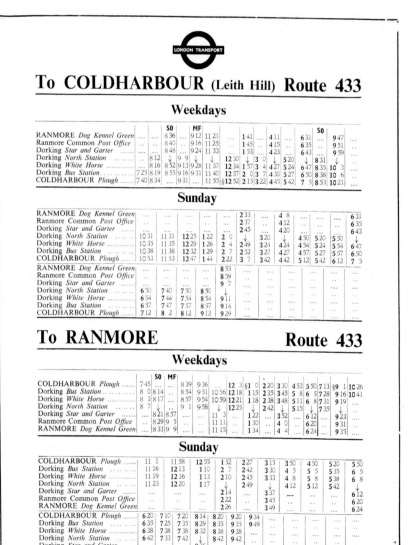

GUILDFORD

ORIGINAL ALLOCATION:-
GS 30, 31, 33, 35, and 39

Transferred from Aldenham unlicensed on 26th November 1953 and licensed for service the following day. All five C class Cubs were withdrawn and delicensed on 27th November.

ROUTES OPERATED:-
448 and 448A

27th November 1953 to 11th August 1964
London Transport majority share handed to Tillingbourne Valley 11th August 1964

425
Peak hour short journeys. 11th August 1964

432
School journeys to and from Horsley. Exact dates unknown

436
Peak hour duplicate journeys Guildford – Woking Exact dates unknown. Running number GF7

PEAK VEHICLE REQUIREMENT   4 GS – unchanged throughout entire period of operation

GS 39 was one of Guildford's original allocation and entered service on 27th November 1953. The bus still has the paper pay as you enter label in the windscreen and the front grabrails have not yet been fitted below the windscreen. The date of the theatre advert on the left suggests therefore that this picture was probably taken in September 1954 since the grab handles were all fitted later that year. *Southdown Enthusiasts Club*

The origins of bus routes to the east of Guildford are quite complex and it is worth including a brief summary of how London Transport became involved in them. The 1930 Transport Act set up Regional Traffic Commissioners and central-ised licensing system for bus routes, whereas prior to this, local councils had that responsibility. Guildford Council's Watch Committee had a policy of encouraging competition and granted licences to several different operators for routes within and radiating from the town. Tillingbourne Motor Services began a route from Guildford via Merrow over the North Downs at Newlands Corner to Gomshall in 1924, extending it to Peaslake in 1925 and again to Ewhurst in 1926. Aldershot & District (A&D) ran the 25 from Guildford along the Tillingbourne Valley through Chilworth and Albury, joining the main road at Silent Pool near Shere. The route ran on via Gomshall to Dorking. A&D soon countered the Tillingbourne service by starting the 25B to Peaslake and Ewhurst running along the same road as the 25 as far as Gomshall then following the Tillingbourne route to Ewhurst. The London General Omnibus Company did not approve of these routes in what they saw as 'their area', and through their subsidiary East Surrey began running in competition to A&D's 25 between Dorking and Guildford in 1928. At the same time East Surrey started route 44 which exactly paralleled Tillingbourne's route from Guildford to Ewhurst. Brown Motor Services were also running their route along the same roads as A&D's 25 as far as Abinger Hammer.

A&D withdrew the 25B leaving the service to Ewhurst to Tillingbourne and East Surrey. In 1930 with the impending Traffic Act, the four operators agreed a co-ordinated timetable through Chilworth and Albury, and later the same year East Surrey and Tillingbourne co-ordinated the route to Peaslake and Ewhurst. Under the new system, licences were granted for existing services, following which there was little change until the 1933 Traffic Act came into force and set up the London Passenger Transport Area (LPTA) and 'Special Area'. Guildford was on the boundary line of this area which crossed the Ewhurst route between Merrow and Newlands Corner, but included Chilworth and Shalford along the other routes. Since A&D's 25 to Dorking crossed into the 'Special Area' again near Wootton, it withdrew, leaving the Guildford – Dorking service to LT which it numbered 425. On 3rd August 1933, LT renumbered its route to Ewhurst 448. Other than the section of the 448 from Guildford to just beyond Merrow, the route lay outside the 'Special Area', but within the larger LPTA. London Transport therefore had no automatic right to acquire Tillingbourne, and its offers to do so were refused. In an attempt to exert their authority, LT reacted to Tillingbourne's rebuff by imposing restrictions on them carrying any local passengers from Merrow in and out of Guildford. This led to an immediate protest from local passengers who were inconvenienced by the restriction, such that LT were forced to relent, subsequently granting a licence to Tillingbourne to carry what were termed 'special passengers' between Guildford and Merrow. This was renewed annually until the 1969 Transport (London) Act removed the need. In March 1934, LT acquired the service operated by Magnet Motors who had also run a few journeys to Peaslake. LT became the sole operator of the limited service beyond Peaslake to Ewhurst and the 448 timetable became operated one third by Tillingbourne and two thirds by LT to a timetable which remained almost unchanged until August 1964 when LT withdrew. Tillingbourne continued with their hourly service to Albury and Farley Green, and the final act of co-ordination occurred in April 1935 when LT and Tillingbourne agreed to accept each other's return tickets between Guildford, Albury, Shere, Gomshall and Peaslake.

The 448 required four buses, the narrow lane from Gomshall up to Burrows Cross resulting in a restriction to the use of small buses, remaining in force until LT withdrew in August 1964. GS 30, 31, 33, 35 and 39 arrived on 26th November 1953 replacing all the Cubs, an allocation which remained unchanged until GS 31 was exchanged with GS 66 from Amersham on 23rd July 1956.

On 9th August 1950, London Transport began a new town service in Guildford serving a small development of new houses in Pewley Way close to the town centre. The timetable provided a limited weekday service for shopping during the day with a couple of evening journeys. The journey time was only 11 minutes and provided seven journeys during the week and ten on Saturdays. Although the route had nothing in common with the 448, London Transport numbered it 448A since their contribution to the 448 resulted in some buses having extended layovers in Guildford, and the 448A timetable was arranged so that it could be run by buses in between trips on the 448. The 448A timetable would remain completely unaltered until August 1964, Tillingbourne continuing the same timetable for a further 14 months before they withdrew the route.

After the introduction of the GSs, the 448 timetable saw a regular 30 minute headway throughout the day right up to the last departure from Guildford at 10.28pm. There were five journeys beyond Peaslake to Ewhurst which left Guildford between the normal 30 minute headway, all being run by London Transport, while the main Peaslake service continued the pre-war arrangement of Tillingbourne running one third and London Transport two thirds. The Sunday service was – even by the standards of the time – extremely good. The first departure from Guildford was at 9.28am after which the timetable was exactly the same as each weekday until the last departure at 10.28pm, the only small variation being the omission of the first Ewhurst journey in the morning.

GS 39 pulls out from the island opposite the Bulls Head at Ewhurst on one of the five journeys which ran beyond Peaslake. Comparison with the picture of the same bus on Page 77 shows that it now has the grab handles fitted and the paper PAYE label has been replaced with the transfer in the front quarter light. The Aldershot & District bus waits at the terminus before returning to Guildford via Cranleigh on route 23. It was one of a batch of 16 new East Lancs lowbridge bodied Dennis Lance K3s delivered in 1949/50. They were of an improved design with Dennis's own engines, five-speed gearboxes and lower saloon heaters, and had a long life with the company. *Mick Webber*

To PEASLAKE & EWHURST

Route 448

Operated jointly with Tillingbourne Valley Services Ltd.

NOTE. Between Coverwood and the Foot of Pitch Hill, passengers may board buses and be set down only at Woolpit (St. Thomas's School Gates).

Weekdays

P.M. times are in heavy figures

			TV		MF	MF					SO	TV	SO		TV			TV
Guildford Bus Station, Onslow Street ...	628	658	728	...	750	758	828	858	928	958	1028	1058	1128	1158	1216	1258	128
Guildford Horse and Groom	631	7 1	731		753	8	831	9 1	931	10 1	1031	11 1	1131	12 1	1219	1 1	131
Merrow Church............................	641	711	741		8 3	811	841	911	941	1011	1041	1111	1141	1211	1229	1 11	141
Newlands Corner	645	715	745		8 7	815	845	915	945	1015	1045	1115	1145	1215	1233	115	145
Shere Telephone Exchange..................	653	723	753	...	815	823	853	923	953	1023	1053	1123	1153	1223	1241	123	153
Gomshall Compasses	656	726	756	8 0	818	826	856	926	956	1026	1056	1126	1156	1226	1244	126	156
Peaslake War Memorial..................	7 8	738	8 8	8 12	830	838	9 8	938	10 8	1038	11 8	1138	12 8	1238	1256	138	2 8
Ewhurst Bulls Head	.			825	.		.	.	.		.					1 9	.

			TV			TV		TV			TV			TV			TV
Guildford Bus Station, Onslow Street ...	146	228	258	328	358	428	458	516	531	558	631	7 1	728	831	858	958	1028
Guildford Horse and Groom	149	231	3 1	331	4 1	431	5 1	519	534	6 1	634	7 4	731	834	9 1	10 1	1031
Merrow Church............................	159	241	3 11	341	4 11	441	5 11	529	544	611	644	714	741	844	911	1011	1041
Newlands Corner	2 3	245	315	345	415	445	515	533	548	615	648	718	745	848	915	1015	1045
Shere Telephone Exchange..................	211	253	323	353	423	453	523	541	556	623	656	726	753	856	923	1023	1053
Gomshall Compasses	214	256	326	356	426	456	526	544	559	626	659	729	756	859	926	1026	1056
Peaslake War Memorial..................	226	3 8	338	4 8	438	5 8	538	556	611	638	711	741	8 8	911	938	1038	11 8
Ewhurst Bulls Head	239		.	.	.	.	.	6 9	.	.	.	.	.	924	.	.	.

Sundays

•—Additional journeys on Bank Holiday Sundays and Mondays only

								TV				TV			TV		
Guildford Bus Station, Onslow Street ...	928	...	•1128	...	1216	...	1258	...	128	146	228	258	328	358	428	458	516
Guildford Horse and Groom	931	.	•1131	.	1219	.	1 1	.	131	149	231	3 1	331	4 1	431	5 1	519
Merrow Church............................	941	.	•1141	.	1229	.	1 11	.	141	159	241	3 11	341	4 11	441	5 11	529
Newlands Corner	945	.	•1145	.	1233	.	115	.	145	2 3	245	315	345	415	445	515	533
Shere Telephone Exchange..................	953	.	•1153	.	1241	.	123	.	153	211	253	323	353	423	453	523	541
Gomshall Compasses	956	.	•1156	.	1244	.	126	.	156	214	256	326	356	426	456	526	544
Peaslake War Memorial..................	10 8	.	•12 8	.	1256	.	138	...	2 8	226	3 8	338	4 8	438	5 8	538	556
Ewhurst Bulls Head	.	.	.	.	1 9	.	.	.	.	239	.	.	.	.	.	.	6 9

	TV			TV			TV		
Guildford Bus Station, Onslow Street ...	558	631	7 1	728	...	831	858	...	1028
Guildford Horse and Groom	6 1	634	7 4	731	.	834	9 1	.	1031
Merrow Church............................	611	644	714	741	.	844	911	.	1041
Newlands Corner	615	648	718	745	.	848	915	.	1045
Shere Telephone Exchange..................	623	656	726	753	.	856	923	.	1053
Gomshall Compasses	626	659	729	756	.	859	926	.	1056
Peaslake War Memorial..................	638	711	741	8 8	.	911	938	.	11 8
Ewhurst Bulls Head	.	.	.	.	.	924	.	.	.

MF—Monday to Friday.   **TV**—Operated by Tillingbourne Valley Services Ltd.   **SO**—Saturday only

NOTE: While every effort will be made to keep to the timetables, London Transport does not undertake that its buses will be operated in accordance with them, or at all. London Transport will not be responsible for any loss, damage or inconvenience caused by reason of any operating failure or in consequence of any inaccuracies in the timetables.

LONDON TRANSPORT, 55 BROADWAY, S.W.I. ABBey 1234

20.3.57

F4800(A)

Waterlow & Sons Limited, London and Dunstable

Agreements with the Union laid down minimum layover periods for buses at termini of three minutes for crew buses and five minutes for omo buses – the additional time in that case to allow the driver time to complete the waybill and change front and rear blinds. An exception to this was where an omo journey used a 'lazy' blind display which did not need changing. To fit in with the Tillingbourne timetable, only three minutes were allowed at Ewhurst and Peaslake, an extremely unusual arrangement which continued until London Transport withdrew from the route. Perversely, the 448A which used a 'lazy' blind display was always allowed five minutes' layover at Pewley Way.

Between Peaslake and Ewhurst passenger traffic was extremely limited with very few houses along the way. The road from Coverwood down Pitch Hill into Ewhurst was steep and narrow such that, other than the gates at Woolpit school, passengers were not permitted to board or alight. The terminus at Peaslake required a turn from the village street by the War Memorial, then a reverse round the small road island, buses then standing at the shelter just off the main road for the return. The turn at Ewhurst required a reverse off the main road opposite the Bulls Head pub to stand on the stop which was also used by the 449, Aldershot and District's service 23 from Guildford via Cranleigh and for a short period in 1955 by the 852. In 1950 this was altered so that buses ran clockwise round the island opposite the pub to stand.

Morning departures into Guildford for early shoppers carried heavy loads, and buses left Peaslake at 8.11am and 8.33am, as well as the 8.28am from Ewhurst duplicated from Peaslake at 8.41am. Four journeys were therefore provided in this 30 minute period, and further duplicates ran during the day, all of which were provided by London Transport. The 1955 public timetable showed duplicates at 8.41am from Peaslake every day, and from Guildford at 3.28pm every day and 12.58pm and 2.28pm on Saturdays. These duplicates ran all the way to Peaslake and also duplicated the return journey. Other unscheduled duplicates were run '*to instructions*' on an ad-hoc basis where traffic might be busiest. In 1959, the 8.41am duplicate from Peaslake was timed to run at 8.43am, two minutes behind the journey from Ewhurst, an arrangement which lasted until Tillingbourne took over the whole route. There was however a curious alteration in June 1959 to this journey. Instead of running as a 448 to Guildford, the 8.43am followed the normal 448 route to Silent Pool but then ran via the 425 route through Albury and Chilworth to Guildford. The reason behind this is unknown, and there seems no logical explanation, particularly as there was no return journey via the same routeing in the afternoon. By October 1960, this journey had reverted to operating as a 448 once again.

In addition to the duplicates, an additional journey ran at 3.53pm from Guildford, five minutes in front of the regular 3.58pm, but was withdrawn in the winter 1958 schedules. The other timetabled duplicates were gradually removed, all except the morning Peaslake bus being withdrawn by 1960. Because of the requirement to use GSs on the route, certain journeys which carried exceptional loads still saw unscheduled duplicates. Reducing passengers beyond Gomshall however resulted in a morning and evening peak duplicate being curtailed there. In 1964, a new terminal working was approved at Gomshall. The morning bus set down passengers at the stop on the main road just before the end of Queen Street about 200 yards before the Compasses Inn. The bus then turned right along Queen Street to run round to Tower Hill on the normal line of route. There was a short stand time on the stop at Tower View from where the bus then ran down to The Compasses and back to Guildford. The evening journey worked in the reverse direction, terminating at Tower Hill before running back along Queen Street to the main road for the return. A revised schedule was sent to the Aldenham blind shop on 9th May 1964, the new panels requiring Gomshall shown twice with the two different qualifying points (Tower Hill and Queen Street) complete with two intermediate points. This was only three months before London Transport withdrew and although it is not recorded if this duplicate ran five days a week, the new blind was little used.

The first signs of reducing traffic were recognised in the winter 1956 schedules when the 9.58am and 10.58am journeys from Guildford and returns from Peaslake were reduced to operate on Saturdays only. In the significant reductions with the winter 1958 schedules the Sunday service to Ewhurst was abandoned and the Peaslake timetable reduced to every 45 minutes, thus eliminating two GSs from Guildford's Sunday run out. Other than these small cuts and the gradual reduction in duplicates, the timetable then remained unchanged until London Transport withdrew. Tillingbourne's journeys remained completely unchanged throughout the period of joint operation.

The scheduling of GSs on duplicates was not confined to the 448 however. Gradual timetable cuts on other routes which accelerated from the early 1960s gave rise to an occasional lack of capacity on a few peak journeys. One GS was therefore regularly rostered to run a duplicate to Woking and back each morning on the 436, while a school journey to Horsley on the 432 also saw regular use of a GS to run the duplicate. Since these never appeared in the public timetable and no records remain, the exact timing of these is unknown. Running number GF7 was regularly used for the 436 duplicate, but that used on the 432 is not known.

By the mid-1960s, losses on rural routes were becoming an increasing concern. The GS fleet was also in decline since the routes they operated were bearing the majority of service cuts, and in order to improve efficiency in scheduling, RFs were replacing GSs where possible. Despite declining passengers, reasonable loads were still being carried on the 448 such that timetable cuts would have thrown up some capacity issues at certain times due to the limited seating capacity of the GSs. RFs could have allowed cuts given their greater capacity, but since they were not permitted beyond Gomshall, the GSs had to remain running a timetable which could otherwise have been cut back. The 425 and 432 schedules did not allow any time to run the 448A even on a reduced timetable although it carried fewer and fewer passengers. In any event, the 448 schedules would have become much less efficient without operation of the 448A, so that both routes had continued with little alteration. With increasing losses, London Transport approached Tillingbourne in 1964 to see if they were prepared to take over their part of the 448 and the whole of the 448A. The agreement which led to London Transport handing over their operation on 12th August 1964 is covered in detail in *Green All Over* and does not need to be repeated here. London Transport's last day was a Tuesday to accord with the standard roster week, which ran from Wednesday to Tuesday, revised rosters without the 448 and 448A starting from the next day. Tillingbourne's subsequent operation of the 448 and 448A is covered in chapter eight.

Guildford's original allocation was all included in the first overhaul programme for late 1956 or early 1957, GS 30 being the first to go on 12th October 1956. Five days later GS 25 was allocated fresh from overhaul as cover. GS 30 returned on 28th November, releasing GS 33 but which went to Amersham once completed.

On 19th July 1964, GS 35 has left Peaslake and is approaching Burrows Cross on a return trip to Guildford. The bus was officially allocated to Dorking at this time so perhaps has been borrowed to cover some engineering work on Guildford's other GSs. Three weeks after this was taken, London Transport handed over their share of the 448 to Tillingbourne Valley who continued to use their own GSs on the route for a further six years. *Peter Mitchell*

GS 35 went for overhaul on 27th December returning on 13th February 1957, and GS 39 on 29th January, returning on 29th March. GS 32 was transferred to Amersham on 13th February for use as a float bus, returning on 1st May along with GS 33 transferred back from Amersham. GS 66 was delicensed on 18th May, went for overhaul three days later and returned at the end of July, although the exact date is not recorded. Guildford's allocation remained more stable compared to other garages, and no further changes were made until GS 39 was transferred to Stevenage on 7th May 1959. GS 27 was transferred temporarily on 29th November 1960 from Chelsham to release GS 25 for its second overhaul. It returned on 3rd February 1961, was relicensed on 1st March, in turn releasing, GS 27 for its second overhaul.

The final allocation was GS 25, 26, 35 and 36 and all were delicensed on 13th August 1964. GS 25 remained there until sold direct to Tillingbourne Valley on 27th October when it resumed work on the 448, 448A and their other routes. GS 26, 35 and 36 were all relicensed, GS 26 and 36 being transferred to Dunton Green on 1st November and GS 35 to Windsor on 1st September.

Of the two bus stations in Guildford, London Transport's in Onslow Street was somewhat more basic than the larger one at Farnham Road. Apart from the 425, all of London Transport's routes radiated from Onslow Street which was shared with the town services operated by Aldershot & District, Safeguard, and Tillingbourne. GS 21 is loading for a journey to Peaslake, while GS 36 appears to have returned from a journey up to Pewley Way. GS 21 received its second overhaul in June 1961 and on return was allocated to Guildford on 1st September, remaining at Guildford until operation of the 448 was taken over by Tillingbourne. GS 36 arrived at Guildford on 22nd December 1956 and remained there until the end of service. It too was delicensed on 13th August 1964, but enjoyed a long and varied life before becoming one of the last sold in 1973. *S J Butler collection*

GUILDFORD GS SCHEDULES – OCTOBER 1960

MONDAY TO FRIDAY

ROUTE	TIME DEPART	FROM	TO	ROUTE NUMBER	TIME DEPART	FROM	TO
RUNNING NUMBER GF 6				**RUNNING NUMBER GF 8**			
LIGHT	6.50 am	Lees Road Garage	Onslow Street	LIGHT	7.25 am	Lees Road Garage	Onslow Street
448	6.58 am	Onslow Street	Peaslake	448	7.32 am	Onslow Street	Ewhurst
448	7.41 am	Peaslake	Onslow Street	448	8.28 am	Ewhurst	Onslow Street
448	8.28 am	Onslow Street	Peaslake	448A	9.34 am	Onslow Street	Pewley Way
448	9.11 am	Peaslake	Onslow Street	448A	9.50 am	Pewley Way	Onslow Street
LIGHT	9.53 am	Onslow Street	Lees Road Garage	LIGHT	10.05am	Onslow Street	Lees Road Garage
LIGHT	11.20am	Lees Road Garage	Onslow Street	LIGHT	12.16pm	Lees Road Garage	Onslow Street
448	12.11 pm	Peaslake	Onslow Street	448A	12.26 pm	Onslow Street	Pewley Way
448	1.46 pm	Onslow Street	Ewhurst	448A	12.42 pm	Pewley Way	Onslow Street
448	2.42 pm	Ewhurst	Onslow Street	448	12.58 pm	Onslow Street	Peaslake
448	3.58 pm	Onslow Street	Peaslake	448	1.41 pm	Peaslake	Onslow Street
448	4.41 pm	Peaslake	Onslow Street	448A	2.26 pm	Onslow Street	Pewley Way
448	5.31 pm	Onslow Street	Peaslake	448A	2.42 pm	Pewley Way	Onslow Street
448	6.14 pm	Peaslake	Onslow Street	448	3.28 pm	Onslow Street	Peaslake
LIGHT	6.57 pm	Onslow Street	Lees Road Garage	448	4.11 pm	Peaslake	Onslow Street
				448	4.58 pm	Onslow Street	Peaslake
RUNNING NUMBER GF 21				448	5.41 pm	Peaslake	Onslow Street
LIGHT	6.20 am	Lees Road Garage	Onslow Street	448	6.31 pm	Onslow Street	Peaslake
448	6.28 am	Onslow Street	Peaslake	448	7.14 pm	Peaslake	Onslow Street
448	7.11 am	Peaslake	Onslow Street	448A	7.59 pm	Onslow Street	Pewley Way
448	7,58 am	Onslow Street	Peaslake	448A	8.15 pm	Pewley Way	Onslow Street
448	8.41 am	Peaslake	Onslow Street	448	8.31 pm	Onslow Street	Ewhurst
448	9.28 am	Onslow Street	Peaslake	448	9.27 pm	Ewhurst	Onslow Street
448	10.11 am	Peaslake	Onslow Street	448	10.28 pm	Onslow Street	Peaslake
448A	11.26 am	Onslow Street	Pewley Way	448	11.11 pm	Peaslake	Onslow Street
448A	11.42 am	Pewley Way	Onslow Street	LIGHT	11.54 pm	Onslow Street	Lees Road Garage
448	12.16 pm	Onslow Street	Ewhurst				
448	1.12 pm	Ewhurst	Onslow Street	**RUNNING NUMBER GF 7**			
448	2.28 pm	Onslow Street	Peaslake	*LIGHT*		*Lees Road Garage*	*Onslow Street*
448	3.11 pm	Peaslake	Onslow Street	*436*		*Onslow Street*	*Woking*
LIGHT	3.53 pm	Onslow Street	Lees Road Garage	*436*		*Woking*	*Onslow Street*
				LIGHT		*Onslow Street*	*Lees Road Garage*
LIGHT	5.06pm	Lees Road Garage	Onslow Street	*Exact times of 436 morning peak duplicates not known*			
448	5.16 pm	Onslow Street	Ewhurst	*LIGHT*	*3.20 pm*	*Lees Road Garage*	*Onslow Street*
448	6.12 pm	Ewhurst	Onslow Street	*448*	*3.28 pm*	*Onslow Street*	*Peaslake*
LIGHT	7.08 pm	Onslow Street	Lees Road Garage	*448*	*4.11 pm*	*Peaslake*	*Onslow Street*
				Times in italics: bus runs as duplicate to GF 8. This was in the public			
LIGHT	9.20 pm	Lees Road Garage	Onslow Street	timetable until October 1957, operated to instructions thereafter.			
448A	9.26 pm	Onslow Street	Pewley Way	448A	5.35 pm	Onslow Street	Pewley Way
448A	9.42 pm	Pewley Way	Onslow Street	448A	5.51 pm	Pewley Way	Onslow Street
LIGHT	9.56 pm	Onslow Street	Lees Road Garage	LIGHT	6.05 pm	Onslow Street	Lees Road Garage

GUILDFORD GS SCHEDULES – OCTOBER 1960

SATURDAY

ROUTE NUMBER	TIME DEPART	FROM	TO
RUNNING NUMBER GF 6			
LIGHT	6.50 am	Lees Road Garage	Onslow Street
448	6.58 am	Onslow Street	Peaslake
448	7.43 am	Peaslake	Gomshall
448	8.00 am	Gomshall	Ewhurst
448	8.28 am	Ewhurst	Onslow Street
448A	9.26 am	Onslow Street	Pewley Way
448A	9.42 am	Pewley Way	Onslow Street
448A	10.56 am	Onslow Street	Pewley Way
448A	11.10 am	Pewley Way	Onslow Street
448	11.28 am	Onslow Street	Peaslake
448	12.11 pm	Peaslake	Onslow Street
448	1.46 pm	Onslow Street	Ewhurst
448	2.42 pm	Ewhurst	Onslow Street
448	3.58 pm	Onslow Street	Peaslake
448	4.41 pm	Peaslake	Onslow Street
448	5.31 pm	Onslow Street	Peaslake
448	6.14 pm	Peaslake	Onslow Street
LIGHT	6.57 pm	Onslow Street	Lees Road Garage

ROUTE NUMBER	TIME DEPART	FROM	TO
RUNNING NUMBER GF 7			
LIGHT	*12.50 pm*	*Lees Road Garage*	*Onslow Street*
448	*12.58 pm*	*Onslow Street*	*Peaslake*
448	*1.41 pm*	*Peaslake*	*Onslow Street*
448	*2.28 pm*	*Onslow Street*	*Peaslake*
448	*3.11 pm*	*Peaslake*	*Onslow Street*

Times in italics:- bus runs as duplicate to GF 8 and GF 21 This was in the timetable until October 1957, operated to instructions thereafter.

ROUTE NUMBER	TIME DEPART	FROM	TO
448A	5.35 pm	Onslow Street	Pewley Way
448A	5.51 pm	Pewley Way	Onslow Street
LIGHT	6.05 pm	Onslow Street	Lees Road Garage

GF 7 was available to run additional journeys on 425 to Chilworth until lunchtime but details of these are not known

ROUTE NUMBER	TIME DEPART	FROM	TO
RUNNING NUMBER GF 8			
LIGHT	10.50 am	Lees Road Garage	Onslow Street
448	10.58 am	Onslow Street	Peaslake
448	11.41 am	Peaslake	Onslow Street
448A	12.26 pm	Onslow Street	Pewley Way
448A	12.42 pm	Pewley Way	Onslow Street
448	12.58 pm	Onslow Street	Peaslake
448	1.41 pm	Peaslake	Onslow Street
448A	2.26 pm	Onslow Street	Pewley Way
448A	2.42 pm	Pewley Way	Onslow Street
448	3.28 pm	Onslow Street	Peaslake
448	4.11 pm	Peaslake	Onslow Street
448	4.58 pm	Onslow Street	Peaslake
448	5.41 pm	Peaslake	Onslow Street
448	6.31 pm	Onslow Street	Peaslake
448	7.14 pm	Peaslake	Onslow Street
448A	7.59 pm	Onslow Street	Pewley Way
448A	8.15 pm	Pewley Way	Onslow Street
448	8.31 pm	Onslow Street	Ewhurst
448	9.27 pm	Ewhurst	Onslow Street
448	10.28 pm	Onslow Street	Peaslake
448	11.11 pm	Peaslake	Onslow Street
LIGHT	11.54 pm	Onslow Street	Lees Road Garage
448A	8.15 pm	Pewley Way	Onslow Street
RUNNING NUMBER GF 21			
LIGHT	6.20 am	Lees Road Garage	Onslow Street
448	6.28 am	Onslow Street	Peaslake
448	7.11 am	Peaslake	Onslow Street
448	8.28 am	Onslow Street	Peaslake
448	9.11 am	Peaslake	Onslow Street
448	9.58 am	Onslow Street	Peaslake
448	10.41 am	Peaslake	Onslow Street
448A	11.26 am	Onslow Street	Pewley Way
448A	11.42 am	Pewley Way	Onslow Street
448	12.16 pm	Onslow Street	Ewhurst
448	1.12 pm	Ewhurst	Onslow Street
448	2.28 pm	Onslow Street	Peaslake
448	3.11 pm	Peaslake	Onslow Street
448A	3.56 am	Onslow Street	Pewley Way
448A	4.12 pm	Pewley Way	Onslow Street
448A	4.44 pm	Onslow Street	Pewley Way
448A	5.00 pm	Pewley Way	Onslow Street
448	5.16 pm	Onslow Street	Ewhurst
448	6.12 pm	Ewhurst	Onslow Street
LIGHT	7.-8 pm	Onslow Street	Lees Road Garage
LIGHT	9.20 pm	Lees Road Garage	Onslow Street
448A	9.26 pm	Onslow Street	Pewley Way
448A	9.42 pm	Pewley Way	Onslow Street
LIGHT	9.56 pm	Onslow Street	Lees Road Garage

LEATHERHEAD

ORIGINAL ALLOCATION

GS 5   Transferred from Aldenham for training on 14th October 1953 – licensed for service 6th November 1953

GS 17   transferred from Aldenham for service 6th November 1953

ROUTE 481   6th November 1953 – 9th December 1958
                         10th December 1958 – 25th October 1961 Peak hour and duplicates only

         422 & 462   Peak and special duplicates 6th November 1953 – 1st December 1967

PEAK VEHICLE REQUIREMENT

2 GS   6th November 1953 – 9th December 1958

1 GS   10th December 1958 – 1st December 1967

Leatherhead received GSs in November 1953 for use on the 481. The route had been started only six months before, on 6th May that year, to serve the estate at The Wells on Epsom Common just outside the town. The name had originally come from salt wells, later to become part of a farm. The area had been developed as a new housing estate in the 1920s and 30s and until 1953 had never had a bus service. The 481 was a short route taking only nine minutes from the station to the estate where buses ran clockwise round a loop. The timetable ran to a general 30 minute headway each weekday with one gap of over an hour mid-morning when traffic was quieter. The bus left Leatherhead garage at 6.44am to run light to Wells Estate from where it worked the first journey into Epsom at 7.04am. It remained out all day and operated the complete timetable until the last journey from Epsom to The Wells at 8.32pm, from where it ran light back to Leatherhead arriving at 8.57pm. Driver duties for the 481 involved travelling as passengers to and from Epsom by the 408 route, and the bus was allocated running number LH59.

The development of the Wells Estate is referred to in the text, but the road across Wells Common from the maim Epsom to Leatherhead road remained as open common land for many years. GS 17 was allocated to Leatherhead at the same time as GS 5, and on 16th July 1955 comes across Wells Common on a journey back to Epsom Station
Peter Mitchell

When the route began, a second bus was allocated for special duplicates, presumably because of some journeys where the 20 seat capacity of the Cub was inadequate. This practice continued after the allocation of GS 5 and 17, the duplicate remaining in the allocation until December 1967.

GS 5 was delicensed on 1st January 1956, and despatched to Chiswick for overhaul on 29th February. It was replaced by GS 84 on 1st January 1956, sent from Reigate where it had languished out of use since delivery. It was noted in the daily movement records as '*new bus licensed*', and was the last GS to enter service two years after it had been delivered.

GS 17 went for overhaul on 31st May 1956, being replaced by GS 12 from overhaul on 6th June. After overhaul, GS 5 went to Hertford, and GS 17 to Hemel Hempstead. GS 12 was transferred to Crawley on 16th January 1959. GS 30 came from Windsor on 28th January – noted as 'float bus' – and was delicensed six days later, GS 13 having arrived on 31st January having been made redundant at Swanley following the October 1958 cuts when route 479 had been withdrawn. GS 30 remained out of use at Leatherhead until relicensed on 25th March. It replaced GS 13 to be sent for overhaul on 16th March. GS 30 remained in service until delicensed on 1st September, then being transferred to Dunton Green – again as 'float bus' – on 25th November. GS 13 returned on 19th May and remained at Leatherhead for almost six years before being sent to Hertford at the end of 1964 to become one of that garage's last GSs in service. Hertford sent GS 14 in exchange which remained at Leatherhead until the end of GS operation there on 2nd December 1967. It did not see further revenue earning service with London Transport and remained stored at Leatherhead for more than two years. It passed into London Country's ownership and was moved to Garston in September 1970 and sold the following year.

GS 5 was licensed for service on 6th November 1953 and is clearly very new in this picture. No grab handles have yet been fitted and no paper "pay as you enter" label has been stuck on the windscreen. The picture illustrates a background of bleak housing and concrete roads which were typical of many new council estates built in the decade after the war but which fulfilled a desperate need for the replacement of sub-standard housing and a population moving out from London. *Maurice Doggett*

GS 30 was used as a float bus in the south area and arrived at Leatherhead from Windsor on 28th January 1959 as cover for GS 13 which was called in for overhaul. As this picture was taken in the summer, it will probably have been between 17th July and 1st September on which date it was delicensed once again and transferred to Dunton Green. On fine Sundays, the 422 was frequently duplicated and this bus waits at Leatherhead station for a journey to Boxhill carrying running number LH201. Headley Common *en route* was a popular destination for day trippers and the terminus at Boxhill was about half a mile from the summit and viewpoint. *Steve Fennell collection*

Facing page The 442 route was one of those introduced perhaps more in hope than expectation of reasonable passenger numbers. Apart from Stoke Poges village, il offered no facility not covered by other routes and crew operation soon proved optimistic. It was converted to omo on 14th August 1954, and almost four years later GS 78 appears to be completely empty in Stoke Poges on a journey back to Windsor. By this date, the timetable had been reduced to a few peak and shopping journeys, and two months later the route would be finally abandoned. *Peter Mitchell*

The narrow estate roads in The Wells were initially thought to be unsuitable for large buses, and RFs were not approved for the route until 10th December 1958 when the GS was formally replaced with an RF. Due to this restriction there had been no cross working from other routes on the 481, the allocated GS being fully employed all day running a timetable which changed little throughout the 1950s. Since buses worked in a loop round the estate, and the 481 used a 'lazy blind' display, there was no need to change the blind at all during the day, and in 1958, the timetable was altered so that the previous five minute layover at The Wells was omitted, buses running non-stop round the estate, but taking a longer layover at Epsom station between journeys. In 1957, two later journeys were added in the evening so that the last departure from Epsom station was at 9.32pm to Wells Estate from which the bus ran light back to Leatherhead garage. The restriction to GS operation having been lifted, a further late evening journey was added by using an RT from the 418 which worked the 9.31pm journey from Bookham station through Epsom to West Ewell. From here it operated the 10.22pm back through Epsom to Leatherhead garage, but completing a double run en-route via Wells Estate as a 481.

Until December 1958, the second GS was permanently allocated for duplicates on the 481, but following conversion to RF, one GS was retained although noted only as a *Special Duplicate* in the allocation book. It did however operate timetabled journeys in the morning peak. In the October 1962 schedules it left Leatherhead garage at 8.03am to run to The Wells to work the 8.21am into Epsom three minutes behind the RF, effectively as a timetabled duplicate. It returned from Epsom, again three minutes behind the RF, to work another journey in from The Wells, finishing at Epsom station at 8.58am. From here, the driver took a relief break before taking over at 9.21am on the 419 while that driver took the GS empty back to the garage for his break. The running number LH63 was used for this duty. For the remainder of the day, it remained allocated for duplicates as required. The running number allocated to the duplicate workings was LH201, journeys being run on 481, 422 to Boxhill and 462 to Fetcham. No records have been found of the actual timings of these journeys, but they would have been run in peak hours and at school times. The Saturday allocation of the GS duplicate was withdrawn in the schedules of 25th October 1961, but an RF was again allocated for 481 Saturday duplicates from 22nd May 1963. In June 1962, the formal allocation was reduced to one GS Monday to Friday for duplicates only, the allocation remaining until withdrawn with the 1967 winter schedules.

WINDSOR

ORIGINAL ALLOCATION
GS 77, 78, and 80 Licensed and transferred from Aldenham 12.7.54

ROUTE 442   14th July 1954 – 14th December 1958
       445   14th July 1954 – 30th December 1966
       459   15th October 1958 – 3rd March 1960

PEAK VEHICLE REQUIREMENT
2 GS until 14th December 1958, 1 GS until 30th December 1966

Given that the GSs were intended for minor rural routes, their allocation to Windsor was perhaps unexpected, but by 1954 passenger numbers were falling away and economies were being sought. Windsor operated two short routes to places which were for the most part served frequently by others, and although both routes were crew operated, passenger levels were appreciably lower than Windsor's other routes.

The 442 was one of the new routes introduced in June 1948 to meet the exponential rise in passenger numbers in the immediate post-war years, and provided the village of Stoke Poges with a service for the first time. Leaving Slough along the same road as the 353 and the town services to the growing Manor Park estate, it passed the edge of the estate before reaching Stoke Poges village itself a short distance further on. From here it continued to Farnham Royal located on the main road from Slough to Beaconsfield. It ran to an approximately hourly headway Monday to Saturday, while on Sundays the same headway operated seven journeys from early afternoon to mid evening. The total journey time from Slough station to Farnham Royal was only 17 minutes and resulted in the inefficient use of the bus and crew rostered to run it. The large area of woodland at Burnham Beeches had been commandeered by the War Office during the war, but was opened again to the public in 1948. This immediately became an extremely popular place for weekend visitors, and on Monday to Saturday, the 442 was extended every two hours there from Farnham Common during the summer period. A different route numbered 474 ran on Sundays direct from Slough to Burnham Beeches and enjoyed and hourly headway in the morning, increasing to half hourly in the afternoon. Both the 442 and 474 were operated with RTs, and in its first few years, the 442 carried enough passengers to justify this, but by 1954, numbers had fallen back to the extent that a GS would provide enough capacity.

From its inception, the 442 provided only a very limited facility to places not served by other routes. The centre of Stoke Poges village was only a few hundred yards from the main road between Slough and Gerrards Cross on the 353 which enjoyed a half hourly headway all day six days a week, and hourly all day Sunday. The short distance from the village to Farnham Royal used a lane which passed a golf course and was typified by a number of large houses producing minimal traffic. Farnham Royal was served by the 441 route which ran as many as many as five or six journeys an hour seven days a week. The 442 therefore was largely superfluous from its inception, and went into a rapid decline following conversion from RT to GS, the principal reduction being the withdrawal of the summer extension to Burnham Beeches which was not reinstated in 1954 when GSs replaced RTs. Within two years, the 442 Monday to Friday timetable had been reduced to only five journeys to Farnham Royal. There were two departures at 8.06am and 8.51am, and then no service until three journeys from mid-afternoon, the bus returning to Windsor garage just after 8.00pm. The Saturday timetable had been reduced to just two afternoon journeys which allowed just under an hour and a half for shopping in Slough. Such a skeleton timetable was unsustainable, and the 442 was abandoned completely after 13th October 1958 as part of the savage cuts following the seven week strike earlier that year.

The 445 was Windsor's second route, and linked Windsor to the riverside village of Datchet, running a short way beyond to Datchet Common to turn by the Rising Sun pub. The journey time from Windsor Castle (where most journeys terminated) was just 14 minutes and was crew operated with RFs. The timetable ran to a 30 minute headway all day during the week requiring two buses which

Crew operation of the 445 was converted to omo on the same date as the 442. This picture of GS 77 illustrates the genteel riverside nature of Datchet village in the 1950s and is little changed today. The terminus at The Rising Sun pub at Datchet Common is a few minutes further on, and the bus passes a single parked car in a village street which is now barely passable with parked cars. *Alan Cross*

ran to an extremely inefficient schedule whereby one bus arrived back at Windsor three minutes after the departure of the second bus, and then stood at the Castle terminus for 27 minutes before its next departure. In this way, each bus and crew ran in service for only 28 minutes each hour! Operation was more efficient on Sundays when one bus ran to a 40 minute headway all day.

Although the 445 provided a useful link to and from Windsor – especially at weekends when large numbers of visitors would arrive – Slough grew in importance from about 1950, and by 1951 the 460 and 484 routes ran three of four journeys an hour from Datchet to Slough six days a week, even Sunday having a 30 minute service in the afternoon. By 1954, passenger numbers no longer justified crew operation, and GSs replaced the RFs on 14th July that year on the same day that the RT on the 442 was replaced.

GS 77, 78, and 80 were taken from store at Garston where they had remained since delivery. Two buses were required for service (one for each of route 442 and 445) plus one engineering spare. GS 80 was transferred to Hitchin on 30th October 1956 when timetable reductions reduced the allocation to two GS. Although there was in theory no engineering spare after the transfer of GS 80, the 442 timetable required a bus for only a very limited period during the week and for only a short period Saturday afternoon. Windsor's allocation remained unchanged until 24th November 1959 when GS 30 arrived from Amersham to release GS 77 for its first overhaul. GS 78 was sent to Chiswick for overhaul on 7th January 1959, GS 77 following soon after. GS 40 came from Garston on 1st January 1959 to replace GS 78 for overhaul on 7th January, returning to Dunton Green on 4th March. GS 40 was delicensed on 1st March, moved to storage at Guildford for several months, returning again to Windsor for service on 13th January 1960. Its stay this time was extremely short. It was withdrawn only two weeks later, which proved to be the end of its service life. On 5th August that year it was noted in the fleet records as one of five GS *'stored unlicensed for disposal'* and was one of the pair sold to West Bromwich early in 1961. After all these changes, Windsor's allocation consisted of just GS 77 which became a casualty of the October 1962 changes when GS 20 arrived from Crawley on 9th October. GS 77 was delicensed and transferred to Reigate on 23rd November where it remained in store for eighteen months until sold in May 1964.

The 30 minute weekday headway on the 445 – apart from being inefficient – was also too generous, and with the winter 1954 schedules was reduced to generally hourly, although a 45 minute headway was operated on Saturday in the afternoon. The hourly headway on Sundays did not begin until mid-afternoon. To allow for omo working, the running time was increased by two minutes, but the hourly headway still required 18-minute stand time at Datchet Common and ten at Windsor Castle. One scheduling oddity to balance a crew working was the 10.38pm each evening from Windsor bus station to Datchet and back, worked by an RT from the 335 allocation. With the drastic reduction of the 442 timetable referred to above, the GS from that worked one morning journey on the 445 and most of the evening timetable, while the bus which had worked most of the 445 all day was rostered to run the last journey to Farnham Royal on the 442.

London Transport sought many other economies in the October 1958 schedules, and one which was perhaps unexpected was the retention of the GS following the withdrawal of the 442. This bus which was used to replace the crew RF on the 459 between Uxbridge and Richings Park at Iver. The route had been run by the Central area before the war but withdrawn as part of wartime cost-saving measures, and when reintroduced ran via a different route from Uxbridge to be operated remotely from Windsor garage by the Country area. The hourly weekday timetable was soon reduced to a peak hour service during the week, although it retained an hourly service all day Saturday. The Sunday timetable had been an early casualty in the winter 1952 schedules. The GS was rostered every day on running number WR25 and left Windsor garage at 6.16am as a 458 to Uxbridge. On Saturdays, the bus ran the hourly timetable all day, arriving back at Uxbridge at 10.22pm, then working the 10.30pm 458 back to Windsor, timed to run only three minutes behind the previous journey, running effectively as a duplicate.

GS operation on the 459 remained for only five months from October 1958. GS 78 has pulled in to the parade of shops in front of Uxbridge Underground station on a journey to Richings Park. The bus stop was for the 607 trolleybus route to Shepherds Bush, 709/710/711 Green Lines to London and the 457/457A to Slough, and although the trolleybus terminus was a short distance from the station, a turning circle and passing loop had been installed here. The clothing of the waiting passengers, and the Austin A35 car behind the bus are all very redolent of the time. This picture was taken in November or December 1958, as GS 78 was delicensed on 1st January 1959 and sent to Works for overhaul a week later. It returned for further service at Dunton Green on 4th March.
Peter Grace

Nevertheless, the running time to Windsor for the GS was still two minutes longer than the crew RF it followed to comply with the Union agreement on running times for omo workings. One wonders if, in practice, the GS driver sometimes followed right behind the RF and avoided carrying any passengers at all back to Windsor! The Monday to Friday schedule allowed for the bus to return to Windsor in the off peak period, and after the two morning trips to Richings Park, the bus worked the 9.24am 458 back to Windsor. The afternoon working was different, the GS running the 1.52pm 457 journey to Iver Heath from where it ran to Richings Park for the four afternoon journeys. The bus finished at Iver at 6.51pm when it worked the 6.56pm 458 journey from there back to Windsor. GS operation on the 459 did not last long however. Although passenger numbers had declined, the capacity of the GS proved inadequate on some journeys, and it was replaced after a little more than four months with an RF from 4th March 1959.

In a further economy – despite the link between Windsor and Datchet – the 445 Sunday service was withdrawn in October 1958, the evening service also being withdrawn during the week at the same time after the 6.06pm from Windsor Castle. The Saturday headway remained unchanged including the late evening journey from the 335 allocation which continued until the winter 1963 schedules. An additional departure from Datchet Common to Windsor at 6.03pm during the week operated as a means of running a 460 peak hour trip back to the garage.

GS operation on the 445 continued until the winter schedules were introduced on 31st December 1966. The Monday to Friday timetable remained little changed throughout the 1960s with a crew operated morning positioning journey for the 484 added from 1964. The need for a facility to go shopping in Windsor reduced significantly, and in 1965 the Saturday timetable was reduced to operate only until lunchtime, the bus finishing its day at 1.45pm back at the garage. On 31st December 1966, the GS was replaced by an RF and, for the remainder of the 1960s, the 445 gradually withered away to a skeleton timetable. GS 20 was delicensed in September 1964 to be replaced by GS 35 which had been withdrawn at Guildford after the 448 and 448A had been transferred to Tillingbourne Valley some weeks earlier. It remained until February 1966 when it was demoted for use as Abbey Wood's staff bus. GS 42 was transferred from Garston to replace it and remained until the last day of operation, and on 31st December 1966 was transferred to Dorking.

The crew duties for May 1955 overleaf show the crew rosters for the 442 and 445 at the time. WR5 ran all of the 442, and WR7 most of the 445. Duty 354 worked WR5 on both the 442 and the 445 evening service as described above. WR6 was used for the 445 on Sunday but WR7 started at the same time and ran as a duplicate to WR6 on the 3.15pm from Windsor. It also worked an additional duty late in the evening, running two journeys to Datchet in between those run by WR6. These Sunday journeys on WR7 were not included in the public timetable and were therefore extra scheduled workings. This duty was withdrawn with the start of the 1955 winter schedules. The driver on duty 359 worked the whole of the scheduled 445 except during his relief period when the driver from duty 360 travelled to Windsor Castle to take over the bus, returning later to work the 9.15pm to Datchet on WR7. Note that drivers were allowed two minutes to and from the parked bus at Windsor to give time to walk from the canteen or office to the stand in the bus station. The bus on WR5 was left at Slough station by the driver on duty 352, to be taken over by duty 354 later.

MONDAY TO FRIDAY

Duty No.	Start Time	Route	Running Number	Time	Place	Time	Place	Finish Time	Relief Period	Total Time Worked
351	6.47am	445	WR7	7.02	WR	9.51*	WI			
		445	WR7	10.36	WI	1.41	WI			
			Walk	1.41	WI	1.56	WR	2.11pm	43m	6h 41m
352	7.11am	442	WR5	7.26	WR	9.27	WR			
		353	Travel	9.34	WR	9.38	WC			
		445	WR7	9.52	WI	10.36	WI			
			Walk	1036	WI	10.51*	WR			
		442	WR5	12.35	P	1237	WR			
			WR5	1237	WR	2.30	SR			
			Walk	2.30	SR	2.36	SL			
		353	Travel	2.39	SL	2.49	WI			
		445	WR7	3.13	WI	3.56	WI			
			Walk	3.56	WI	4.11	WR	4.26pm	1h44m	7h 32m
353	1.19pm	353	Travel	1.34	WR	1.38	WC			
		445	WR7	1.41	WC	3.11	WI*			
		445	WR7	3.56	WI	8.30	WR	8.45pm	43m	6h 43m
354	3.19pm	353	Travel	3.34	WR	3.48	SK			
			Walk	3.48	SK	3.54	SR			
		442	WR5	3.55	SR	4.37	SR*			
		442	WR5	5.56	SR	6.40	SR			
		442/5	WR5	7.14	SR	1045	WR	11.00pm	1h19m	6h 22m

SATURDAY

Duty No.	Start Time	Route	Running Number	Time	Place	Time	Place	Finish Time	Relief Period	Total Time Worked
355	6.47am	445	WR7	7.02	WR	10.36	WI*			
		445	WR7	12.06	WI	3.15	WR	3.30pm	1h 28m	7h 15m
356	10.12am	457	Travel	10.27	WR	10.31	WC			
		445	WR7	10.36	WI	12.06	WI			
		353	Travel	12.19	WI	12.23	WR			
		442	WR5	12.37	WR	2.30	SR*			
		442	WR5	3.55	SR	4.53	WR	5.08pm	1h 23m	5h 33m
357	1.30pm	445	WR7	1.45	WR	4.45	WR*			
		445	WR7	5.30	WR	7.41	WI			
		353	Travel	7.49	WI	7.53	WR	8.08pm	48m	5h 55m
358	3.45pm	445	WR7	4.00	WR	6.15	WR			
			WR7	6.15	WR	6.17	P*			
		353	Travel	7.34	WR	7.38	WC			
		445	WR7	7.49	WI	10.45	WR	11.00pm	1h 15m	6h 00m

SUNDAY

359	3.00pm	445	WR6	3.15	WR	6.56	WI*			
		445	WR6	8.26	WI	10.00	WR	10.15pm	1h 28m	5h 47m
360	3.00pm	445	WR7	3.15	WR	4.00	WR			
			WR7	4.00	WR	4.02	P*			
		417	Travel	6.43	WR	6.47	WC			
		445	WR6	6.56	WI	8.26	WI			
		417	Travel	8.35	WI	8.39	WR			
		445	WR7	9.15	WR	1045	WR	11.00pm	2h 41m	5h 19m

LOCATION CODES :-	WR	Windsor Bus Station	SK	Slough, Windsor Road Granada Cinema
	WC	Windsor Castle Hill Northbound	SR	Slough Station
	WI	Windsor Castle Hill Southbound	P	To or from parking of bus
	SL	Slough, Windsor Road Bus Shelter	*	Denotes the start of a relief period during the duty

Before the 1962 reallocations, GS 20 had been Hertford's training bus for a short period but was sent to Garston on 1st September. It was soon relegated as a "heater float" bus and went to Amersham, Grays and Crawley before being transferred to Windsor on 9th October where it remained until it was delicensed there on 7th September 1964. It was its last period in service and was sold early in 1965. It has just pulled out from the stand at Windsor Castle for a journey to Datchet with a Post Office Morris Commercial van behind.

4 North West Operations

GS 28 arrived at High Wycombe from overhaul two weeks before the start date of the 442 route on 3rd October 1965, and a few weeks later on 30th October the bus appears to have a reasonable load on a journey through Hicks Farm Estate. The unedifying architecture of many new estates of the period is well illustrated by the blocks of flats in the background. The 442 was High Wycombe's only omo duty that could not be combined with any others until one-man conversions on route 305 and 455 resulted in more efficient rosters.
Peter Mitchell

HIGH WYCOMBE

INITIAL ALLOCATION   GS 28 from overhaul 15th September 1965
Licensed for service 1st October 1965

ROUTE OPERATED   442 3rd October 1965 – 16th February 1968

Route 442 was introduced on 3rd October 1965 in order to provide a service to Hicks Farm estate to the east of High Wycombe town centre. Only a short section covered roads with no previous bus service, part of the route running along the road to Micklefield estate already being part of the 326 route. The 442 timetable was designed to suit daytime shopping, running on weekdays only to a 30 minute headway. The first departure from High Wycombe garage was at 10.00am, the last at 5.35pm, buses running in a loop through Hicks Farm, alternate journeys running either clockwise or anti-clockwise. High Wycombe was administratively in the South West District when the route started, hence the number 442.

High Wycombe's operations had always been 100% crew operated so that the 442 became the only omo duty in the roster. The duty was allocated to drivers in strict order of seniority and received the enhanced rate of pay for omo working. Some of them had perhaps not driven a manual crash gearbox bus, so required some training before the route began. The decision to operate the route with a GS seemed perverse given the policy of replacing them where possible on other routes, but by late 1965 omo conversions had gathered pace resulting in a shortage of omo RFs around the fleet. Since traffic potential on the new 442 was not likely to be great and crew working was not feasible, then a small capacity GS was more sensible in the circumstances. Since the 442 omo duty required only one driver all day and could not be worked from any other roster, the timetable had to allow time for a meal relief break during the day, resulting in a 90 minute gap in service between 12.30pm and 2.00pm from High Wycombe, although this probably caused minimal inconvenience to potential shoppers.

GS 28 had been overhauled in August 1965, after which it was transferred to High Wycombe on 15th September 1965 to allow type training before the 442 commenced operation. On 7th October 1967, GS 21 was replaced at St Albans when the 382 was converted to RF. It was sent to High Wycombe to replace GS 28 which was delicensed and returned to store at Garston. GS 21's tenure at High Wycombe however was short lived when the 442 was converted to RF operation on 17th February 1968. After a short period in store, GS 28 saw further service in 1968 at Northfleet and would later spend more than four years as a staff bus, not being finally delicensed until February 1973. GS 21 however was not so fortunate, its short spell on the 442 proving to be its last period in service.

In 1968 when the 305 was converted to omo, joint rosters could be arranged with the 442. Two earlier journeys were added on Monday to Friday and the 90 minute lunchtime meal relief break was eliminated so that the 442 timetable ran all day.

AMERSHAM

INITIAL ALLOCATION

For training:-	GS 4	23rd November 1953
For service:-	GS 55 and 60	16th December 1953
	GS 34, 50 and 64	17th December 1953
	GS 52, 56, 65 and 66	18th December 1953
	GS 61 and 62	21st December 1953
	All entered service on	21st December 1953

ROUTES OPERATED

348, 348A, 373, 397, 398, 398A	21st December 1953 – 23rd October 1962
332	16th October 1957 – 23rd October 1962
	(Schooldays only)

394, 394A – School journeys and duplicates plus one evening journey

PEAK VEHICLE REQUIREMENT   10

When the first GS allocations were complete, Amersham had the largest, although Hertford would later become the second largest once the second allocation was made there in June 1954. The network of routes operated by both garages were similar in their rural nature, serving many small villages and what were still in 1954 small country towns. In the 1950s, the area to the north and west of Chesham had changed little in the previous 50 years. Amersham and Chesham had seen some housebuilding between the two wars and the Metropolitan line from London increased the number of commuters. The resulting affluence in the area became a significant factor in the gradual decline in passenger numbers.

Amersham's GS routes effectively fell into two separate groups, those radiating from Chesham being generally more rural in nature and requiring the majority of the daily run out. From Amersham itself the only route was the 398 to Beaconsfield plus two journeys numbered 398A diverting from the route at Coleshill to run to Winchmore Hill. The short 373 route from Beaconsfield to Penn was worked remotely by buses running to and from Amersham on the 398.

The Chesham routes were:-

348	Chesham Moor – Chesham – Hivings Hill – Bellingdon – Buckland Common or St Leonards
348A	Chesham Moor – Chesham – Hivings Hill – Pond Park Estate
397	Chesham Moor – Chesham – Hawridge – Cholesbury – Wigginton – Tring

GS 4 was Amersham's training bus, allocated almost one month before its allocation of Cubs was replaced on 21st December 1953. It remained at Amersham until its first overhaul in January 1956. It has apparently worked a journey back to Amersham garage on route 353, but there is no reference in any allocation book or timetable to GSs working journeys on that route. It is most likely therefore that some journeys from the garage to and from Chesham were worked as 353. GS 61 parked behind was also one of Amersham's original allocation, and it had worked back to the garage, perhaps from an early peak hour journey. *Mick Webber*

A brand new GS 62 picks up passengers outside Amersham garage for Beaconsfield on its second day in service, three days before Christmas 1953. It has yet to be fitted with a paper PAYE label in the front windscreen and appears to have a blind from one of the Cubs it replaced, which retained the larger route numbers. Three more new GSs are visible inside the garage. *Alan Cross*

The Amersham routes were:-
373   Beaconsfield – Knotty Green – Penn
398   Amersham Station – Amersham – Coleshill – Beaconsfield
398A Amersham Station – Amersham – Coleshill – Winchmore Hill

The other principal route radiating from Chesham was the 394 with a number of variations numbered 394A, 394B, and 394C which covered some positioning journeys to and from Amersham garage and odd journeys in Chesham which terminated at the Nashleigh Arms north of the Broadway in the town centre – the main stopping point and terminus (394A was Chesham Moor). In 1954 the 394 and variants were crew operated with 15T13s since consistent loads were carried around Chesham, particularly on the road out to Chartridge which had seen much 'ribbon development' of new houses in the 1920s and 1930s. Whilst these routes were not GS operated, at various times a small number of peak and school journeys were run on the 394 with GSs from the other routes. These can be seen from the running number schedules included later in this section.

Whilst 'Chesham Moor' perhaps sounds like a rural location, it was in fact a large council estate on the edge of Chesham which – like all Home Counties towns – saw increased development in the 1950s. Journeys to and from here on the GS routes were limited, the majority being operated by the crew buses on the 394A providing more capacity.

The large village of Penn retained its rural character despite the development of many new houses during the 1950s and 1960s. On 24th March 1962, GS 52 has left the terminus on a 373 back to Beaconsfield with the 'lazy' blind display used on this short route. Seven months after this picture was taken, the 363 from High Wycombe was extended to Beaconsfield to replace the 373 on the same day that Amersham's GSs were all replaced. Unlike many others, GS 52 would remain for a further 12 years being one of the very last in use. *Peter Mitchell*

GS 33 arrived at Amersham from its second overhaul on 1st January 1962 having been fitted with indicators. Ten days later it was transferred to Tring, returning after being replaced there with an RF on 2nd July, only to be replaced again on 24th October along with all Amersham's GSs. A few weeks before the changeover, it picks up passengers at Chesham Broadway for one of the many short journeys to Bellingdon. *Colin Routh*

To the north west of Chesham town centre, a new estate was developed at Pond Park, and the 348 had been introduced in October 1953 shortly before the GSs arrived to provide the link into Chesham. The running time to and from the estate was only ten minutes, and the service was infrequent, only 11 journeys being provided during the week, 14 on Saturdays and no service at all on Sundays. Other than the addition of a couple of school journeys and a late evening Saturday journey, the timetable remained unaltered throughout the period of GS operation. It was only after the changes in September 1962, when RFs replaced GSs, that the 348A had an increase in service, including one Sunday journey into Chesham Broadway at 2.21pm with a return late in the evening at 10.07pm. The purpose of this limited facility is unclear although cinema performances finished by 10.00pm so that the 10.07pm provided a service back to the estate.

After the climb up Hivings Hill from Chesham, the 348 ran into less populated countryside. Bellingdon however was a fairly large spread-out village with a council estate, all of which justified a number of extra journeys from Chesham which turned there, reversing into a side lane just beyond the Bull Inn in the centre of the village. Indeed, around half of the 348 timetable consisted of these short journeys. At busier shopping times on Saturdays, some of these ran within a few minutes of those to or from Buckland Common or St Leonards, and between 4.30pm and 6.45pm during the week there were no fewer than seven departures to Bellingdon as shoppers and commuters returned home. A morning schoolday journey to Bellingdon and the afternoon return were duplicated each day.

GS 56 was part of Amersham's initial allocation and remained there until replaced with RFs in October 1962. It has come in from Penn and stopped in Beaconsfield High Street before running down to the terminus at the Saracens Head. The lack of traffic and parked cars is evident, and the Ford Popular and Standard Vanguard van in the background are very typical of the period. *Peter Jones collection*

GS 65 was part of Amersham's original allocation and remained there until the changeover in October 1962. The driver looks at the photographer as he signals to pull away from the same stop as GS 33 on the previous page on a 348 to St Leonards. The service to this small hamlet was very infrequent, the Saturday service unusually having fewer journeys than during the week. *Peter Aves collection*

The 348 to the new estate at Pond Park on the edge of Chesham started on 7th October 1953 a few weeks before Amersham's Cubs were all replaced. The service was renumbered 348A on 19th May 1954. GS 61 was one of Amersham's original allocation and waits at Chesham Broadway for passengers on the ten-minute journey to the estate. Buses interworked all day between the 348, 348A and 397 from Chesham, some duties also being worked to and from the 398 rosters as shown in the running number schedules on pages 106–108. *Peter Jones collection*

The road beyond the village was not narrow, but had far less passenger traffic. Only a very few houses were passed before the farm and house at Braziers End about a mile beyond Bellingdon, and about another mile further on the route turned right down to a staggered road junction. This was Buckland Common where buses reversed into the lane beside the Rose and Crown pub to stand before the return journey. This had been the sole terminus of the route until an additional leg was added in March 1947 to the small hamlet of St Leonards a mile or so beyond the turning at Buckland Common. The 348 was one of the shorter rural routes with a running time of only 22 minutes from Chesham to Buckland Common or 25 minutes to St Leonards, where buses reversed in a side lane near the church. The village was so small however that it was one of the few places without a timing point in the timetable. Although journeys to St Leonards did not actually serve Buckland Common, the stop at the Rose and Crown was only some 100 yards from the main road so that passengers had only to walk this short distance to catch a bus coming from St Leonards. During the week, of the 14 journeys which continued beyond Bellingdon, seven each ran to either St Leonards or Buckland Common, whereas only six from the total of 17 on Saturdays ran to St Leonards. On Sundays, at a time when leisure traffic could still be buoyant, there were six journeys to Buckland Common and three to St Leonards. This timetabling resulted in uneven gaps to both villages, and the hourly service to Buckland Common on Saturday afternoon meant that anyone catching the 12.34pm from St Leonards could not return from Chesham until 5.00pm. Although there was a late evening departure every day to Buckland Common, the last bus to St Leonards was shortly after 8.00pm, reflecting the limited passenger numbers from this small hamlet.

The 397 had the advantage of a country town at each end of the route, and served a number of villages along the way. The road out from Chesham through Chesham Vale had a number of scattered houses all the way. Climbing steadily through Hawridge the 397 reached Cholesbury where the route turned right at the village green. The lane straight on led to Buckland Common less than half a mile beyond, but London Transport never altered the 348 which – as a 'dead leg' working from Chesham – became less and less efficient to run as passengers fell away. A different routeing to these villages from Cholesbury – perhaps numbered 397A – would have provided a more cost effective way of serving St Leonards and Buckland Common and allowed the 348 to be cut back to Bellingdon, which provided enough revenue to remain worthwhile. It would be a further 20 years before London Country made these changes when a circular routeing from Cholesbury was introduced.

From Cholesbury the 397 road across common land passed by woodland to a T junction where the route turned left and passed the entrance to the famous Champneys health farm. A mile further on the village of Wigginton was reached. This was a larger village providing reasonable traffic and from there a steep hill descended to join the main A41 road into Tring. After dropping passengers in the High Street, a short run through the town led to London Transport's small garage where the last passengers were set down on the main road before the bus turned onto the garage forecourt to reverse.

A town at each end of the 397 provided much greater potential than the 348 and justified an hourly headway all day until late evening. On Sundays, a 90 minute headway ran from lunchtime until late evening. On Saturdays, greater numbers of shoppers travelling into Chesham justified an increased service so that eight additional short journeys were run to and from Cholesbury about half way along the route, the 1.25pm from Chesham to Tring and the 2.06pm return being duplicated. A short journey from Cholesbury was timed to depart at 2.22pm just five minutes in front of the duplicated journey from Tring, since these two buses might not have sufficient capacity left on board to pick up people all the

GS 60 has arrived at Chesham Moor on a journey from Tring. The driver checks the ticket machine so that he can complete his waybill before reversing into Bois Lane to stand. It has running number MA 24, so this will be a Saturday when most 397 journeys from Tring ran to Chesham Moor, and will depart as a 348 to either St Leonards or Buckland Common. *John Hambley collection*

way into Chesham. The duplicate bus from Tring was later timed to run two minutes behind the regular departure, and in the cuts of October 1958, other than two early morning trips, all of the Saturday short journeys to Cholesbury were withdrawn in a response – even then – to a reduction in shoppers who had begun to use cars instead. Although not in the public timetable, a duplicate bus might be run on one of the late afternoon returns from Chesham but this too ceased with the 1958 cuts.

On returning to Chesham, having run the duplicate 348 morning schoolday journey to Bellingdon, the bus then ran light to Cholesbury to run from there as a duplicate to the service bus into Tring. Both buses then ran together to form the 9.15am from Tring back to Chesham. The timetable on the 397 was run entirely by Amersham, but in 1956 the duplicate referred to above was withdrawn and replaced by Tring's GS from the 387 which ran a journey from Wigginton at 9.03am four minutes behind the through journey from Chesham. On schooldays, the bus ran in service to Wigginton (although not shown in the timetable) and during school holidays instead ran light to the village. There was also an afternoon schoolday return from Tring to Wigginton which equally did not appear in the public timetable.

The 348, 348A and 397 were all interworked, buses running journeys on all three routes. The Monday to Friday schedules for winter 1960 are shown overleaf, from which readers can see that the bus working MA45 ran morning and afternoon school journeys. These journeys were worked under contact to Buckinghamshire County Council and the blind showed only 'School Special' as illustrated in the picture of GS 42.

As far as can be determined, this display was unique to that duty and not repeated at any other garage where GSs ran such journeys. The schedule also shows the early morning 394 journeys worked by MA25, and the 394 schoolday journeys worked by MA41. MA18 ran morning peak journeys on 348 and 348A before returning to Amersham garage to work the Beaconsfield routes for the rest of the day. After the first 348 journey to Buckland Common, MA24 ran to the Nashleigh Arms then to Quill Hall Estate to spend the remainder of the day on the Beaconsfield routes. One scheduling oddity is the 5.43pm 348 journey from Quill Hall Estate to the Nashleigh Arms run by MA25. The bus ran light from Chesham Broadway to work this journey, which appears to be an evening return to the morning 7.26am Nashleigh Arms to Quill Hall Estate worked by MA24. The purpose of this is unclear but it is likely it ran for the use of a few people who lived in Chesham and worked in the estate.

It will be seen that most – but not all – buses worked in service to and from Amersham garage. Drivers for those buses which did not return to the garage during the day travelled by 353 or 362 to and from Chesham Broadway to change over.

The 332 route number was introduced from 16th October 1957 for journeys which served the schools on Stanley Hill in Amersham. In 1962, GS 64 is about to leave Amersham garage showing the rather crowded blind display for these journeys. It is allocated to MA31, so it is operating the single morning journey at 8.54am from the garage to Quill Hall. The two afternoon journeys were allocated to MA 21. *Alan Cross*

AMERSHAM GS SCHEDULES – WINTER 1960
MONDAY TO FRIDAY

ROUTE NUMBER	TIME DEPART	FROM	TO	ROUTE NUMBER	TIME DEPART	FROM	TO
RUNNING NUMBER MA 18				**RUNNING NUMBER MA 21**			
348	6.23 am	Amersham Garage	Bellingdon	398	6.16 am	Amersham Garage	Beaconsfield
348	6.59 am	Bellingdon	Chesham Bdy	373	6.48 am	Beaconsfield	Penn
348A	7.19 am	Chesham Bdy	Pond Park Estate	373	7.09 am	Penn	Beaconsfield
348A	7.34 am	Pond Park Estate	Chesham Bdy	373	7.32 am	Beaconsfield	Penn
348A	7.51 am	Chesham Bdy	Pond Park Estate	373	7.53 am	Penn	Beaconsfield
348A	8.06 am	Pond Park Estate	Chesham Bdy	373	8.17 am	Beaconsfield	Penn
LIGHT	8.19 am NSch	Chesham Bdy	Amersham Garage	373	8.38 am	Penn	Beaconsfield
348A	8.27 am Sch	Chesham Bdy	Pond Park Estate	398	9.53 am	Beaconsfield	Quill Hall Estate
348A	8.42 am Sch	Pond Park Estate	Amersham Garage	398	10.37 am	Quill Hall Estate	Beaconsfield
398	9.14 am	Amersham Garage.	Coleshill Magpies	373	11.21 am	Beaconsfield	Penn
398	9.27 am	Coleshill Magpies	Quill Hall Estate	373	11.42 am	Penn	Beaconsfield
398	9.57 am	Quill Hall Estate	Amersham Garage	373	12.05 pm	Beaconsfield	Penn
SPREADOVER BUS				373	12.26 pm	Penn	Beaconsfield
398	4.07 pm	Amersham Garage	Beaconsfield	398	12.47 pm	Beaconsfield	Quill Hall Estate
373	4.39 pm	Beaconsfield	Penn	398	1.31 pm	Quill Hall Estate	Coleshill Church
373	5.00 pm	Penn	Beaconsfield	398	1.57 pm	Coleshill Church	Quill Hall Estate
373	5.23 pm	Beaconsfield	Penn	398	2.23 pm	Quill Hall Estate	Beaconsfield
373	5.45 pm	Penn	Beaconsfield	398	3.07 pm	Beaconsfield	Amersham Garage
373	6.11 pm	Beaconsfield	Penn	332	3.49pm Sch	Amersham Garage	Quill Hall Estate
373	6.32 pm	Penn	Beaconsfield	332	4.02pm Sch	Quill Hall Estate	Amersham Garage
398	6.53 pm	Beaconsfield	Quill Hall Estate	332	4.15pm Sch	Amersham Garage	Quill Hall Estate
398	7.48 pm	Quill Hall Estate	Beaconsfield	332	4.28pm Sch	Quill Hall Estate	Amersham Garage
373	8.36 pm	Beaconsfield	Penn	398	4.45 pm	Amersham Garage	Quill Hall Estate
373	9.05 pm	Penn	Beaconsfield	398	5.02 pm	Quill Hall Estate	Beaconsfield
398	9.38 pm	Beaconsfield	Quill Hall Estate	373	5.46 pm	Beaconsfield	Penn
398A	10.22 pm	Quill Hall Estate	Winchmore Hill	373	6.07 pm	Penn	Beaconsfield
398A	10.54 pm	Winchmore Hill	Amersham Garage	373	6.44 pm	Beaconsfield	Penn
				373	7.05 pm	Penn	Beaconsfield
RUNNING NUMBER MA 19				373	7.46 pm	Beaconsfield	Penn
398	6.51 am	Amersham Garage	Beaconsfield	373	7.57 pm	Penn	Beaconsfield
373	7.23 am	Beaconsfield	Knotty Green	398	8.18 pm	Beaconsfield	Amersham Garage
373	7.36 am	Knotty Green	Beaconsfield	**RUNNING NUMBER MA 22**			
373	7.49 am	Beaconsfield	Penn	397	6.46 am	Amersham Garage	Cholesbury
373	8.10 am	Penn	Beaconsfield	397	7.24 am	Cholesbury	Chesham Bdy
398	8.31 sm	Beaconsfield	Quill Hall Estate	348	7.46 am	Chesham Bdy	Bellingdon
398	9.15 am	Quill Hall Estate	Amersham Garage	348	8.06 am	Bellingdon	Chesham Bdy
398	1.01 pm	Amersham Garage	Beaconsfield	397	8.34 am	Chesham Bdy	Tring
373	1.33 pm	Beaconsfield	Penn	397	9.15 am	Tring	Chesham Bdy
373	1.55 pm	Penn	Beaconsfield	348	9.59 am	Chesham Bdy	Buckland Common
373	2.30 pm	Beaconsfield	Penn	348	10.28 am	Buckland Common	Chesham Bdy
373	3.00 pm	Penn	Holtspur	397	11.24 am	Chesham Bdy	Tring
373	3.30 pm	Holtspur	Penn	397	12.04 pm	Tring	Chesham Moor
373	3.56 pm	Penn	Penn	348	12.55 pm	Chesham Moor	Buckland Common
398	4.22 pm	Holtspur	Amersham Garage	348	1.32 pm	Buckland Common	Chesham Bdy
398	5.10 pm	Amersham Garage	Quill Hall Estate	**PARK AT CHESHAM OR LIGHT TO / FROM GARAGE – UNKNOWN**			
398	5.27 pm	Quill Hall Estate	Coleshill Magpies	348	3.20 pm	Chesham Bdy	Bellingdon
398	5.52 pm	Coleshill	Quill Hall Estate	348	3.40 pm	Bellingdon	Chesham Moor
398	6.27 pm	Quill Hall Estate	Coleshill Church	397	4.10 pm	Chesham Moor	Tring
LIGHT	6.52 pm	Coleshill Church	Amersham Garage	397	5.04 pm	Tring	Chesham Moor
				348	6.05 pm	Chesham Moor	Bellingdon
				348	6.25 pm	Bellingdon	Amersham Garage

RUNNING NUMBER MA 24

348	6.10 am	Amersham Garage	Buckland Common
348	6.53 am	Buckland Common	Chesham Bdy
LIGHT	7.18 am	Chesham Bdy	Nashleigh Arms
348	7.26 am	Nashleigh Arms	Quill Hall Estate
398A	7.51 am	Quill Hall Estate	Winchmore Hill
398A	8.23 am	Winchmore Hill	Quill Hall Estate
398	8.55 am	Quill Hall Estate	Beaconsfield
373	10.01 am	Beaconsfield	Penn
373	10.22 am	Penn	Beaconsfield
398	10.43 am	Beaconsfield	Quill Hall Estate
398	11.27 am	Quill Hall Estate	Coleshill Church
398	11.53 am	Coleshill Church	Amersham Garage
398	1.33 pm	Amersham Garage	Beaconsfield
398	2.05 pm	Beaconsfield	Amersham Garage
398	3.08 pm	Amersham Garage	Quill Hall Estate
398A	3.29 pm	Quill Hall Estate	Winchmore Hill
398A	4.02 pm	Winchmore Hill	Quill Hall Estate
398	4.43 pm	Quill Hall Estate	Beaconsfield
398	5.21 pm	Beaconsfield	Quill Hall Est.ate
398	6.05 pm	Quill Hall Estate	Amersham Garage

RUNNING NUMBER MA 23

348	7.18 am	Amersham Garage	Bellingdon
348	7.38 am	Bellingdon	Chesham Bdy
348A	8.21 am	Chesham Bdy	Pond Park Estate
348A	8.37 am	Pond Park Estate	Chesham Bdy
348	8.57 am	Chesham Bdy	Bellingdon
348	9.17 am	Bellingdon	Amersham Garage
397	3.08 pm	Amersham Garage	Tring
397	4.04 pm	Tring	Chesham Bdy
397	4.57 pm	Chesham Bdy	Cholesbury
397	5.19 pm	Cholesbury	Chesham Bdy
348	5.42 pm	Chesham Bdy	Bellingdon
348	6.02 pm	Bellingdon	Chesham Bdy
348	6.31 pm	Chesham Bdy	St Leonards
348	7.01 pm	St Leonards	Amersham Gar.

RUNNING NUMBER MA 25

394	6,33 am	Amersham Garage	Chartridge
394	7.04 am	Chartridge	Hyde End
394	8.01 am	Hyde End	Chartridge
397	8.40 am	Chartridge	Cholesbury
397	9.19 am	Cholesbury	Chesham Bdy
348A	9.42 am	Chesham Bdy	Pond Park Estate
348A	10.07 am	Pond Park Estate	Chesham Bdy
397	10.24 am	Chesham Bdy	Tring
397	11.04 am	Tring	Chesham Moor
348	11.54 am	Chesham Moor	St Leonards
348	12.32 pm	St Leonards	Chesham Bdy
397	1.22 pm	Chesham Bdy	Tring
397	2.04 pm	Tring	Chesham Bdy
348A	2.45 pm	Chesham Bdy	Pond Park Estate
348A	3.00 pm	Pond Park Estate	Chesham Bdy
348A	3.15 pm	Chesham Bdy	Pond Park Estate
348A	3.30 pm	Pond Park Estate	Chesham Bdy
348A	3.45 pm	Chesham Bdy	Pond Park Estate

348A	4.00pm NSch	Pond Park Estate	Chesham Bdy
397 Sch	4.00pm Sch	Pond Park Estate	Cholesbury
397	4.33pm Sch	Cholesbury	Chesham Bdy
348A	5.06 pm	Chesham Bdy	Pond Park Estate
348A	5.21 pm	Pond Park Estate	Chesham Bdy
LIGHT	5.32 pm	Chesham Bdy	Quill Hall Estate
348	5.43 pm	Quill Hall Estate	Chesham Nash Arms
348	6.08 pm	Chesham Nash Arms	Amersham Garage

RUNNING NUMBER MA 31

398	6.33 am	Amersham Garage	Coleshill Magpies
398	6.46 am	Coleshill Magpies	Quill Hall Estate
398	7.25 am	Quill Hall Estate	Amersham Garage
348	7.50am Sch	Amersham Garage	Chesham Bdy
LIGHT	8.10am Sch	Chesham Bdy	Amersham Garage
332	8.54am Sch	Amersham Garage	Quill Hall Estate
332	9.07am Sch	Quill Hall Estate.	Amersham Garage
LIGHT	12.05 pm	Amersham Garage	Chesham Bdy
397	12.24 pm	Chesham Bdy	Tring
397	1.04 pm	Tring	Chesham Moor
348	1.55 pm	Chesham Moor	Buckland Common
348	2.30 pm	Buckland Common	Chesham Bdy
348	3.00 pm	Chesham Bdy	St Leonards
348	3.30 pm	St Leonards	Chesham Bdy
348	4.05 pm	Chesham Bdy	Bellingdon
348	4.25 pm	Bellingdon	Chesham Bdy
348	4.45 pm	Chesham Bdy	Bellingdon
348	5.05 pm	Bellingdon	Chesham Bdy
397	5.29 pm	Chesham Bdy	Tring
397	6.08 pm	Tring	Chesham Moor
348	7.58 pm	Chesham Moor	St Leonards
348	8.36 pm	St Leonards	Chesham Bdy
348A	9.06 pm	Chesham Bdy	Pond Park Estate
348A	9.21 pm	Pond Park Estate	Chesham Bdy
397	9.36 pm	Chesham Bdy	Tring
397	10.15 pm	Tring	Amersham Garage

RUNNING NUMBER MA 41

348	6.30 am	Amersham Garage	St Leonards
348	7.18am Nsch	St Leonards	Amersham Garage
348	7.18am Sch	St Leonards	Chesham Bdy
394	7.53am Sch	Chesham Bdy	Chartridge
394	8.10am Sch	Chartridge	Chesham Bdy
LIGHT	8.30am Sch	Chesham Bdy	Pond Park Estate
348A	8.46am Sch	Pond Park Estate	Chesham Bdy
397	9.08am NSch	Amersham Gar.age	Tring
397	9.24am Sch	Chesham Bdy	Tring
397	10.04 am	Tring	Chesham Moor
348	10.55 am	Chesham Moor	Buckland Common
348	11.30 am	Buckland Common	Chesham Bdy
348A	12.01 pm	Chesham Bdy	Pond Park Estate
348A	12.16 pm	Pond Park Estate	Chesham Bdy
LIGHT	12.40 pm	Chesham Bdy	Amersham Garage
394	3.31pm Sch	Amersham Garage	Chesham Nash Arms
394	3.57pm Sch	Chesham Nash Arms	South Heath
LIGHT	4.30pm Sch	South Heath	Chesham Bdy
394	4.30pm NSch	Amersham Garage	Chesham Bdy
348	5.18 pm	Chesham Bdy	St Leonards

348	5.48 pm	St Leonards	Chesham Bdy

PARK CHESHAM BDY 6.13 PM – 7.13 PM

LIGHT	7.16 pm	Chesham Bdy	Chesham Moor
348	7.27 pm	Chesham Moor	Buckland Common
348	8.02 pm	Buckland Common	Chesham Bdy
397	8.34 pm	Chesham Bdy	Tring
397	9.13 am	Tring	Chesham Moor
348	10.22 pm	Chesham Bdy	Buckland Common
348	10.49 pm	Buckland Common	Amersham Garage

RUNNING NUMBER MA 45

348A	6.18 am	Amersham Garage	Pond Park Estate
348A	6.49 am	Pond Park Estate	Chesham Bdy
348	7.10 am	Chesham Bdy	Bellingdon
348	7.30 am	Bellingdon	Chesham Bdy
348	7.52 am	Chesham Bdy	Bellingdon
348	8.12 am	Bellingdon	Chesham Bdy
Schools	Schools dup	Pond Park Estate	Chesham Bdy
348	9.00 am	Chesham Bdy	St Leonards
348	9.32 am	St Leonards	Chesham Bdy

PARK AT CHESHAM OR LIGHT TO / FROM GARAGE – UNKNOWN

348	11.42 am	Chesham Bdy	Bellingdon
348	12.02 pm	Bellingdon	Chesham Bdy
348	12.42 pm	Chesham Bdy	Bellingdon
348	1.02 pm	Bellingdon	Chesham Bdy
348	1.17 pm	Chesham Bdy	St Leonards
348	1.52 pm	St Leonards	Chesham Bdy
397	2.24 pm	Chesham Bdy	Tring
397	3.04 pm	Tring	Chesham Bdy
348A	3.46pm Sch	Chesham Bdy	Pond Park Estate
Schools	4.01pm	Pond Pk Est School Special – route unknown	
348	4.51 pm	Chesham Bdy	Bellingdon
348	5.11 pm	Bellingdon	Chesham Bdy
348A	5.40 pm	Chesham Bdy	Pond Park Estate
348A	5.55 pm	Pond Park Estate	Chesham Bdy
348A	6.10 pm	Chesham Bdy	Pond Park Estate
348A	6.25 pm	Pond Park Estate	Chesham Bdy
348	6.50 pm	Chesham Bdy	Bellingdon
348	7.10 pm	Bellingdon	Chesham Bdy
397	7.34 pm	Chesham Bdy	Tring
397	8.13 pm	Tring	Amersham Garage

MA 45 DISPLAYED 'SCHOOL SPECIAL' BLIND WITH NO ROUTE NUMBER FOR MORNING AND AFTERNOON JOURNEYS AS SHOWN

NSch	Not schooldays
Sch	Schooldays only

The schedule includes workings on route 332, the number having been introduced on 16th October 1957 for journeys from Amersham station via Stanley Hill to serve the schools there. At the same time, the 398 and 398A were extended from Amersham garage to Quill Hall Estate then being developed. Previously the route notionally ran to Amersham station but until this extension, the service up the hill from the garage to the station had been limited to only three morning journeys before 9.30am with one additional late evening journey on Saturday. If these journeys were intended for potential passengers wishing to catch the Metropolitan line towards London, there were no afternoon return journeys to either Coleshill or Beaconsfield until the 1957 extension. Before this, passengers would have had to catch a 362 or 353 for the short journey down to Amersham garage to catch the 398 from the stop on Gore Hill opposite the garage.

The minimal service on the 398A to Winchmore Hill is referred to in the text. GS 52 was one of Amersham's original allocation, and received its first overhaul in 1957, returning to Amersham until the end of service on 23rd October 1962. The driver signals to pull away from the stop at Gore Hill on the 3.29pm journey from Quill Hall estate with apparently few passengers. The journey was timed to pick up those school children in Coleshill who lived along the narrow lanes to Winchmore Hill.
Alan Cross

Beaconsfield was an important – though small – country town. It was popular with weekend visitors, had always been a little more affluent than similar towns in the Country area, and a worthwhile destination. Operation of the 332, 373, 398 and 398A was less complex that the Chesham based routes. The 373 schedule was arranged to work from the 398, a duty on the 373 consisting in most cases of two or three journeys to Penn and back before returning as a 398 to Amersham. Two buses were required to run the 373 timetable during the morning and evening peak since there were a number of commuters who used the route to travel to and from Beaconsfield station. The Beaconsfield terminus for the 373 and 398 was at the Saracens Head hotel situated on the cross roads with the main A40 which ran through the town. Buses crossed the roundabout here to turn across the main road to Slough and stand outside the hotel. Connections here were available on the 455 or 711 Green Line route to Uxbridge and on into London. The 441, 455, and 711 between them provided six journeys an hour into High Wycombe.

The nature of the 373 was less rural. The journey time to Penn was only 17 minutes and the road there had seen much housebuilding in the 1920s and 1930s. Penn was a large and expanding village, its main link to High Wycombe enjoying a 20 or 30 minute headway on the 363 into High Wycombe. Other than a number of commuters, the only purpose of the 373 outside peak times was to provide a shopping service into Beaconsfield. The need to run so many positioning journeys on the 398 meant that the timetable to and from Amersham was more frequent than could be justified once passenger numbers declined. The 373 and resultant positioning journeys were withdrawn in the October 1962 changes, the 363 being extended from Penn to Beaconsfield, although on a less frequent timetable.

GS 31 was transferred from Guildford to Amersham on 23rd July 1956 to replace GS 66, which went to Guildford. It was called in for overhaul in October 1957, and returned on 24th November 1957. It is picking up at the stop at the bottom of Gore Hill opposite Amersham garage on one of the few short journeys to Coleshill Church, only seven minutes from this stop. During the week there was only one evening peak journey which turned there, but five on Saturday including one late evening journey. On Saturday 12th April 1958, it picks up five passengers, and given the direction of the shadows on this sunny day this is the 5.02pm journey. *Buses of Yesteryear*

At Amersham, the stop for the 398 and 398A was at the bottom of Gore Hill almost opposite Amersham garage. There was a steady climb up the hill on the busy main road to Beaconsfield, and at the top the routes turned right by the water tower into the lane through the village of Coleshill. The road was narrow in places, and at the far end the lane came back onto the main road by the Magpies pub. Occasional short journeys turned in the village where they reversed at the War memorial by the Church. A morning and evening peak journey ran to the Magpies but, because there was no safe turning point here, buses ran in a loop either direct along the main road then back through the village or vice versa. In 1959 the B473 junction was improved with a short section of new road creating a short loop round which buses could safely turn. Once back on the B473 it was a short run into Beaconsfield where the route turned right into the residential Ledborough Lane towards the station and High Street and from there down to the Saracens Head terminus. In 1955, the journey time from Amersham garage to Beaconsfield was 30 minutes, but was reduced by three minutes after the Quill Hall extension was introduced, presumably because the previous running time had proved more than generous.

In 1955, the 398A ran only two journeys on Monday to Friday. The route turned down a narrow lane in Coleshill village which soon became single track in places and was probably the reason for the route's restriction to GS operation. These two journeys, although they ran every day, were timed to suit children going to Coleshill village school and who were almost the sole purpose of the route. The terminus at Winchmore Hill involved a loop working round the Common, and was less than 200 yards from the main road served frequently by the 362 between High Wycombe, Amersham and Chesham. The timetable changes which came about with the extension to Quill Hall also added a late evening journey to Winchmore Hill, but this must have been completely pointless. Nevertheless, this late journey survived the conversion to RF operation in October 1962 (at which time the restriction to GS operation was lifted) but was withdrawn the following year.

Amersham's first allocation of GSs has been noted, 12 buses being allocated to cover a maximum run out of ten which applied only on Monday to Friday. Without the need for school journeys at weekends, the Saturday run out was eight, with six Sunday. The daily vehicle movement sheets record that ten C class Cub were delicensed at Amersham on 21st December and sent to Garston for storage pending disposal, the GSs taking over that day. On 5th January 1954, GS 60 was sent to Tring for a short period but soon returned to Amersham.

Although running numbers changed somewhat up to 1962, there were few major timetable changes, some of the reductions which came from the 1958 winter schedules having been referred to above. On 23rd October 1962, the complete replacement of Amersham's GSs by some the former Green Line RF coaches, which had been made redundant after the first RMCs entered service, was part of the first major reduction in GS operation. The GSs, although rugged and reliable with good fuel consumption were nonetheless non-standard and could be readily disposed of to small independent operators. Apart from the 398A, none of Amersham's single deck routes were restricted to GS operation by 1962 so that replacement with RFs was a practical operational change. The replacement took place with the winter schedules and were accompanied by some timetable reductions. The Sunday service on the 398 was withdrawn as was that on the 348 beyond Bellingdon. The 397 route number was abandoned, the 348 and

348A simply being extended from Chesham to Tring on much the same timetable. A two-hourly Sunday service ran between Tring and Bellingdon which could be operated by one bus. With slightly greater interworking between all routes, Amersham's allocation was reduced by one RF overall.

GS 62 was exchanged with GS 69 on 30th September 1954 from Garston, Amersham's allocation then remaining unchanged until 1956 when the first programme of overhauls commenced. GS 75 which had been stored at Garston since delivery was licensed and transferred to Amersham on 1st January 1956 to release GS 4 for overhaul, going to Chiswick three days later. On 15th March it went to Chelsham where it remained until October 1962. On 16th July GS 16 arrived fresh from overhaul and on 23rd July GS 66 was exchanged with GS 31 from Guildford, the reason for this being unclear. GS 16 moved on to Epping on 1st September, GS 31 going for overhaul on 5th October to be replaced temporarily by GS 24 which had just been overhauled. GS 31 returned on 24th November releasing GS 24 to Dunton Green. At various times in 1957, GS 34, 50, 52, 55, 61, 64 and 65 all went for overhaul, all being returned to Amersham. The last of the original allocation, GS 61 went for overhaul on 20th November, returning on 10th January 1968 and relicensed for service on 1st February. GS 16, 26, 32 and 33 were transferred to Amersham for short periods as cover.

By 1959, Amersham's allocation had been reduced to 11 buses covering a maximum run out of ten Monday to Friday, nine Saturday and only three Sunday, reflecting the severe reduction in services that day. The allocation remained stable for over two years, consisting of GS 31, 34, 50, 52, 55, 56, 60, 64, 65, 69 and 75. GS 61 was chosen as one of those hired to Great Yarmouth and was delicensed on 7th September 1961. It was the end of its revenue earning service with London Transport, and when returned from Great Yarmouth on 5th August 1959 it remained in store for almost two years before being sold to Corvedale Motors at Ludlow in April 1961.

The major changes which took place on 24th October 1962 are described in chapter six. Amersham's entire allocation of GSs was replaced by RFs, and the driver rosters combined to cover all omo workings. The majority of Amersham's GSs went for further service, GS 69 and 75 being the only two that were withdrawn and stored, both being sold in 1963. During 1962, and in preparation for the October changes, Amersham's allocation saw frequent transfers to and from other garages. Two of the original allocation, GS 50 and 60, went for their second overhaul early in 1962, both returning for service at Garston, although GS 50 returned unlicensed to Amersham on 26th March where it remained out of use for a month before going to Garston. During 1962, GS 20, 30, 33, 39, 42, 51 were all allocated for short periods, GS 62 from the original allocation also returning on 18th September as a stopgap for three weeks before relegation as a staff bus at Tring on 9th October, two weeks before the changeover to RF. To augment Amersham's existing allocation, RFs 299, 301, 305, 306 and 307 were transferred on 23rd October to replace the GSs the following day.

Thus one of the Country area's largest GS operations came to an abrupt end, the changeover proving to be the beginning of the steady decline which would see all but five GSs removed from service during the next six years.

GS 33 replaced GS 51 at Tring on12th January 1962. It was replaced by an RF on 23rd May 1962. Until this date, Tring also had T 790 allocated for the 352 at weekends as well as some peak journeys on the 387 during the week. T 790 was finally delicensed and transferred to Garston on 8th June, but GS 33 remained until transferred to Amersham on 2nd July. At some point in the early spring of 1962, GS 33 has just left the terminus by the pond to run a journey back to Beaconsfield Road in Tring. It is noticeable that there are no passengers. The seven journeys to Aldbury on Saturday were all one-man operated, but three of the ten journeys on Monday to Friday were crew operated from the 301 allocation. *D. Pearson*

TRING

INITIAL ALLOCATION
GS 68 and 70 arrived 1st January 1954

ROUTES OPERATED
387 January 1954 (exact date uncertain) – 23rd May 1962
397 School journeys Tring – Wigginton. Exact dates unknown

PEAK VEHICLE REQUIREMENT
One bus (two when 397 morning school journey operated)

The location of Tring garage meant that it had always been a small outpost near the Country area's north-western boundary. The overriding reason for its location was to provide an allocation for the 301/302 trunk routes and the 706/707 Green Line routes and had minimal allocation otherwise. One bus was required for the 352 between Berkhamsted and Dunstable which ran only at weekends, while a second bus ran the 387 linking a residential area near the town centre to the railway station located about 1.5 miles from the town. A few journeys ran beyond the station to the small but picturesque village of Aldbury where buses turned round by the pond and village green. Journey time from Beaconsfield Road to the station was only 12 minutes with a further five allowed for those journeys running on to Aldbury.

One bus operated the entire 387 timetable with the exception of some additional journeys on Monday to Friday. A second bus operated between 7.09am and 8.59am in the morning and between 4.02pm and 7.58pm, providing extra facilities for commuters to and from Tring station, and remained crew operated. This had been a Q type and later CR, whilst the bus operating all day had been a Cub. Running numbers were TG1 for the Cub, and TG2 for the additional bus with one journey from TG5 by a bus from the 301 allocation.

GS 68 and 70 were licensed on 1st January 1954 and transferred from Aldenham to Tring. GS 60 was transferred from Amersham on 5th January, and may have been used for training for a brief spell before returning to Amersham. Although the exact date of the GSs entering service is not known, London Transport's daily movement sheets record that the three Cubs at Tring were withdrawn and delicensed on 26th January, and were the last in service anywhere. The GSs therefore entered service on this date if not earlier. The GS retained the running number TG1, the crew-operated peak duty being covered by a T type retaining running number TG2. Small changes in rosters resulted in some evening 387 journeys being operated by an RT from the 301 allocation. None of the 387 journeys justified crew operation, but with the exception of TG2 all of Tring's crew duties were on the 301/302 in a joint allocation with Hemel Hempstead, where buses swapped between each garage on a daily basis and crews worked on buses from both garages during the day. Crew working on the 387 was therefore a useful method of balancing some duties. Rigid speed schedules allowed 10 minutes from the garage to the station for the GS, but only eight minutes for the crew operated journeys.

The service to Aldbury was both sparse and irregular, providing only eight journeys Monday to Friday and seven Saturday, four of the Monday to Friday journeys being part of the crew roster. One early morning Saturday return to the station was crew operated. A limited Sunday service ran in the afternoon and evening when only two journeys served Beaconsfield Road, and eight ran to the station, four of which ran on to Aldbury. One morning journey ran from Tring garage to the station at 8.36am which was run with an RT from the 301, as was the 2.24pm. The GS was rostered from 2.54pm until 10.26pm and operated as a duty for one driver.

An additional schoolday duplicate into Tring and back on the 397 is referred to in the section on Amersham, Tring using the spare GS to operate a journey to Wigginton at 8.50am, returning two minutes behind the through journey operating in from Amersham. This did not appear in the allocations and the running number is not known. In 1960 an afternoon school journey was also added from Tring to Wigginton, the bus running light back to the garage. The timing of this allowed it to be worked by TG1 between journeys on the 387. These 397 school journeys remained in the schedules until the winter schedules of 1962, at which time the reduced 387 timetable eliminated the need for the second crew operated bus. Much later during the London Country period, a crew operated RF was allocated to work much of the Saturday morning timetable, and crew operated journeys from the 301 remained in the schedules.

The 387 Sunday service was a victim of the extensive winter 1958 cuts, but the remaining timetable changed little, although new speed schedules in October 1958 resulted in the running time between the garage and the station to be cut by one minute for the GS. The mix of crew and omo working on the 387 came to an end on 23rd May 1962 when timetable changes and schedule reductions resulted in a single omo RF replacing the T and GS. GS 33 was transferred to Amersham until the whole GS allocation there was replaced on 24th October.

Of the two allocated in 1954, GS 70 was transferred to Garston on 10th July 1956 but not replaced, since a spare bus was borrowed from Amersham or Hemel Hempstead if necessary. GS 16 was transferred from Garston on 1st November 1957 (noted as 'float bus' in the records) but was delicensed and moved to Hemel Hempstead on 9th December. GS 33 transferred from Amersham on 1st February 1958 to release GS 68 for overhaul, which returned on 3rd April although not relicensed until 1st May. In turn GS 33 was then delicensed and stored out of use until licensed again on 20th August, thus allowing GS 68 to become one of the five GSs hired by Great Yarmouth. GS 33 then remained as Tring's sole GS until withdrawn on 23rd May 1962, the only change being GS 51 transferred briefly from Amersham to cover GS 33's overhaul in December 1961.

HEMEL HEMPSTEAD

INITIAL ALLOCATION
GS 17 (allocated 11th July 1956), GS 83 (allocated 1st July 1956)

ROUTES OPERATED
316   11th July 1956 – 5th May 1964
316B   6th May 1964 – 2nd October 1965
317 / 317A 8th July 1959 – 21st May 1963 and 6th May 1964 – 2nd October 1965

PEAK VEHICLE REQUIREMENT Two buses

The 316 had its origins in a route jointly operated by Rover Bus and Chesham & District, the latter's share being acquired by Amersham & District in 1932 who numbered the route as 16. London Transport in turn acquired Amersham & District's share in 1934, renumbering it into their 300 series as 316, whilst Rover Bus retained their share. The route had been busy during the War since it served the airfield at Bovingdon and passenger levels remained high in post-war years, particularly on Saturdays. The timetable – though irregular – provided two journeys an hour for much of the day, including Sundays. The actual routes taken by London Transport and Rover Bus varied slightly on leaving Hemel Hempstead, but from Boxmoor station followed the same roads as far as Lye Green at which point London Transport ran via Codmore Cross to join the 362 route into Chesham, missing out the centre of Lye Green village itself. Between Bovingdon and Lye Green, many Rover Bus journeys ran via Whelpley Hill, and from Lye Green village ran via a more direct route into Chesham via Nashleigh Hill and Berkhamsted Road. Rover also operated an infrequent service via Latimer and Flaunden, running into Chesham via a different route.

GS 42 comes across the bridge over the Grand Union Canal in Fishery Road, Hemel Hempstead on a 316 to Chesham. London Transport's operation of the route was always the minority share, requiring only one bus all day with a second after lunchtime. GS 42 went to Hemel Hempstead as part of the major reallocations in October 1962, and remained until LT's share of the 316 was handed over to Rover Bus in May 1964. After many periods as a training bus, staff bus, and periods of service at Dorking and Windsor, GS 42 became one of the last two in revenue earning service at Garston in March 1972 when it was the last bus back to Garston shortly after GS 33. *Lyndon Rowe*

London Transport's allocation was crew operated with two single deckers which had been either Q or T. In 1954, the 316 was chosen to test the viability of omo with larger buses, and on 22nd July that year RF 700 was transferred from Reigate as a training bus. On 11th August, the 316 was converted to omo when RF 700 was joined by omo RF 517 and 647, which had been running on the 419 from Leatherhead. The trial on the 316 was a success, so much so that RF 649 was also converted in October to allow RF 700 to return to Leatherhead to operate again on the 419.

The frequency of the timetable, combined with the gradual reduction in traffic rendered the higher capacity of the RFs unnecessary, and given that there were surplus GSs around the fleet, the 316 was converted to GS operation on 11th July 1956.

GS 83 had been delicensed at Dorking on 6th June and moved to Reigate. It was relicensed for service and transferred to Hemel Hempstead on 1st July, initially for use as a training bus, since Hemel Hempstead's drivers were not then familiar with the GS. GS 17 had gone from Leatherhead for overhaul on 31st May, and arrived from Works on 12th July to commence operation on the 316 with GS 83. London Transport's contribution to the 316 consisted of one bus running approximately every two hours all day, the second bus commencing mid-afternoon and running until early evening. The bus operating all day ran as HH80, the second as HH81. In October 1956, the route was extended a short distance from the new town centre to Highfield where buses reversed at Bathurst Road. Running time between Hemel Hempstead and Chesham was 41 minutes, and since additional running time to Bathurst Road was only four minutes, the extension was easily accommodated without changes to the timetable. On 10th June 1959, a further short extension beyond Bathurst Road to St Paul's Road was added, taking one minute longer. At the same time, the journeys up to St Paul's Road were reduced to operate only on Saturdays, but two school journeys to Blessed Cuthbert Mayne School situated off Gadebridge Road close to the new town centre were added during the week.

With a general two hour round trip for each bus, the running time necessitated long layovers at each end. In Chesham, buses were not permitted to stand on the Broadway in excess of a few minutes since buses frequently ran through or terminated there and the stops easily became congested. Buses with a longer layover therefore had to operate in a lengthy loop to the north of the Broadway and stand at a stop some distance from the terminus.

Both GSs were also required on Sundays using the same running numbers. One return journey to Chesham was run in the morning, both buses being required after lunch to run an hourly headway until late evening. With Rover Bus there were no less than 25 journeys on Sunday between Hemel Hempstead and Chesham, only a few less than during the week. London Transport's Sunday run out somewhat surprisingly survived the significant cuts in the October 1958 schedules, but from May 1959, it was reduced to one bus running every two hours in the afternoon and evening only. In the October 1960 schedules, London Transport's Sunday journeys were withdrawn, and Rover Bus cut their timetable back significantly to 15 journeys. The Sunday service on the 362/362A was diverted to Ley Hill to replace the section no longer served by the 316.

In the schedules from 4th April 1959, an additional GS was allocated for duplicates on the 316 which operated as HH209 on Saturdays only, presumably because passengers on some shopping journeys were too great for one bus. The actual timing of these journeys is not recorded. GS 28 arrived from Garston 14th January, initially to allow GS 83 to go for overhaul, but was retained when GS 83 returned on 25th March to provide the additional bus then scheduled.

The allocation of a GS to the 317/A in July 1959 perhaps seemed illogical. The routes worked a joint RF roster with the 307 and 337, but with falling traffic – particularly on the route to Berkhamsted – a GS provided small savings in costs. Passenger levels on the narrow lanes through the village of Nettleden were especially low, and the rosters were arranged so that the majority of the 317A was GS operated. It was replaced by an RF in the 1963 summer schedules, but reinstated a year later when operation on the 316 ceased. GS 51 transferred to Hemel Hempstead as part of the October 1962 changes, and would be its last GS. The remaining GS workings were replaced by RF on 3rd October 1965, GS 51 being delicensed the following day. It remained stored out of use for over two years before being sold in 1968. It has arrived at Hemel Hempstead bus station. Since Little Gaddesden appears on the blind as an intermediate point, this may have been the afternoon journey which served Ringshall just beyond there, since there were no 317A journeys from Berkhamsted. *S J Butler collection*

On 8th July 1959, one RF allocated to the 317 and 317A was replaced with a GS which operated as HH76 Monday to Friday and HH74 on Saturdays. The precise reason for this is unclear other than a small saving in costs could be made, and passenger loads on several journeys were small. The special duplicate bus remained in the allocation book specifically for the 316. The allocation then consisted of GS 17, 28, and 83 and there is no record of a fourth bus being allocated during 1959. At the time, operation on 317 and 317A was limited to HH74 Monday to Friday only, the bus being available to operate as HH209 for 316 Saturday duplicates. Operation on the 316 remained unchanged until 6th May 1964 when London Transport withdrew from the route completely. It was perhaps surprising that the duplicate HH209 remained allocated until this date despite the obvious reduction in traffic.

Following withdrawal from the 316, in a change which seemed contrary to policy at the time, one GS was retained and added to the 317 and 317A. The former section of the 316 from the town centre to St Paul's Road had adequate alternate journeys on the 301C, but a new route numbered 316B was introduced providing five journeys on Saturdays when the 301C did not serve that section. The 316B also continued the two previous 316 schoolday journeys to Blessed Cuthbert Mayne School. The 307, 316B, 317, 317A and 337 were then worked by a pool of five RF and one GS Monday to Friday and by four RF and two GS on Saturdays. The GSs were confined to the 316B, 317 and 317A which had a mix of RF and GS workings. Reductions in the winter 1964 schedules removed the second GS on Saturdays after which the schedules remained unchanged for a further year. The introduction of winter timetables on 3rd October 1965 brought widespread cuts across the whole Country area, and the remaining GS was replaced by an RF.

GS 80 was transferred from Garston on 1st November 1959. GS 26 had been one of two buses delicensed at Chelsham on 1st October 1959, and taken to Reigate for storage. It went to Harrow Weald garage as a staff bus on 15th February 1960 but stayed for only one week before being relicensed for service at Hemel Hempstead on 1st March. GS 19 was taken from temporary store at Romford on 1st May to release GS 17 for overhaul. Two months later GS 19 was also sent for overhaul on 6th July but returned to service at Dunton Green. When GS 17 returned from overhaul on 1st August, GS 26 was once again stood down, stored at Garston, but returned to Hemel Hempstead on 1st January 1961. GS 26 spent time at eight different garages during its service life, often used as a float bus to release others for overhaul. It was itself overhauled for a second time in October 1961, later spending longer periods at Guildford and Dunton Green before withdrawal in April 1965.

In the major changes of October 1962, GS 68, 80 and 83 were all withdrawn and transferred to Garston where they remained in store awaiting sale. They were replaced by GS 42, 51, and 55 from Amersham, having been replaced by the conversions to RF there. GS 17 remained at Hemel Hempstead until delicensed and stored at Garston in April 1963. GS 42 was sent to Harlow for six days on 6th June 1964, and on return to Hemel Hempstead was noted as 'delicensed, stored bus'. On 14th August it was relicensed and transferred to Garston. GS 55 was transferred to Garston in March 1963, and GS 51 – Hemel Hempstead's last GS – was delicensed on 4th October 1965, the day after it was replaced by an RF.

HEMEL HEMPSTEAD GS SCHEDULES – SEPTEMBER 1961
MONDAY TO FRIDAY

ROUTE NUMBER	TIME DEPART	FROM	TO	ROUTE NUMBER	TIME DEPART	FROM	TO
		RUNNING NUMBER HH 76				**RUNNING NUMBER HH 80**	
317A	8.59 am	TWO WATERS GAR.	LITTLE GADDESDEN	316	6.23am	TWO WATERS GAR.	BOVINGDON
317A	9.37 am	LITTLE GADDESDEN	TWO WATERS GAR.	316	6.41am	BOVINGDON	HEMEL HEMPSTEAD
317	11.00 am	TWO WATERS GAR.	BERKHAMSTED STN	LIGHT	7.04am	HEMEL HEMPSTEAD	TWO WATERS GAR.
317	12.13 pm	BERKHAMSTED STN	TWO WATERS GAR.	316	7.59am	TWO WATERS GAR.	CHESHAM BROADWAY
317A	1.35 pm	TWO WATERS GAR.	LITTLE GADDESDEN	316	9.45am	CHESHAM BROADWAY	St PAULS ROAD
317A	2.09 pm	LITTLE GADDESDEN	TWO WATERS GAR.	316	10.25am	St PAULS ROAD	CHESHAM BROADWAY
317A	4.14 pm	TWO WATERS GAR.	RINGSHALL	316	11.26am	CHESHAM BROADWAY	St PAULS ROAD
317A	4.52 pm	RINGSHALL	HEMEL HEMPSTEAD	316	12.25pm	St PAULS ROAD	CHESHAM BROADWAY
317	5.26 pm	HEMEL HEMPSTEAD	BERKHAMSTED STN	316	1.32pm	CHESHAM BROADWAY	St PAULS ROAD
317	6.35 pm	BERKHAMSTED STN	HEMEL HEMPSTEAD	316	2.25pm	St PAULS ROAD	CHESHAM BROADWAY
317A	7.45 pm	HEMEL HEMPSTEAD	LITTLE GADDESDEN	316	3.35pm	CHESHAM BROADWAY	St PAULS ROAD
317A	8.14 pm	LITTLE GADDESDEN	TWO WATERS GAR.	316	4.42pm	St PAULS ROAD	CHESHAM BROADWAY
317	9.10pm	TWO WATERS GAR.	RINGSHALL	316	5.42pm	CHESHAM BROADWAY	St PAULS ROAD
317	9.59pm nW	RINGSHALL	TWO WATERS GAR.	316	6.42pm	St PAULS ROAD	CHESHAM BROADWAY
317	9.59pm W	RINGSHALL	HEMEL HEMPSTEAD	316	7.40pm	CHESHAM BROADWAY	HEMEL HEMPSTEAD
317	10.31pm W	HEMEL HEMPSTEAD	GREAT GADDESDEN	316	8.47pm	HEMEL HEMPSTEAD	CHESHAM BROADWAY
317	10.51pm W	GREAT GADDESDEN	TWO WATERS GAR.	316	10.08pm	CHESHAM BROADWAY	TWO WATERS GAR.
						RUNNING NUMBER HH 81	
				LIGHT	3.36pm	TWO WATERS GAR.	HEMEL HEMPSTEAD
		W:- WEDNESDAY ONLY		316	3.47pm	HEMEL HEMPSTEAD	CHESHAM BROADWAY
		nW:- NOT WEDNESDAY		316	4.38pm	CHESHAM BROADWAY	HEMEL HEMPSTEAD
		The HEMEL HEMPSTEAD terminus was the bus station.		316	5.23pm	HEMEL HEMPSTEAD	BOXMOOR STATION
				316	5.37pm	BOXMOOR STATION	HEMEL HEMPSTEAD
				316	5.51pm	HEMEL HEMPSTEAD	CHESHAM BROADWAY
				316	6.45pm	CHESHAM BROADWAY	St PAULS ROAD
				316	7.42pm	St PAULS ROAD	CHESHAM BROADWAY
				316	8.40pm	CHESHAM BROADWAY	HEMEL HEMPSTEAD
				316	9.47pm	HEMEL HEMPSTEAD	BOVINGDON
				316	10.11pm	BOVINGDON	HEMEL HEMPSTEAD
				LIGHT	1033pm	HEMEL HEMPSTEAD	TWO WATERS GAR.

HEMEL HEMPSTEAD GS SCHEDULES – SEPTEMBER 1961
SATURDAY

ROUTE NUMBER	TIME DEPART	FROM	TO	ROUTE NUMBER	TIME DEPART	FROM	TO
		RUNNING NUMBER HH 74				**RUNNING NUMBER HH 80**	
317	6.42 am	TWO WATERS GAR.	BERKHAMSTED STN	316	6.23am	TWO WATERS GAR.	BOVINGDON
317	7.45 am	BERKHAMSTED STN	TWO WATERS GAR.	316	6.41am	BOVINGDON	HEMEL HEMPSTEAD
317A	8.59 am	TWO WATERS GAR.	LITTLE GADDESDEN	LIGHT	7.04am	HEMEL HEMPSTEAD	TWO WATERS GAR.
317A	9.37 am	LITTLE GADDESDEN	TWO WATERS GAR.	LIGHT	8.01am	TWO WATERS GAR.	HEMEL HEMPSTEAD
317	11.00am	TWO WATERS GAR.	BERKHAMSTED STN	316	8.12am	HEMEL HEMPSTEAD	CHESHAM BROADWAY
317	12.13pm	BERKHAMSTED STN	TWO WATERS GAR.	316	9.20am	CHESHAM BROADWAY	St PAULS ROAD
317A	1.35 pm	TWO WATERS GAR.	LITTLE GADDESDEN	316	10.25am	St PAULS ROAD	CHESHAM BROADWAY
317A	2.09 pm	LITTLE GADDESDEN	TWO WATERS GAR.	316	11.26am	CHESHAM BROADWAY	St PAULS ROAD
317	3.55pm	TWO WATERS GAR.	GREAT GADDESDEN	316	12.25pm	St PAULS ROAD	CHESHAM BROADWAY
317	4.20pm	GREAT GADDESDEN	BOXMOOR STATION	316	1.40pm	CHESHAM BROADWAY	St PAULS ROAD
317A	4.48pm	BOXMOOR STATION	LITTLE GADDESDEN	316	2.42pm	St PAULS ROAD	CHESHAM BROADWAY
317A	5.26pm	LITTLE GADDESDEN	TWO WATERS GAR.	316	3.35pm	CHESHAM BROADWAY	St PAULS ROAD
317	7.02pm	TWO WATERS GAR.	BERKHAMSTED STN	316	4.42pm	St PAULS ROAD	CHESHAM BROADWAY
317	8.13 pm	BERKHAMSTED STN	TWO WATERS GAR.	316	5.35pm	CHESHAM BROADWAY	St PAULS ROAD

316	6.42pm	St PAULS ROAD	CHESHAM BROADWAY
316	7.40pm	CHESHAM BROADWAY	HEMEL HEMPSTEAD
316	8.47pm	HEMEL HEMPSTEAD	CHESHAM BROADWAY
316	10.08pm	CHESHAM BROADWAY	TWO WATERS GARAGE

RUNNING NUMBER HH 209

316	Duplicates to operate per schedule
	Exact timing not known but operated only on Saturday

RUNNING NUMBER HH 81

LIGHT	1.29pm	TWO WATERS GAR.	St PAULS ROAD
316	1.42pm	St PAULS ROAD	CHESHAM BROADWAY
316	2.40pm	CHESHAM BROADWAY	St PAULS ROAD
316	3.42pm	St PAULS ROAD	CHESHAM BROADWAY
316	4.35pm	CHESHAM BROADWAY	St PAULS ROAD
316	5.42pm	HEMEL HEMPSTEAD	CHESHAM BROADWAY
316	6.40pm	CHESHAM BROADWAY	St PAULS ROAD
316	5.51pm	St PAULS ROAD	CHESHAM BROADWAY
316	6.45pm	CHESHAM BROADWAY	St PAULS ROAD
316	7.42pm	St PAULS ROAD	CHESHAM BROADWAY
316	8.40pm	CHESHAM BROADWAY	HEMEL HEMPSTEAD
316	9.47pm	HEMEL HEMPSTEAD	BOVINGDON
316	10.11pm	BOVINGDON	HEMEL HEMPSTEAD
LIGHT	10.33pm	HEMEL HEMPSTEAD	TWO WATERS GAR.

HEMEL HEMPSTEAD GS SCHEDULES – 6TH MAY 1964

MONDAY TO FRIDAY

ROUTE NUMBER	TIME DEPART	FROM	TO
		RUNNING NUMBER HH 76	
LIGHT	6.10 am	TWO WATERS GAR.	HEMEL HEMPSTEAD
317	6.22 am	HEMEL HEMPSTEAD	BOXMOOR STATION
317	6.35 am	BOXMOOR STATION	BERKHAMSTED STN
317	7.45 am	BERKHAMSTED STN	TWO WATERS GAR.
317A	8.59 am	TWO WATERS GAR.	LITTLE GADDESDEN
317A	9.37 am	LITTLE GADDESDEN	TWO WATERS GAR.
317	11.00 am	TWO WATERS GAR.	BERKHAMSTED STN
317	12.13 pm	BERKHAMSTED STN	TWO WATERS GAR.
317A	1.35 pm	TWO WATERS GAR.	LITTLE GADDESDEN
317A	2.09 pm	LITTLE GADDESDEN	TWO WATERS GAR.
316B	3.25 pm Sch	TWO WATERS GAR.	CUTHBERT MAYNE SCH
316B	3.46 pm Sch	CUTHBERT MAYNE SCH	TWO WATERS GAR.
317A	4.14 pm	TWO WATERS GAR.	RINGSHALL
317A	4.52 pm	RINGSHALL	HEMEL HEMPSTEAD
317	5.26 pm	HEMEL HEMPSTEAD	BERKHAMSTED STN
317	6.35 pm	BERKHAMSTED STN	HEMEL HEMPSTEAD
317A	7.45 pm	HEMEL HEMPSTEAD	LITTLE GADDESDEN
317A	8.14 pm	LITTLE GADDESDEN	TWO WATERS GAR.

Sch		Schooldays only	

SATURDAY

ROUTE NUMBER	TIME DEPART	FROM	TO
		RUNNING NUMBER HH 74	
317	6.42 am	TWO WATERS GAR.	BERKHAMSTED STN
317	7.45 am	BERKHAMSTED STN	TWO WATERS GAR.
317A	8.59 am	TWO WATERS GAR.	LITTLE GADDESDEN
317A	9.37 am	LITTLE GADDESDEN	BOXMOOR STATION
316B	10.14 am	BOXMOOR STATION	ST PAUL'S ROAD
316B	10.31 am	ST PAUL'S ROAD	TWO WATERS GAR.
317A	1.35 pm	TWO WATERS GAR.	LITTLE GADDESDEN
317A	2.09 pm	LITTLE GADDESDEN	TWO WATERS GAR.
316B	4.10 pm	TWO WATERS GAR.	ST PAUL'S ROAD
316B	4.30 pm	ST PAUL'S ROAD	TWO WATERS GAR.
316B	6.27 pm	TWO WATERS GAR.	ST PAUL'S ROAD
316B	6.47 pm	ST PAUL'S ROAD	BOXMOOR STATION
317	7.05 pm	BOXMOOR STATION	BERKHAMSTED STN
317	8.13 pm	BERKHAMSTED STN	TWO WATERS GAR.
		RUNNING NUMBER HH 90	
LIGHT	7.10 am	TWO WATERS GAR.	HEMEL HEMPSTEAD
317	7.20 am	HEMEL HEMPSTEAD	BOXMOOR STATION
317	7.33 am	BOXMOOR STATION	BERKHAMSTED STN
LIGHT	8.33 am	BERKHAMSTED STN	BOXMOOR STATION
317	8.52 am	BOXMOOR STATION	BERKHAMSTED STN
317	10.35 am	BERKHAMSTED STN	TWO WATERS GAR.
317	1.00 pm	TWO WATERS GAR.	BERKHAMSTED STN
317	2.20 pm	BERKHAMSTED STN	TWO WATERS GAR.
317	3.55 pm	TWO WATERS GAR.	GREAT GADDESDEN
317	4.20 pm	GREAT GADDESDEN	BOXMOOR STATION
317A	4.48 pm	BOXMOOR STATION	LITTLE GADDESDEN
317A	5.21 pm	LITTLE GADDESDEN	TWO WATERS GAR.

There was no Sunday service on the 317/317A

GARSTON

INITIAL ALLOCATION   See below

ROUTES OPERATED

309`	19th May 1954 – 14th February 1969
309A	4th November 1964 – 14th February 1969
319 group	11th July 1956 – 14th October 1958
336A	February 1954 – 30th March 1972
361	19th May 1954 – 13th October 1959

PEAK VEHICLE REQUIREMENT   Four buses

At the time the GSs arrived, Garston's allocation for small single deckers was for a single bus for the 336A Loudwater Estate service at Rickmansworth. The route had its origins in 1928 when the developer of the estate had started a bus service as a link to the station at Rickmansworth. The basic service pattern provided journeys for commuters in the morning and evening, with a number of journeys to allow time for shopping in Rickmansworth during the day, a general pattern which continued – albeit with fewer journeys – for the next 44 years until the route was finally abandoned. On the formation of the London Transport Passenger Board in 1933, the Loudwater route was entirely within the newly created 'Special Area'. The service was running at a loss, and despite the powers granted to them to acquire it, London Transport initially refused an offer to purchase it. Discussions became extremely acrimonious, London Transport retaliating to the estate owner's unwillingness to negotiate the sale of the route by refusing to allow the service to use the station forecourt at Rickmansworth which London Transport controlled. There were no further developments until 1949 when the executors of the estate owner who had died asked London Transport to take over the route. By then however, it was estimated to be losing more than £1000 a year – approximately £30,000 per annum now – a considerable sum. No other operator was prepared to take over, so agreement was finally reached, London Transport assuming control on 7th June 1950 and a C class Cub being allocated. The bus was out-stationed on the estate, and the existing driver who lived locally was retained. The route was numbered 336A but apart from the fact that it paralleled the 336 for a short distance along the A404 from Rickmansworth, it had nothing at all in common with that route. By 1950, the introduction of a number of new routes had resulted in a shortage of spare route numbers and this is thought likely to be the reason for the choice of 336A.

There appears to be some doubt as to the exact date when the Cub was replaced with a GS on the 336A. Although the last C class Cubs in service are recorded as those withdrawn at Tring in January, there is no definitive record of the 336A being changed before this. The large number of GSs sent to Garston for storage is described in chapter one, but the daily movement sheets do not record any of them being licensed for service there in January. GS 67 and 69 were transferred from Aldenham to Garston on 22nd January and 24th February 1954 respectively but not recorded as licensed for service until 1st May. GS 71, 76 and 77 were among 13 further GSs transferred unlicensed from Aldenham on 10th February and at some point were also licensed for service there, but again the exact date is not recorded. This may have been a clerical error in the records.

There was no service on the 336A after the bus returned from Loudwater at 12.17pm on Saturday, when it was returned to Garston for refuelling and routine maintenance and could be exchanged for the spare bus as necessary. An arrangement was made to fuel the bus in Rickmansworth during the week, and the driver paid his daily takings in at the ticket office at Rickmansworth station.

Reference is made in chapter one to the intention to use a number of GSs to convert some lightly used crew operated routes to one man operation. Having remained in store since delivery from Aldenham on 10th February 1954, GSs 71, 75 and 76 were licensed for service on 19th May 1954, taking over operation of routes 309 and 361 that day and converting them from crew operation with 15T13s. The 309 had originally run between Uxbridge via Denham and Harefield to Rickmansworth, but with the rapid post war growth in passenger numbers the limited capacity of the single deckers became inadequate, and was a particular problem between Harefield, Denham and Uxbridge as numbers of commuters grew. On 6th May 1953 therefore, the 309 was reduced to operate only between Rickmansworth and Harefield, the service on to Uxbridge being converted to double deck by extending the 347. This route had begun only 14 months earlier and had already been extended from Watford to Hemel Hempstead to replace another single deck crew route where capacity had become an issue. The road through Woodcock Hill to Harefield enjoyed less traffic, the truncated 309 thus becoming a semi-rural minor route.

The ten-minute journey from Rickmansworth took the 336A into the narrow lanes of the private Loudwater Estate. On 26th November 1965, GS 17 stands in the village in surroundings typical of the route. That the route lasted until March 1972 was remarkable given its constant losses, but the fact that a member of London Transport's senior management lived in Loudwater and used the route to catch the Metropolitan Line into London was an important factor in retaining it until he retired. *Peter Mitchell*

The 361 ran between Rickmansworth and Chorleywood but via an indirect route. After the War, Chorleywood was an expanding village and enjoyed a frequent train service to Rickmansworth and central London on the Metropolitan Line. In October 1958, the 336 was diverted from the main A404 through the village and offered a direct link to Rickmansworth with a journey time of around 10 minutes, while the 335 and 703 provided two or three journeys each hour along the A404, although missing out the village centre. Although the village street and shops were on the road along the south side of the station, many of the houses were to the south a little way from the centre. The 361 turned at Green Street a few yards from station and shops, leaving the village via Shire Lane before running into Heronsgate Lane which became quite narrow, having a couple of single track sections before reaching the main Uxbridge road at Mill End where it joined the frequent service on the 321 into Rickmansworth. Curiously, the 361 timetable included a timing point at the 'Whip and Collar' pub at Mill End where there was compulsory stop used by all routes, but this same point never appeared in the 321 timetable.

In 1954 the 309 operated to a general hourly headway requiring one bus all day. The 361 journey time was 19 minutes, again requiring one bus running back and forth all day. With a five minute layover at each end, the frequency was 48 minutes for most of the day, slightly longer where a couple of journeys were extended in Chorleywood to turn at The Gate Inn on the A404. The bus for the 309 ran in service, leaving Garston Garage at 5.40am Monday to Friday, 6,38am Saturday and 12.39pm Sunday, when there were only seven journeys in the afternoon and evening. On Monday to Friday the bus ran light back to Garston at 10.30pm, since a 321 departure was timed to leave Rickmansworth station at 10.31pm. On Saturday and Sunday evenings however when passenger numbers would be higher, the bus ran in service at 10.30pm, timed to leave between the 10.27pm and 10.34pm 321 journeys on Saturday and between the 10.18pm and 10.38pm journeys on Sunday.

GS 75 was one of 16 surplus GSs transferred unlicensed to Garston in February 1954. It is recorded as being licensed for service on 19th May and remained at Garston before being transferred to Amersham on 1st January 1956. With no grab handles fitted, this picture was therefore taken in 1954 as it waits in the car park above Rickmansworth station for a journey to Chorleywood on the 361. The 'lazy' blind is rather cramped, LT STN as the qualifying point for Rickmansworth being barely readable. Chorleywood Stn on the blind was slightly misleading since buses reversed at the junction of Station Road and Green Street some 200 yards from the station.
Mick Webber

Although the 361 timetable required only one bus, additional journeys operated on Monday to Friday in the morning peak and for schools. The first bus left Garston at 5.53am to operate the main service, a second bus departing at 7.43am to operate as a duplicate on the 8.24am to Chorleywood, the duplicate running on to 'The Gate Inn' for school children, although the journey ran all year round. On return to Rickmansworth, a second duplicate was operated on the 9.22am to Chorleywood. The second bus was then parked at Rickmansworth out of service all morning while the driver returned to Garston. This arrangement provided a spare bus in the event of breakdown, but was returned in service back to Garston at 12.37pm by one of the 309 or 361 drivers at the end of their shift. On school-days, the bus left Garston again at 2.20pm to work the 3.41pm to Chorleywood and back followed by duplicate evening peak journeys before returning to Garston at 7.33pm.

In July 1956, the 319 route and its many variants were converted from crew RF to omo RF. Two years earlier in May 1954, these variants had been part of the 318, but in a complicated change were transferred to the 319 along with a section of the previous 318. The 319 route number had been used up to this point for the route from Hemel Hempstead via Nettleden to Little Gaddesden. It was renumbered 317A in these changes, and would see a brief spell of GS operation some years later. In the conversion to omo RF, one GS was also allocated to the 319 schedules from 11th July 1956. Its Monday to Friday allocation was to the two 319D schoolday journeys to Langleybury School. It was also rostered on Saturday when Garston worked only the 319 to Chipperfield, the two morning works journey variants being operated by Hemel Hempstead. It is not known which actual journeys were worked on Saturday. The GS was withdrawn from the 319 from 29th October 1958.

On 16th October 1957, a couple of 309 journeys on Wednesday and Sunday were extended from the Kings Arms in the village centre to the Hospital, and cross working on Sunday between the two routes was introduced from that date. Although the timetables for both routes could be worked by one bus, two were scheduled. After the first 361 journey, the bus operated additional 309 journeys for visitors to Harefield Hospital, following which it ran light back to Garston. The 309 timetable for the Sunday evening was then arranged to allow operation of the remaining 361 timetable between 309 journeys before running back to Garston at 10.30pm. This arrangement did not last long however as the 361 Sunday service was withdrawn in the winter 1958 schedules. At the same time, the 309 was extended a short distance in Harefield from the Kings Arms past the Hospital to turn at the 'Vernon Arms' at Hill End a few minutes from the village.

A more fundamental change took place on 14th October 1959 when the 361 was withdrawn completely and replaced by extending the 309 to Chorleywood. The terminus at Green Street was replaced by an extension up to some new houses which were being built at Furze View, and the extended route had a running time of 40 minutes from there to Hill End. Three buses remained rostered on Monday to Friday, two Saturday and one Sunday. Whereas the previous 361 timetable had operated to the same general (if somewhat odd) frequency, the new timetable on the extended 309 was completely irregular throughout the day during the week. On Saturday however, each bus completed a round trip in 90 minutes, so there was a regular 45 minute headway all day, alternate journeys at Harefield terminating every 90 minutes at either Hill End or St Mary's Road. In a reversal of the previous year, a Sunday service was again run to Chorleywood, providing five

In July 1968, GS 33 stands at the terminus at Furze View in Chorleywood waiting to operate back to Harefield. The short extension to Furze View from the village centre had been made in October 1959. By the time this picture was taken, only one GS remained rostered to the 309 and 309A, and seven months later it would be replaced by an RF, bringing GS operation on the route to an end. *Peter Aves collection*

journeys between lunchtime and late evening. The Sunday service on the whole route was however withdrawn in the winter 1963 schedules, but the weekday timetable was little changed. Two years before this, Saturday morning shopping traffic on the 336A had fallen to the point where passengers were almost non-existent, the service being withdrawn after the last Saturday of operation on 21st October 1961.

Running numbers for Garston's GSs changed during the 1950s. Initially, the 309/361 were allocated GR62, 63, and 64, the 336A GR68. GR68 later became GR58. From the October 1959 changes when the 309 and 361 were combined into one route, the 309 became GR2, 3, and 4, the 336A becoming GR1, these running numbers remaining unchanged throughout the rest of GS operation. GR1 remained in use by LCBS until the final withdrawal of the 336A on 30th March 1972.

A fundamental change took place on 3rd November 1964 when the 703 Green Line route was withdrawn, its passengers having seriously declined in the previous few years as improvements on the Metropolitan Line gave a faster more frequent service to London. The only local link lost by the withdrawal of the 703 was that from Amersham and Rickmansworth to Mount Vernon Hospital and Northwood. Although the previous hourly Green Line service was no longer required, there remained a need for a limited service for shoppers and hospital visitors. On 4th November, therefore, the 309A was introduced, running seven journeys to Northwood during the week and six on Saturdays. One additional journey ran on Wednesday afternoon from Rickmansworth for hospital visitors. The Saturday service was provided at the expense of a reduction from 18 to 12 journeys between Rickmansworth and Harefield, although most of the Monday to Friday journeys were operated by the bus which was otherwise spare during the off peak period. The running number schedules which came into force on 4th November show an uncomplicated allocation, but of note is the scheduling of some buses, after completing a journey, to run light to a different location to take up service again.

After the mid-1960s, the 309 began to suffer a decline in passengers in common with all such minor routes. The winter 1964 timetable remained unchanged after the widespread cuts which came with the winter 1965 cuts, but six months later with the introduction of the 1966 summer schedules, the last two evening journeys to both Harefield and Chorleywood were cut during the week although the Saturday service continued unchanged. Although the 1967 summer schedules on 13th May included no major changes, minor timetable alterations allowed the allocation to be reduced to two buses Monday to Friday, and at the same time the allocation was altered to one GS and one RF, removing two GSs from the 309.

GARSTON GS SCHEDULES – 4TH NOVEMBER 1964

MONDAY TO FRIDAY

RUNNING NUMBER GR 1

ROUTE	TIME DEPART	FROM	TO
336A	7.31am	LOUDWATER Village	RICKMANSWORTH Stn.

THEN ALL JOURNEYS UNTIL

ROUTE	TIME DEPART	FROM	TO
	10.33am	RICKMANSWORTH Stn.	LOUDWATER Village
	11.15am	LOUDWATER Village	RICKMANSWORTH Stn.
	12.06pm	RICKMANSWORTH Stn.	LOUDWATER Village
	2.15pm	LOUDWATER Village	RICKMANSWORTH Stn.
	3.35pm	RICKMANSWORTH Stn.	LOUDWATER Village

THEN ALL JOURNEYS UNTIL

ROUTE	TIME DEPART	FROM	TO
	6.32pm	LOUDWATER Est Office	RICKMANSWORTH Stn.
	6.49pm	RICKMANSWORTH Stn.	LOUDWATER Village

RUNNING NUMBER GR 3

ROUTE	TIME DEPART	FROM	TO
309	5.49am	GARSTON GARAGE	HAREFIELD Truesdale Dr.
309	6.47am	HAREFIELD Truesdale Dr.	CH' WOOD The Gate
309	7.36am	CH' WOOD The Gate	RICKMANSWORTH Car Pk
309	8.08am	RICKMANSWORTH Car Pk	CH' WOOD Furze View
309A	8.34am	CH' WOOD Furze View	NORTHWOOD STN.
309A	9.16am	NORTHWOOD STN.	RICKMANSWORTH Car Pk

BUS PARKED AT RICKMANSWORTH 9.30AM – 12.09PM

CHANGE OF DRIVER

ROUTE	TIME DEPART	FROM	TO
309A	12.09pm	RICKMANSWORTH Car Pk	NORTHWOOD STN.
309A	12.30pm	NORTHWOOD STN.	RICKMANSWORTH Car Pk
309	1.04pm NTh	RICKMANSWORTH Car Pk	CH' WOOD Furze View
309	1.04pm Th	RICKMANSWORTH Car Pk	CH' WOOD The Gate
LIGHT	1.31pm Th	CH' WOOD The Gate	CH' WOOD Furze View
309	1.45pm	CH' WOOD Furze View	HAREFIELD St Marys Road
309	2.32pm	HAREFIELD St Marys Road	CH' WOOD Furze View
309	3.15pm W	CH' WOOD Furze View	HAREFIELD HOSPITAL
309	3.59pm W	HAREFIELD HOSPITAL	CH' WOOD Furze View
309	3.15pm NW	CH' WOOD Furze View	HAREFIELD Kings Arms
309	3.59pm NW	HAREFIELD Kings Arms	CH' WOOD Furze View
309	4.41pm	CH' WOOD Furze View	HAREFIELD Kings Arms
LIGHT	5.22pm	HAREFIELD Kings Arms	RICKMANSWORTH Car Pk

BUS PARKED AT RICKMANSWORTH 5.38PM – 6.39PM

ROUTE	TIME DEPART	FROM	TO
309	6.39pm	RICKMANSWORTH Car Pk	CH' WOOD Furze View
309	7.05pm	CH' WOOD Furze View	HAREFIELD Kings Arms
309	7.53pm	HAREFIELD Kings Arms	CH' WOOD Furze View
309	8.43pm	CH' WOOD Furze View	HAREFIELD St. Marys Road
309	9.28pm	HAREFIELD St Marys Road	CH' WOOD Furze View
309	10.11pm	CH' WOOD Furze View	GARSTON GARAGE

RUNNING NUMBER GR 2

ROUTE	TIME DEPART	FROM	TO
LIGHT	5.42am	GARSTON GARAGE	RICKMANSWORTH Car Pk
309	6.17am	RICKMANSWORTH Car Pk	CH' WOOD Furze View
309	6.43am	CH' WOOD Furze View	HAREFIELD Kings Arms
309	7.29am	HAREFIELD Kings Arms	CH' WOOD Furze View
309	8.10am	CH' WOOD Furze View	HAREFIELD Truesdale Dr.
309	8.59am	HAREFIELD Truesdale Dr.	CH' WOOD Furze View
309	9.45am	CH' WOOD Furze View	RICKMANSWORTH Car Pk

CHANGE DRIVER AT RICKMANSWORTH

ROUTE	TIME DEPART	FROM	TO
309A	10.20am	RICKMANSWORTH Car Pk	NORTHWOOD STN.
309A	10.41am	NORTHWOOD STN.	RICKMANSWORTH Car Pk
309	11.00am	RICKMANSWORTH Car Pk	CH' WOOD Furze View
309	11.45am	CH' WOOD Furze View	HAREFIELD St Marys Road
309	12.32pm	HAREFIELD St Marys Road	CH' WOOD Furze View
309	1.15pm W	CH' WOOD Furze View	HAREFIELD HOSPITAL
309	1.15pm NW	CH' WOOD Furze View	HAREFIELD Hill End
309	2.03pm W	HAREFIELD HOSPITAL	CH' WOOD Furze View
309	2.01pm NW	HAREFIELD Hill End	CH' WOOD Furze View
309	2.45pm	CH' WOOD Furze View	HAREFIELD Hill End
309	3.31pm	HAREFIELD Hill End	CH' WOOD The Gate
309	4.18pm	CH' WOOD The Gate	RICKMANSWORTH Car Pk

CHANGE DRIVER AT RICKMANSWORTH

ROUTE	TIME DEPART	FROM	TO
309	4.50pm	RICKMANSWORTH Car Pk	CH' WOOD Furze View
309	5.20pm	CH' WOOD Furze View	HAREFIELD St. Marys Road
309	6.05pm	HAREFIELD St. Marys Road	CH' WOOD Furze View
309A	6.48pm	CH' WOOD Furze View	NORTHWOOD STN.

MEAL RELIEF BREAK AT NORTHWOOD

ROUTE	TIME DEPART	FROM	TO
309A	8.15pm	NORTHWOOD STN.	GARSTON GARAGE

RUNNING NUMBER GR 4

ROUTE	TIME DEPART	FROM	TO
309A	7.06am	GARSTON GARAGE	NORTHWOOD STN.
LIGHT	7.56am	NORTHWOOD STN.	HAREFIELD St Marys Road
309	8.14am	HAREFIELD St Marys Road	CH' WOOD The Gate
309	9.02am	CH' WOOD The Gate	HAREFIELD Hill End
309	9.51am	HAREFIELD Hill End	CH' WOOD Furze View
309	10.35am	CH' WOOD Furze View	HAREFIELD Hill End
309	11.21am	HAREFIELD Hill End	CH' WOOD Furze View
309	12.05pm	CH' WOOD Furze View	GARSTON GARAGE
309A	2.38pm W	GARSTON GARAGE	NORTHWOOD STN.
309A	3.28pm W	NORTHWOOD STN.	CH' WOOD Furze View
309	4.08pm W	CH' WOOD Furze View	HAREFIELD Hill End
309	4.54pm W	HAREFIELD Hill End	RICKMANSWORTH Car Pk
LIGHT	3.01pm NW	GARSTON GARAGE	RICKMANSWORTH Car Pk
309	3.36pm NW	RICKMANSWORTH Car Pk	CH' WOOD Furze View
309	4.02pm NW	CH' WOOD Furze View	HAREFIELD Hill End
309	4.51pm NW	HAREFIELD Hill End	RICKMANSWORTH Car Pk
309A	5.17pm	RICKMANSWORTH Car Pk	NORTHWOOD STN.
309A	5.38pm	NORTHWOOD STN.	RICKMANSWORTH Car Pk
LIGHT	5.56pm	RICKMANSWORTH Car Pk	CH' WOOD Furze View
309	6.14pm	CH' WOOD Furze View	HAREFIELD Kings Arms
309	7.08pm	HAREFIELD Kings Arms	CH' WOOD Furze View
309	7.50pm	CH' WOOD Furze View	GARSTON GARAGE

W = Wednesday only: NW = Not Wednesday

Th = Thursday only. NTh = Not Thursday

1. Journeys operating on Wednesday were for visiting times at Harefield Hospital and Mount Vernon Hospital at Northwood

2. The reason for the different terminus on the 1.04pm by GR 2 from Rickmansworth on Thursday is not known

3. Driver changes at Rickmansworth where the bus was parked for a period are shown. All other changes were on through journeys at Rickmansworth

4. The bus on GR 1 for the 336A was not scheduled to return to Garston but was exchanged at Rickmansworth with GR 2 or 3 to allow routine maintenance

GARSTON GS SCHEDULES – 4TH NOVEMBER 1964

SATURDAY

ROUTE NUMBER	TIME DEPART	FROM	TO	ROUTE NUMBER	TIME DEPART	FROM	TO
		RUNNING NUMBER GR 2				**RUNNING NUMBER GR 3**	
309	6.38am	GARSTON GARAGE	HAREFIELD Kings Arms	309	7.23am	GARSTON GARAGE	HAREFIELD Kings Arms
309	7.29am	HAREFIELD Kings Arms	CHORLEYWOOD	309	8.18am	HAREFIELD Kings Arms	CHORLEYWOOD
309	8.17am	CHORLEYWOOD	HAREFIELD St Marys Road	309	9.05am	CHORLEYWOOD	HAREFIELD Hill End
309	9.14am	HAREFIELD St Marys Road	CHORLEYWOOD	309	9.51am	HAREFIELD Hill End	CHORLEYWOOD
309A	9.57am	CHORLEYWOOD	NORTHWOOD STN	309	10.25am	CHORLEYWOOD	HAREFIELD Hill End
309A	10.45am	NORTHWOOD STN.	CHORLEYWOOD	309	11.21am	HAREFIELD Hill End	CHORLEYWOOD
309A	11.25am	CHORLEYWOOD	NORTHWOOD STN	309	12.15pm	CHORLEYWOOD	HAREFIELD Hill End
309A	12.20pm	NORTHWOOD STN	CHORLEYWOOD	309	1.01pm	HAREFIELD Hill End	CHORLEYWOOD
309A	1.05pm	CHORLEYWOOD	NORTHWOOD STN	309	1.45pm	CHORLEYWOOD	HAREFIELD Hill End
309A	1.53pm	NORTHWOOD STN.	CHORLEYWOOD	309	2.31pm	HAREFIELD Hill End	CHORLEYWOOD
309A	2.32pm	CHORLEYWOOD	NORTHWOOD STN	309	3.15pm	CHORLEYWOOD	HAREFIELD Hill End
309A	3.21pm	NORTHWOOD STN.	CHORLEYWOOD	309	4.01pm	HAREFIELD Hill End	CHORLEYWOOD
309A	4.01pm	CHORLEYWOOD	NORTHWOOD STN.	309	4.45pm	CHORLEYWOOD	HAREFIELD Hill End
309A	4.50pm	NORTHWOOD STN.	CHORLEYWOOD	309	5.36pm	HAREFIELD Hill End	CHORLEYWOOD
309A	5.30pm	CHORLEYWOOD	NORTHWOOD STN.	309	6.20pm	CHORLEYWOOD	HAREFIELD Hill End
309A	6.20pm	NORTHWOOD STN.	CHORLEYWOOD	309	7.06pm	HAREFIELD Hill End	CHORLEYWOOD
309	7.00pm	CHORLEYWOOD	HAREFIELD Kings Arms	309	7.50pm	CHORLEYWOOD	GARSTON GARAGE
309	7.54pm	HAREFIELD Kings Arms	CHORLEYWOOD				
309	8.38pm	CHORLEYWOOD	HAREFIELD Hill End				
309	9.24pm	HAREFIELD Hill End	CHORLEYWOOD				
309	10.08pm	CHORLEYWOOD	GARSTON GARAGE				

1. Saturday operation was extremely simple:- GR2 ran all the 309A journeys to and from Northwood, with early and late 309 journeys to Harefield. GR3 ran a general 90 minute headway between Harefield and Chorleywood all day.

2. All driver changes were at Rickmansworth, drivers travelling to and from Garston by 321 or 385

3. 4th November was the first Saturday of operation on the 309A, six journeys to Northwood replacing the former hourly 703 Green Line service

4. The terminus at Chorleywood throughout the day on Saturdays was Furze View

GS 57 carries running number GR4 which was a Monday to Friday spreadover duty. As this picture appears to have been taken during the daytime, the bus is probably working the 12.05pm journey from Chorleywood back to Garston garage. It will not be required again until mid-afternoon. After nine years at Northfleet and a brief spell at Crawley, it was transferred to Garston on 11th March 1963 and stayed for four years before a final period back at Northfleet. *Alan Cross*

It was the 1968 winter schedules which brought significant cuts to the 309. The Saturday service had been almost unaltered since November 1964 when the 309A was added, but from 5th October the service to Chorleywood was cut from 15 to 11 journeys Monday to Friday and halved from 18 to nine journeys Saturday. Between Rickmansworth and Harefield, the service was cut from 13 to eight journeys Monday to Friday, and from 12 to six on Saturday. This latter change allowed operation by only one RF, the GS being reduced to operation on Monday to Friday. Revised schedules on 15th February 1969 replaced the remaining GS with an RF, thus bringing GS operation on the 309 to an end. GS 34 spent more than four years at Garston, but only as a training bus, before being stood down in July 1969, its later use more infrequent as older drivers with manual gearbox licences retired.

Thus Garston's GS operation was reduced to the single GS for the 336A. Despite a slow reduction in passengers, the timetable at the point when London Country took over had remained unchanged after the final Saturday service in 1961, and would remain so until the last day of operation. One unusual addition to the 336A timetable was the extension of one morning journey from Rickmansworth to Northwood. This was added on 13th May 1967 when the 309 / 309A allocation was reduced to two buses and replaced a 309A journey. With strict adherence to London Transport practice, an additional blind panel was added to the 336A blind so that the journey could work through from Loudwater without a change to 309A at Rickmansworth. This single Northwood journey continued to the last day of operation by which time only three journeys remained between there and Rickmansworth.

Garston's allocation of GSs for service is almost impossible to detail, since changes were made far more frequently than at any other garage. Garston's operational fleet never made use of its total capacity, so that it became the main storage location for spare buses in the northern area. Whilst some GSs remained in store there for longer periods, many others were held in temporary storage for short periods, sometimes as little as a week before being reallocated elsewhere. With so many GSs available, Garston therefore exchanged its operational buses on a frequent basis. It was only in later years when numbers had dwindled significantly that the buses employed remained in service for longer periods. Of the original allocation, GS 75 went to Amersham on 1st January 1956. GS 42 came from Dorking in February 1955 (exact date not recorded) and went for overhaul on 18th December 1956 to be replaced by GS 28 fresh from overhaul. It remained until May 1965, later being overhauled and chosen to go to High Wycombe to start the 442 route. GS 33 came from its last overhaul on November 1965 and remained in service until the last day of operation. GS 17 replaced GS 28 and was intended to remain until the end, but suffered engine failure in March 1971. GS 42 had been demoted to training duties, but was sent to Garston to replace GS 17, remaining with GS 33 until the last day.

The last months of the 336A have been covered in detail in many other publications, but on the evening of 30th March 1972, GS operation came to an end. GS 42 was the allocated service bus that day but, wisely, staff put out GS 33 as duplicate, and on that final day, the 336A carried more passengers than it had probably enjoyed for the previous year. Both buses were scheduled to run light from Rickmansworth back to Garston, but the driver put up the 309 blind at Rickmansworth and ran in service back to the garage!

ST ALBANS

INITIAL ALLOCATION   GS 72

ROUTES OPERATED
Special Duplicate 9th December 1959 – use and routes unknown
382 13th April 1960–22nd May 1963, 1st February 1965–13th November 1967

Facing page On 1st February 1967, GS 21 was transferred from the 399 at Grays to St Albans for the 382 where it remained until replaced with an RF on 7th October the same year. By 1967 the 382 timetable had been reduced to only four journeys with no service in the morning into St Albans after the first journey from Codicote just after 8.00am. The next bus was just after 1.00pm and provided an afternoon shopping facility with two return journeys in late afternoon. When the GS was replaced the timetable was cut further to only two journeys during the week and three Saturday. On a wet day, GS 21 has arrived at Codicote and the driver reads his paper before setting the blind for the return trip. This stop was also used by the 315 works journeys from Kimpton into Welwyn Garden City and by Birch service 203 between Bedford and London. *Colin Rivers collection*

St Albans would perhaps never have had any GSs scheduled had it not been for a developing shortage of omo RFs which came about as omo conversions gathered pace throughout the 1960s. Most of these were straight conversions from crew operated RF to omo, but included a smaller number of conversions from crew double deck. The 382 was an extremely minor route serving no purpose other than a limited shopping service from some sparsely populated countryside between Welwyn and St Albans. Codicote – the outer terminus of the 382 – was a larger village on the hourly Birch Brothers 203 route from London to Bedford and Rushden giving a link to Hitchin and Welwyn, whilst Birch's other route 206 provided a limited service to Luton so that the demand for shopping into St Albans must have been limited even in the early 1950s. From Codicote, the 382 paralleled the Birch routes to Welwyn which had frequent services to Welwyn Garden City and Stevenage, and in the early 1950s an almost hourly service on the 388 to Hertford. The small hamlet of Lemsford was then the main point for likely passengers, after which the route passed few houses until the outskirts of St Albans were reached. In 1955, the 382 timetable operated four journeys Monday to Friday, seven Saturday and there was no Sunday service. It was converted from crew RF to omo on 17th October 1957, the running time being increased from 41 to 42 minutes in strict adherence to a new omo speed schedule!

Increases in Monday to Friday omo RF rosters at St Albans combined with falling traffic on the 382 resulted in a GS being allocated to the 382 from 13th April 1960, Saturday operation retaining the RF. Although this was the formal allocation to the 382, a GS had been allocated to St Albans a little earlier. The amendment dated 9th December 1959 to the allocation book of 14th October notes the addition of one GS to St Albans as a 'Special Duplicate'. It is not known why this was required. GS 72, which had been of those hired to Great Yarmouth, was stored at Gillingham Street (Victoria) on its return on 5th August 1959, being transferred to Grays a month later. In November it was relicensed for service and transferred to St Albans. It is unlikely that the 382 required any duplication but there is photographic evidence of GS workings on the 365. This route carried higher loads to and from Luton during peak times, and it may well have been necessary for some duplication. Luton garage ran 365 works journeys from Batford to the Vauxhall Works in Luton, and it is possible, though unlikely, that the GS was used to duplicate these, running through to and from St Albans.

When formal operation on the 382 began, the timetable remained unchanged from 1955. The GS was rostered only for the 382, there being no cross working to or from other routes, a pattern which continued unchanged until 22nd May 1963 when the GS was replaced again by an RF as service cuts across the Country area reduced some of the earlier shortages. Perhaps surprisingly, a later scheduling change returned GS operation to the 382 on 1st February 1965, this time remaining allocated until 7th November 1967 when an omo RF finally replaced the GS for the last time.

In the October 1962 changes, GS 52 went from Amersham to St Albans on 24th October to replace GS 72 which had been selected as one of the 20 GSs earmarked for disposal and was delicensed and moved for storage at Garston. GS 48 had been sent from Northfleet for overhaul on 29th August 1962. On return from Works, it went to St Albans on 29th October, being licensed for service the next day. GS 51 was then delicensed having operated on the 382 for only one week and moved to Garston. On 21st November it went for overhaul. GS 48 remained until transfer to Leatherhead on 23rd May 1963 at the end of the first period of operation on the 382. The supplementary circular dated 3rd February 1965 to the November 1964 allocation book notes the addition of one GS at St Albans. The allocation also changed such that the GS was rostered on Saturdays. GS 54 had been operating the 389 experimental service at Harlow and was transferred to St Albans when the 389 was withdrawn on Friday 12th February. Whether another GS was sent to St Albans for 10 days until GS 54 arrived is not recorded, but it is more likely that GS 54 took over the 382 on the following Wednesday 17th February, Wednesday being the start of the normal 'roster week'. Since spare buses could be used from nearby Garston if necessary, GS 54 remained the only bus allocated until replaced by GS 21 on 1st February 1967. GS 54 replaced GS 21 at Grays on the 399 for three months until that route was withdrawn. It went to Northfleet where it would be one of the last in service there. GS 21 remained until the allocation was once again changed back to RF for the last time on 7th October 1967.

5 North East Operations

HITCHIN and STEVENAGE

INITIAL ALLOCATION (HITCHIN)
GS 2   12th October 1953 (for training)
GS 8   14th October 1953 (for training)
Both licensed for service 1st November 1953
GS 63   1st January 1954

INITIAL ALLOCATION (STEVENAGE)
GS 2, 5, and 15 from Hitchin 29th April 1959

ROUTES OPERATED
383   1st November 1953 – 7th June 1961 (Saturday)
         1st November 1953 – 21st October 1961 (Mon-Fri)
364   1st November 1953 – 21st October 1961
         (Tuesday and Saturday short journeys to Preston)
807   17th October 1956 – 8th October 1963
         303/384 positioning journeys for 383 and 807

GS 2 entered service at Hitchin on 2nd November 1953. It stands next to C 31 from Hertford which has run in from Datchworth on the 329A. Given that Hertford's Cubs on the 329A were replaced one week later on 9th November then this picture was taken either on Tuesday 3rd or Saturday 7th. One of Hitchin's RFs waits on the left for a journey to Luton on the 364, while the double decker on the right is a Leyland PD2 of Birch Brothers who ran rural routes into Hitchin from their garage at Henlow near Hitchin. *Michael Wickham*

London Transport's garage at Hitchin was its most northerly outpost, and compared to other garages was small and somewhat dilapidated with limited facilities. It was only when Stevenage began to be developed from the late 1940s that Hitchin's allocation began to increase. By the latter half of 1953, before the GSs arrived, its peak vehicle requirement was 19 buses, 11 of which ran to Stevenage each day for works contracts to the expanding industrial area and what were then limited town services. The only omo single deck bus was for the 383 which had started from 18th February 1948 and had become the source of an extremely acrimonious dispute between London Transport and Smith's Coaches of Buntingford who covered much the same route as the 383 from Weston to Hitchin. The details of this dispute have been recorded in detail elsewhere, but in the end London Transport won a Traffic Court judgement to allow them to operate the route.

The 383 timetable consisted of a service to Weston roughly every two hours, in between which were short journeys to Purwell Lane Estate at Walsworth just east of the town where new housing had been developed. The single bus rostered spent lengthy periods on the stand at St Mary's Square between trips since the journey time to Weston was only 23 minutes each way and 11 minutes to Purwell Lane Estate. St Mary's Square was Hitchin's main market place, and London Transport's services reversed onto a stand at one end of the square. The garage was about 300 yards from here and crews walked to and from it to change over. After Walsworth, the 383 carried on for about two miles before reaching Willian where the 384 came in from Letchworth. Until the A1 Great North Road was diverted in 1960 as part of the Stevenage by-pass, the 384 turned right at Willian along a single track lane to reach the original A1, where it turned south towards Graveley and Stevenage. The 383 continued through Willian to a junction with the road from Letchworth which led on to the A1 a few hundred yards further on. In the days with far less traffic, the 383 simply turned right at the T junction here onto the A1, and 400 yards later left at Lannock Hill into the lane up to Willian, about two miles further. This was a gradual climb with no steep sections and on reaching Weston, buses turned left by the Post Office to run round to a shelter in the lane to the rear of the village pub. To this day, the original galvanised tubular aluminium shelter remains in position, though little used with a very infrequent service.

Between November 1953 when the GSs replaced Cubs and 1960, the 383 timetable was virtually unchanged. 9th October 1960 was the last day on which the Sunday service operated, and some weeks later on 21st December the 383 was extended from the town centre to the new Oakfield estate situated along the lane to Great Wymondley. This short extension of only six minutes from St Mary's Square made more efficient use of the bus between the journeys to Weston. The estates provided good passenger loads at certain times, and the timetable then required a second bus during the week in the morning peak and afternoons for school journeys. An additional journey also ran as far as Willian on Tuesday and Friday afternoon, being operated on Tuesday by the bus rostered for the short journeys on the 364 to Preston. On Saturday afternoon, a crew RF ran these 364 journeys, plus two 383 journeys to Purwell Lane Estate, one of which ran as a duplicate to the service bus just after lunch to carry additional shopping passengers into the town.

Hitchin's two Cubs were delicensed on 1st November 1953, GS 2 and 8 taking over the same day. C 13 was withdrawn and delicensed although C 16 was transferred to Tring for a few more weeks in service. One GS worked the 383 every day while the second GS was rostered to a works contract together with the 364 short journeys to Preston on Tuesday and Saturday and one peak 384 journey. Running numbers were HN2 for the 383 and HN102 for the contract work. GS 63 was licensed and sent from Aldenham on 1st January 1954 to provide three GSs – two for service and one engineering spare. GS 3 was transferred from Chelsham to Hitchin on 5th January 1954 for a short period before returning to Chelsham. This may have been to cover a temporary repair or breakdown of either GS 2 or 8 although the reason is not recorded.

GS 2 was transferred to Hertford on 3rd August 1955, but returned on 14th March 1956 after its first overhaul to replace GS 8 which went for overhaul the following day. This left Hitchin with two GSs until GS 80 was transferred from Windsor on 31st October 1956. The 807 had been introduced on 17th October 1956, GS 80 thus providing a spare bus, although the sparse timetable of the 807 meant that the bus was required only for relatively short periods during the day. GS 63 was delicensed for overhaul on 16th October 1957 and replaced by GS 15 from Hertford. On return from overhaul it was stored unlicensed at Luton, although the reason is not recorded. It was relicensed on 25th March 1958 for a short spell at Garston before returning to Hitchin where it remained until delicensed on 7th September, having been one of those earmarked for hire to Great Yarmouth. This was its last period of revenue earning service with London Transport after less than five years, and was sold to Corvedale Motors at Ludlow in April 1961. GS 80 was transferred to Hertford as a float bus on 25th March 1958.

GS 15 was transferred from Hertford to Hitchin on 16th October 1957 to release GS 63 for overhaul. London Transport's terminus in Hitchin was at the end of St Mary's Square where a shelter ran along one end and was filled with stalls of all kinds each week on Tuesday and Saturday's markets. Buses generally reversed onto to the stops but GS 15 has turned to pick up passengers for a 383 to Weston. The Q plate on the bus stop tells passengers to queue that side, although this seems unnecessary.
John Hambley collection

On Monday 29th February 1960, with a sole passenger on board, the driver of GS 2 checks to his right before pulling out on to the Great North Road at Lannock Hill on a journey from Weston. Two hundred yards along the A1, the route turned left into the road to Letchworth and left again into Willian Lane. Later that year, this section of the A1 would be bypassed by the new Stevenage By-Pass which caused the lane almost opposite here to be blocked off. This was used by the 384, but following the opening of the new road, it followed the same road as the 383 into Willian. Further alterations to the road when the Baldock By-Pass was opened have greatly changed the view in the background. *Peter Mitchell*

The requirement for the second GS was removed in the summer schedules of 16th May 1956 when the contract work was altered and converted to double deck and crew RF as Stevenage expanded. The 364 Preston short journeys were converted to RF crew on Saturday. The requirement for a single GS was however short lived, reverting to two on 17th October when route 807 was introduced, and was perhaps the oddest and most pointless Country area route ever begun by London Transport. It ran from Letchworth via Letchworth Gate where factories and offices were located near the A1, before meeting the 383 where it emerged from the lane from Willian. It then followed the 383 to Weston after which it ran along some narrow roads through the tiny hamlet of Friends Green finally to rejoin the A1 Great North Road just north of what was then still the main street in Stevenage. The timetable was principally designed to provide a service for workers in Stevenage's expanding industrial area, with a single return each afternoon into Stevenage for shopping. An early morning journey ran to Stevenage station (then located some distance north of the present station) and via Fairview Road to the factory area at Gunnels Wood. The bus then ran light to Trinity

Church at the south end of Stevenage High Street to work the 7.36am 384B back to Letchworth via Letchworth Gate returning on the 7.59am 384 to Stevenage. These journeys provided an additional service for the morning peak, following which the GS ran light back to Hitchin. There was then no further service until the afternoon when the bus ran to Letchworth to work the 2.37pm into Stevenage with a return at 4.15pm allowing a little over an hour for shopping. On arriving at Letchworth, the bus ran a further 807 back to Gunnels Wood to operate the evening return journey for workers. At a time when factories finished earlier on Fridays, this journey ran 30 minutes earlier that day than on Monday to Thursday. When introduced, an evening service was provided on the 807. The journeys ran on Tuesday and Friday evenings at 8.15pm and 10.05pm from Stevenage with a single journey at 9.12pm from Letchworth but the timing seems to have served little purpose. It was also relatively costly to operate since the bus had to run light to Stevenage for the 8.15pm journey, then light back from Letchworth after completing the 10.05pm. These journeys probably carried few if any passengers and were abandoned in October 1959.

There were no works journeys on Saturdays, the timetable consisting only of the afternoon service, although allowing two hours for shopping with the return at 5.15pm. From Letchworth the bus worked a 6.12pm into Stevenage, returning at 10.00pm presumably for those who had gone into Stevenage to the cinema. Like the service during the week, these were equally costly to operate but continued until finally withdrawn with the 1963 winter schedules.

When Stevenage garage opened on 29th April 1959, GS 2, 5, and 15 were transferred from Hitchin, and scheduling changes meant that the bus for the 383 ran out to Hitchin to take up service. The outward journey in the morning was run 'light', but the bus ran back each evening by working the 10.30pm 303 journey to Stevenage. There were other schoolday positioning journeys operated on the 303, and the Saturday crew working noted above ran to and from Stevenage in service on the 303. Until Hitchin closed, the first 383 ran in service out to Weston each morning to run the first departure back to Hitchin, an increasingly wasteful journey since few if any passengers used it. Once Stevenage opened, the bus ran light via Graveley and the A1 to Lannock Hill to run up to Weston, thus making a small saving in operating costs. The bus then ran the 8.18am from Weston to Hitchin to take up service for the rest of the day.

The running numbers allocated to Stevenage's GS runnings were SV24 for the 383 and SV25 for the 807. The two buses did work journeys on both routes, and the 364 Tuesday short journeys to Preston were worked by SV25 and later SV24 when the schedules changed the afternoon workings. There was a complex working in the afternoon on the 4.06pm 383 journey from Hitchin to Willian. This operated every Tuesday and Friday, but only during school terms on the other three days. On Friday, the bus then ran 'light' from Willian to Letchworth to operate the 4.52pm 807 journey to Stevenage whereas for the remainder of the week, it ran the 4.24pm 383 back to Hitchin, and then a 303 back to Stevenage which ran every Tuesday and only on schooldays Monday, Wednesday and Thursday. The Saturday crew RF referred to above ran journeys on 303, 364, 383 and 384, the duty commencing at lunchtime. The running number for this was SV20, the crew completing the duty by running the 5.12pm 807 to Letchworth and 6.12pm return. There was no need for crew operation of any of these these journeys, but were a means of balancing the Saturday roster and providing a complete shift for one crew.

GS operation on the 383 was relatively short lived however after the transfer to Stevenage. Hitchin's expanding estates led to the smaller capacity of the GSs being inadequate at certain times, particularly on Saturdays. On 7th June 1961 therefore, the Saturday service was converted to RF. In an odd change to allocation however, the RF previously rostered to the 303 on Saturdays was exchanged for the GS which was retained. This arrangement changed once more on 21st October when the GS was replaced on Monday to Friday. The spare GS was again retained and used for duplicate workings on the 303 every day, but was soon replaced with an RF, thereby eliminating the need for the second GS, leaving Stevenage with one GS for the 807. It made little operational sense to retain a single 'non-standard' bus for such limited use. It was not replaced however for a further two years, until 9th October 1963, the general shortage of RFs following widespread omo conversions perhaps being the reason why the 807 retained its GS.

The 807 was not approved for RF operation when introduced due to the narrow roads between from Weston through Friends Green and beyond. The restriction remained noted in the allocation book after RFs replaced GSs but was clearly an error since the Saturday crew RF SV 20 was rostered in 1960 so that the restriction would have been removed by then, although the date seems not to have been recorded.

GS 2 went for its first overhaul on 6th May 1959, returning on 10th July, and relicensed for service on 1st August. GS 5 then went to works, returning on 15th October and relicensed on 1st November. During this period, they were replaced by GS 39 transferred from Dorking on 7th May. This remained until the end of 1961 before transfer to Garston and to overhaul on 1st January 1962. GS 37 spent three weeks at Stevenage in October as a spare bus before going to Hertford on 1st November.

GS 2 transferred to Stevenage when Hitchin garage closed on 29th April 1959, but was immediately delicensed and sent for overhaul on 6th May. It returned on 10th July and was relicensed on 1st August. It was delicensed on 24th October 1962 and sent to Grays as one of those earmarked for sale, where it remained until sold to Southern Motorways on 21st June 1963. Peter Aves has been fortunate enough to drive this bus over the 383 and 807 routes in recent years as part of the Country Bus Rallies fleet when owned by John Huxford. It has arrived at Stevenage bus station on duty SV25 probably having worked the 2.15pm afternoon shopping journey from Letchworth. *J Cowdery*

After operation on the 383 ceased, Stevenage required only one GS. In the changes of October 1962, GS 56 and 64 were transferred from Amersham allowing GS 2 to be delicensed and sent to Grays as one of those earmarked for sale. GS 56 however remained for only one week before being delicensed on 1st November, stored at Grays, and sent for overhaul in January 1963. It nevertheless remained out of use for 18 months until going to Dunton Green for the 471 in October 1964. After GS operation ceased on the 807, GS 64 remained out of use at Stevenage until it went to Hertford on 6th May 1964 where it would see three more years in service before being delicensed. It would pass to London Country, but remained in store until sold to Tillingbourne Valley in April 1971.

The scheduled GS requirement for Hitchin and Stevenage is summarised below:

Allocation book	383			807		303A	Contract	TOTAL	
	MF	Sat	Sun	MF	Sat	MF	Sat		
19th May 1954	1	1	1			1	1	2	Also jnys 364 / 384
18th May 1955	1	1	1			1	1	2	Also jnys 364 / 384
16th May 1956	1	1	1					1	
17th October 1956	1	1	1	1	1		2	2	Also jnys 384
16th October 1957	1	1	1	1				1	
10th December 1958	1	1	1	1	1			2	
14th October 1959	1	1	1	1	1			2	Also jnys 303 / 364 / 384
25th May 1960		1	1	1	1	1		2	Also jnys 303 / 364 / 384
23rd November 1960	1	1	1	1				2	Also jnys 303 / 364 / 384
7th June 1961	1	1		1	1(Sat)			2	Also jnys 303 / 364 / 384
25th October 1961			1	1	1(M-S)			2	Also jnys 384
24th October 1962				1	1			1	Also jnys 384
22nd May 1963				1	1			1	Also jnys 384

- GS operation on the 807 was replaced by RF from 9th October 1963.
- Operation on 303 in 1961 was limited to peak works journeys between Hitchin and Stevenage factory area.
- Journeys on 303 were the evening return from Hitchin after the last 383 plus school journeys.
- Journeys on 364 were a morning schoolday and Tuesday shorts to Preston (also Saturdays until 16th May 1956).
- Journeys on 384 in 1954/1955 were morning peak between Stevenage and Letchworth.
- Journeys on 384 from 1959 were positioning journeys to and from Letchworth for the 807 which changed over time.

HERTFORD

INITIAL ALLOCATION
GS 4 allocated 13th October 1953 – 4th November 1953 for training only.
GS 12, 16, 18, 19 and 22 allocated 4th November 1953
GS 23 allocated 5th November 1953
GS 21 allocated 6th November 1953
All except GS 4 licensed for service 9th November 1953

ROUTES OPERATED

308/308A	7th June 1961 – 22nd November 1968
329, 333, 388	9th November 1953 – 22nd November 1968
331	9th November 1953 – 2nd October 1965 (386 positioning journeys and Saturday journeys to High Cross)
329A	9th November 1953 – 2nd October 1965
333B	9th November 1953 – 15th October 1957
380	7th June 1961 – 21st May 1963
386	21st April 1954 – 22nd November 1968 (Monday to Friday)
	21st April 1954 – 15th October 1958 (Sunday)
386A	21st April 1954 – 12th October 1958
	(Thursday and Sunday – positioning for 386)
388A	15th December 1954 – 21st March 1956
389	21st April 1954 – 16th October 1956

- The 386 remained RF operated on Saturdays although a GS was occasionally used.
- From 7th June 1961 joint GS / RF operation was scheduled on 308, 308A, 329, 331 and 388. The 329A was not approved for GS operation and continued until withdrawn in October 1965. RFs continued to replace GSs on all routes until the final two GSs were withdrawn in November 1968.

GS 10 has stopped in Station Road, Bishop's Stortford to pick up passengers on one of the through journeys to Hitchin. After its first allocation to Chelsham, it went for overhaul on 17th May 1956, returning to Hertford where it was relicensed on 1st July. Since the through service to Hitchin operated only at weekends, and the Saturday service remained crew operated, then this must be one of the Sunday journeys which were abandoned completely in the cuts following the 1958 strike. Given the time on Hampton's clock, then either it is fast, or the driver is late, since departure was scheduled for 4.25pm! The driver has also set the wrong blind, which should have been used for the Tuesday service from Buntingford.
Michael Wickham

Although Hertford did not have the largest GS allocation, its operations were by far the most complex of any garage, a complexity which applied to all its single deck operations.

Hertford was a busy country market town and the single deck routes which radiated from there in all directions, serving what was, despite its proximity to London, a large area, much of which was deeply rural and sparsely inhabited. Many small villages were served, often with a frequent service even by the standards of 1950. Hertford's GS operations were however unique among country area garages since the actual run out of buses allocated to particular running numbers varied almost every day. Additional buses were required for journeys which ran on market days, these being Tuesdays and Saturdays for Hitchin, on Thursdays and Saturdays for Bishops Stortford and Wednesdays for Hertford. Additional shoppers on Saturday and trips to the cinema in the evening also required extra journeys.

The 329 operated just three journeys Monday, Thursday and Friday, six journeys to a two hourly headway Wednesday and Saturday, with two additional short journeys as far as Bulls Green on Saturday. Three Sunday afternoon journeys also operated. The 329 had no service on Tuesdays other than a positioning journey for the 329A which ran remotely from Datchworth to Hitchin on Tuesday and Saturday. The 386 ran from Buntingford to Hitchin on Tuesdays, the bus running to Buntingford as route 331 to take up service. On Thursdays it operated from Buntingford to Bishop's Stortford with positioning journeys via Hadham on the 386A, and on Saturdays two buses ran through journeys between Bishop's Stortford and Hitchin via Buntingford. The two buses scheduled on Sundays ran two journeys into Hitchin and three to Bishop's Stortford. The first ran as a 331 to Buntingford, the second as a 386A to Standon, both buses finishing at Buntingford in the evening before running as 331 back to Hertford.

The service to the tiny hamlet of Chapmore End on the 333 consisted of only two journeys during the week but with an additional journey Wednesday lunchtime, while the Saturday service consisted of five journeys. The 333B timetable serving Ware Park Hospital at Bengeo also had three journeys Wednesday evening for hospital visitors plus three during the day mainly for the convenience of staff. In addition to the staff journeys on Saturdays, there were eight more in the afternoon for visitors, while on Sunday afternoon – which in the 1950s was the main visiting day – there were no fewer than 14 journeys in the afternoon between 1.30pm and 4.15pm. Part of the 389 timetable was duplicated as mentioned later. All this variation resulted in much interworking between routes and different schedules every day.

Hertford's importance meant that the need for small capacity single deckers had been limited. Before the GSs first arrived, six Cubs were rostered Monday to Friday, seven Saturday, and five Sunday. The 386 and 386A were the most isolated routes of all, and operated remotely at some distance from Hertford. Until April 1954 they had been crew operated, since market days in Hitchin and Bishop's Stortford attracted considerable numbers of passengers travelling to market for their shopping. Indeed, the two buses required on Saturdays remained crew operated until the major cuts which followed the 1958 strike. Although the 329 from Nup End into Hertford employed one Cub, the service was mostly crew operated on Wednesday for the additional passengers on Hertford's market day, as was part of the Saturday service.

Hertford received its first GS from Aldenham on 13th October 1953, when GS 4 was sent as a training bus, having been delivered from ECW only the previous day. It remained until 4th November when it was transferred to Amersham for training and later put into service there. GS 12, 16, 18, 19, 21, 22 and 23 were sent from Aldenham between 4th and 6th November, commencing in service on 9th November, replacing all of the Cub allocation. Hertford had an allocation of eight Cubs, three of which were withdrawn on 9th November, but the exact date of withdrawal of the remainder is not recorded in the daily movement records, and it is possible some were retained as spares. The records show however that the remaining five were kept at Hertford out of use until 16th March 1954 when they were transferred to storage at Wood Green. Cubs had also been used on route 372, introduced in May 1948 to provide the first link between Hertford and Welwyn Garden City. The route had quickly become successful, the Cubs having been replaced with crew operated TFs and then RFs before the GSs arrived.

As passenger numbers began to decline, it had always been the intention to convert some lesser crew operated single deck routes to omo. On 21st April 1954, the crew operated journeys on 329 were converted to omo GS operation together with the whole of the 389 and the Tuesday, Thursday and Sunday service on the 386 and 386A, the Saturday service on those latter routes remaining crew operated. This required a maximum of three additional GSs. GS 72, 73 and 74 had been stored at Aldenham since delivery at the end of October 1953 but were all moved to Garston on 10th February 1954. On 8th April, GS 72 was licensed and sent to Epping, but transferred to Hertford on 14th April. Six days later GS 73 and 74 were licensed and sent from Garston to Hertford in readiness for these conversions.

A Hertford GS blind dated June 1961.

From this date, Hertford's schedule requirement became eight Monday to Friday (plus one extra Tuesday and Thursday), ten Saturday and eight on Sunday. A total of ten GSs had been allocated, Saturday being the only day when there was no spare bus. However, the 329, 386, 386A and 389 were all approved for RF operation so that one could be used in the event of a breakdown or emergency. Conversion of the 389 was intended to save costs, but passenger loads on a number of journeys proved too great for the smaller GS. A morning and afternoon journey during the week was therefore duplicated on schooldays, whilst on Saturdays two afternoon departures from Hertford were duplicated all the way to Sawbridgeworth and back as well as an additional journey at lunchtime as far as Gilston, which then formed a duplicate to the bus from Sawbridgeworth on its return to Hertford. This required two buses, fuel and drivers, and was probably more expensive to operate than one crew bus, although there would have been an overall saving in converting the whole route to omo.

The Saturday lunchtime journey to Gilston was timed to leave Hertford at 1.03pm, and ran back from Gilston at 1.45pm three minutes in front of the 1.36pm from Sawbridgeworth. That journey would already have several passengers on board for an afternoon's shopping in Ware or Hertford. On returning to Hertford, the bus then operated as a duplicate to the 2.42pm and 4.42pm journeys to Sawbridgeworth and back. The 388 had been extended to replace the 389 on 17th October 1956, and was cut back again to Hertford on 7th June 1961 when route 380 took over the service to Sawbridgeworth. These Saturday duplicate journeys were withdrawn under the 1958 winter schedules, among the widespread cuts which followed the strike. RF 620 waits behind having arrived on a 342 from Potters Bar. *A D Packer*

To the west of Hertford town centre, new houses were being built at Sele Farm. On 15th December 1954, the 310 was extended from its current terminus at Hertford North station a short distance to turn at the edge of the new development alongside the road to Welwyn. Since at first passenger numbers would be small, the 310 provided a service only at peak times and evenings during the week. With larger numbers of shoppers on Saturdays, the 310 provided a 30-minute service during the day, but nothing on Sundays. To provide an off peak shopping service during the week, route 388A was introduced. At the time there were no spare route numbers, so 388A was being used since the 388 ran along Welwyn Road past the edge of the new estate. The GS which ran the morning and afternoon schoolday duplicate on the 389 was otherwise not required, so it was scheduled to run a 30-minute service between mid-morning and early afternoon. There was then a gap in the timetable to allow the bus to run the 2.39pm 389 schoolday duplicate to Sawbridgeworth and back. Upon its return, three more 388A journeys were run, the bus returning to Fairfax Road garage at 6.15pm. The running number used was HG65 (schooldays), or HG66 (school holidays) and was an economic use of a bus which otherwise stood idle, especially during school holidays. Sele Farm estate grew rapidly however and the 388A ran for the last time on 20th March 1956. The 310 timetable was increased and a Sunday service added, and provided a 30 minute daily headway, increasing to 15 minutes during the day on Saturday. Over the next 20 years, many changes were made to the Sele Farm journeys, other routes having certain peak hour journeys extended there. Because of the complex scheduling, running numbers allocated to the GSs changed many times, those in the range HG60–75 being used from about 1960.

The summer schedules of 16th May 1956 introduced an additional GS on Thursdays, noted in the allocation books as *'special duplicate'*. No specific reference to its purpose has been found, but almost certainly it was used to duplicate the bus for the 386 that day to Bishop's Stortford for market day. The scheduled bus left Hertford at 8.06am running as a 386A via Hadham and Puckeridge to Buntingford before the first 9.22am 386 journey into Bishop's Stortford, which would have become increasingly busy during this period. The scheduled bus would probably have sufficient capacity as far as Standon, so it is likely that the duplicate bus ran out to join it from there into Bishop's Stortford. During the rest of the day, two short journeys to Standon and three to Buntingford were operated, so to what extent the second bus duplicated these is unknown. The first driver on the scheduled bus had a 40-minute break at Bishop's Stortford on arriving with the first journey. The duty then consisted of the first short to Standon, a return to Buntingford, finally coming off at Standon at 3.19pm on the next journey to Buntingford. The 331 timetable was arranged so that the driver travelled back on the 3.21pm to Hertford, the replacement driver having arrived at 3.09pm off the 2.38pm 331 from Hertford. This driver took over the Buntingford journey, returned to Bishop's Stortford, then ran a further short to Standon. A 40-minute break at Bishop's Stortford was taken before running the last journey to Buntingford, finally running the 8.04pm 386A journey back to Hertford.

It was a feature of market day bus services to country towns everywhere that the last journeys did not leave until early evening long after the market traders had packed up and left. Market days were as much a social occasion as for essential shopping, and many pubs would enjoy a good trade well into the evening. The Tuesday 386 timetable into Hitchin included a late departure at 8.10pm, and on Saturdays at 7.00pm from Bishop's Stortford and 7.34pm from Hitchin. It was surely the case that these journeys began to carry fewer and fewer passengers, but they continued in the timetable with little change to the timings until the drastic reductions which came with the 1965 winter schedule.

ROUTE 386 to BUNTINGFORD to BISHOPS STORTFORD

Tuesday and Saturday — Thursday and Saturday

NOTE : Unless travelling to or from a point beyond these limits, a passenger may not board or alight between Throcking Lane and Buntingford *Jolly Sailors*
This service is operated by Pay As You Enter Vehicles. Please have your fare ready as you get on.
A 5/- ROVER TICKET will take you as far as you like on this and on nearly every other Country bus route. Ask the conductor for details.

Tuesday / Thursday

	Tuesday am	Tuesday am	Tuesday pm	Tuesday pm	Tuesday pm	Tuesday pm	Tuesday pm	Thursday am	Thursday am	Thursday pm	Thursday pm	Thursday pm
Hitchin *St. Mary's Square*	11 7	1118	2 8	225	4 4	544	816	....	..	..	..	..
Great Wymondley *Green Man*	1115	1126	216	233	412	552	824	...	..	..	..	..
Titmore Green *Hermit of Redcoats*	1121	....	....	239	....	558	830	...	..	..	..	..
Stevenage *White Lion*	1129	..	..	247	..	6 6	838	...	..	..	..	..
Stevenage *Bus Station*	1133	....	....	251	....	610	842	...	..	..	..	..
Walkern *Post Office*	1149	..	..	3 7	..	626	858	...	..	..	..	..
Cromerhill Common	1154	....	....	312	....	631	9 3	...	..	..	..	..
Ardley	1158	....	....	316	....	635	9 7	...	..	..	..	..
Cottered *Bull*	12 6	....	....	324	....	643	915	...	..	**B**	**B**	..
Buntingford *Jolly Sailors*	P1216	..	..	P334	..	P653	P925	..	941	140	4 0	..
Hare Street	A	..	..	A	..	A	....		947	146	4 6	
Dassells *Hobbs Lane*	....	..	..	....	..	....	....		952	..	151	411
Braughing *Golden Fleece*	....	..	..	....	..	....	....		957		156	416
Puckeridge *Crown & Falcon*	..	..	..	..	..	..	..		10 2	..	2 1	421
Standon *Station*	..	..	..	..	..	..	..		10 5	1144	2 4	424	549
Wellpond Green *Nags Head*	..	..	..	..	..	..	..		1010	1149	2 9	429	554
Little Hadham *Angel*	..	..	..	..	..	..	..		1020	1159	219	439	6 4
Bury Green Road	..	..	..	..	..	..	..		1025	12 4	224	444	6 9
Bishops Stortford *Station Road*	....	..	..	....	..	....	....		1033	1212	232	452	617
Bishops Stortford *Havers Lane Estate*	..	..	..	..	..	..	..		1040	1219	239	459	624

Saturday

	am	am	am	pm	pm	pm	pm	pm	pm	pm
Hitchin *St. Mary's Square*	1113	..	..	1213	2 8	213	4 4	519	741	....
Great Wymondley *Green Man*	1121	..	..	1221	216	221	412	527	749	...
Titmore Green *Hermit of Redcoats*	....	..	..	1227	....	227	....	533	755	...
Stevenage *White Lion*	....	..	..	1235	..	235	..	541	8 3	858
Stevenage *Bus Station*	....	..	..	1239	....	239	....	545	8 7	9 2
Walkern *Post Office*	....	..	..	1255	..	255	..	6 1	..	918
Cromerhill Common	....	..	..	1 0	....	3 0	....	6 6	..	923
Ardley	....	..	..	1 4	....	3 4	....	610	..	927
Cottered *Bull*	....	..	..	112	....	312	....	618	..	935
Buntingford *Jolly Sailors*	....	..	..	122	....	322	....	628	..	945
Hare Street	....	..	..	128	....	328	....	634	..	951
Dassells *Hobbs Lane*	....	..	..	133	....	333	....	639	..	956
Braughing *Golden Fleece*	....	..	..	138	....	338	....	644	..	10 1
Puckeridge *Crown & Falcon*	..	..	..	143	..	343	..	649	..	10 6
Standon *Station*	..	..	10 9	146	....	346	....	652	..	10 9
Wellpond Green *Nags Head*	..	..	1014	151	....	351	....	657	..	
Little Hadham *Angel*	..	..	1024	2 1	....	4 1	....	7 7	..	
Bury Green Road	..	..	1029	C 2 6	....	4 6	....	712	..	
Bishops Stortford *Station Road*	..	..	1037	11 7	214	....	414	....	720	
Bishops Stortford *Havers Lane Estate*	..	..	1044	1114	221	....	421	....	727	

A—Arrives Buntingford Station 2 minutes later.   B—Departs Buntingford *Throcking Lane* 3 minutes earlier.   P—Time at Buntingford *The Crown*.   C—Departs Bishops Stortford *Bricklayers Arms* 3 minutes earlier.

For Additional Service between Stevenage and Walkern see Route 384, between Buntingford and Puckeridge see Route 331, between Little Hadham and Bishops Stortford see Routes 350 · 350A.

LONDON TRANSPORT, 55 BROADWAY, S.W.I ABBey 1234   23.11.60
960/2500W/600 (130)   L563   Kelly & Kelly Ltd, London

This 386 timetable dated 23rd November 1960 differed from previous versions in that the bus on the first journey to Hitchin on Tuesdays then ran the 329A and short journeys from Great Wymondley for the rest of the day. The bus on the 329A morning journey to Hitchin then ran the rest of the 386. Apart from the 9.57am from Buntingford which had run as a 331 from Hertford, the other three journeys terminated at Buntingford station which still had a passengers service. The Thursday journeys ran to Throcking Lane just north of Buntingford High Street to turn. The Saturday service retained RF operations, but the Great Wymondley journeys were run by the GS from the 329A.
Peter Aves collection

The 329A from Datchworth into Hitchin was the Country area's most infrequent route, consisting of just two return journeys on Tuesday and Saturday. The bus was also scheduled to operate three short 386 journeys to Great Wymondley from Hitchin during the day. The 386 timetable was arranged so that the driver had breaks between journeys at Hitchin, as did the driver on the 329A. However, the duties both represented a long day in the period when there were not stricter limits on driver's hours. The bus on the 329A left Hertford at 9.10am, returning to the garage at 6.29pm, that on the 386 leaving Hertford at 8.43am as a 331 to Buntingford, returning as late as 10.05pm at night before running back to Fairfax Road. There was no connecting facility at Buntingford to or from 331 journeys during the day, but it was possible to change drivers at Stevenage White Lion on the 3.52pm from Buntingford. The bus arrived at Stevenage at 4.36pm enabling drivers to travel to and from Hertford on the 390 to change over. It has not been possible to obtain crew rosters, but this was the only occasion during the day when a change on the 386 could be made. Without this, the 386 driver would have been away from Hertford for almost 14 hours so, although it is conjecture, it is most likely that this was the way the roster was constructed.

On Tuesday 7th September 1965, GS 65 has just arrived at Hitchin having worked the 1.21pm 329A from Datchworth. It will now work the 2.08pm 386 short journey to Great Wymondley after which the driver will take his afternoon break. GS 13 is waiting to work the 2.28pm 386 to Buntingford. They carry running numbers HG63 on GS 13 and HG65 on GS 65, details of which can be seen in Hertford's schedules included later. Earlier, Stevenage's RF 590 has worked the 1.07pm 364 short journey to Preston and later will work the 4.06pm 383 journey to Willian which ran only on Tuesday and Friday during school holidays, but every day during school terms. The unidentified RF at the far side is the bus operating the main 383 schedule. This picture was possible for only three more Tuesdays after which the 329A was abandoned and the 386 Tuesday timetable halved with some of the Great Wymondley short journeys being taken over by Stevenage. GS 13 remained at Hertford to become one of the last two in service there, but GS 65 was less fortunate. It remained at Hertford but was involved in a serious accident shortly before the end of GS operation there. It suffered the indignity of being the only GS sold from service for scrap. *Peter Aves*

333B
BENGEO
WARE PARK
HOSPITAL

This E plate for the 333B to Ware Park Hospital is one of the rarest since there were only two of these on stops in Hertford – one in Fore Street and another at The Wash on the bridge over the river. It was in a bin in the yard at Hertford garage in 1965 and given to Peter Aves by one of the garage staff together with several others and a number of fare charts. *Peter Aves collection*

The first operational change – other than the 388A referred to above – came on 17th October 1956 when the 388 was extended over the 389 route to Sawbridgeworth, forming one long route from Welwyn across Hertford. The former time-tables of both routes were virtually unchanged, including the schoolday and Saturday duplicates to Sawbridgeworth. Hertford's overall GS allocation – although adjusted for changes in interworking – remained unchanged until the winter programme of 1957 which brought about the first reductions. The principal cause was the replacement of GSs on the 333 and 333B by RFs since this was a busy local route and passenger numbers were beginning to exceed the capacity of the GSs. All of Hertford's RF routes had been converted to omo by this date (except for one remaining crew duty), and the driver duties on RF and GS routes were combined. With greater interworking across the 17 RFs scheduled, the three GSs allocated to the 333/333B were replaced by 2 RFs, although the timetable changed very little. The only remaining GS journeys scheduled on the 333 were those to Chapmore End where the single track lane into the village made them more suitable even though it was approved for RF operation. The use of GSs on these journeys continued until the end of operations in 1968. These changes reduced Hertford's scheduled GSs by three, which cut the number on Sunday from eight to five. One was saved on Saturday by minor changes to the interworking.

The first change to Hertford's allocation occurred on 3rd August 1955 when GS 2 was transferred from Hitchin, and then on 1st December 1955 GS 73 was loaned to Epping for four weeks. GS 2 did not remain at Hertford for long, being the first to be delicensed and sent to Chiswick on 2nd January 1956 as the first programme of overhauls began. It returned to Hitchin on 14th March allowing GS 8 to go for overhaul. GS 12 was the next of Hertford's initial batch to be sent for overhaul on 16th April 1956. GS 16 went on 25th May, GS 18 on 11th June, GS 19 on 14th June, GS 21 on 6th July, and GS 22 and 23 on 10th and 11th August. They were replaced by GS 5, 9, 10, 14, and 15; GS 18 and 19 returning from overhaul on 26th July and 20th August respectively. During this period, spare 'float' buses were allocated to cover any temporary shortages, but the daily records do not show all of these short term movements. GS 72 and 73 were de-licensed on 16th October 1957, GS 74 on 1st November; GS 44 being transferred from Epping on the same date noted as '*float cover*' in the daily records. GS 80 arrived from Hitchin on 25th March 1958 as a further float bus, GS 72, 73 and 74 going to Chiswick for overhaul on 3rd March, 24th March and 21st April respectively. There is no record of them being used during the previous five months after being delicensed. All three returned to Hertford from overhaul, but when GS 72 returned on 24th April, it was not relicensed and stood idle until 15th August when it was the first of the five buses to be sent on loan to Great Yarmouth. These movements are included here to illustrate the constant re-allocations, and are too complex to include throughout the book. A total of 36 GSs are recorded passing through Hertford in their 15 year period of operation, but this does not include the occasional use of a bus for a few days to cover breakdowns or temporary loans elsewhere. GS 62 for example is not recorded as ever being allocated to Hertford even for a short period, but photographic evidence exists of the bus at Hitchin working the 329A.

The terminus at Chapmore End was next to the small pond at the end of the village, buses turning by reversing on the corner. GS 13 stands by the pond on one of the few journeys which ran there. It has running number HG 72 which was a Saturday working from late 1966 by which time GS operation on Saturday was reduced to only two buses. *J G S Smith*

The long running dispute over pay during the latter part of 1957 carried on into 1958 and, with no resolution, led to the disastrous seven week strike in May and June 1958. Much has been written about this whole unhappy period, but the enormous financial losses combined with the loss of passengers once services returned to normal led to swingeing cuts across London Transport's bus and coach services. Particularly hard hit were the less frequent rural routes. Hertford ran a high proportion of these, and suffered significant cuts when the 1958 winter schedules were introduced on 15th October. The Sunday service on the 329 and 386 was abandoned completely, and the 386A withdrawn. Passengers on Saturdays on the 386 justified the continuing allocation of RFs, but they were converted to omo. On Wednesdays, the lunchtime Chapmore End journey was absorbed into other GS schedules, but the Thursday 386 duplicate was retained. The 388 Saturday duplicate had been withdrawn earlier from 23rd July as part of the immediate cuts following the end of the strike, although the Sunday timetable remained unchanged, including a morning journey to Welwyn and back for churchgoers and people who wanted to travel into Hertford before lunch. Overall, the GS schedule was reduced to five during the week (plus one Tuesday and two Thursday), six on Saturday, and just two Sunday – a significant reduction from the eight scheduled only two years earlier.

The 386 was extended from Bishops Stortford town centre to Havers Lane Estate in June 1959 to provide the new houses with a limited service, and the 350 was similarly extended the following year to provide a daily service. GS 55 transferred from Garston to Hertford on 13th May 1967 and would become one of its last two GSs when finally stood down on 23rd November 1968. It went to Northfleet to become the last GS in service there in October 1969, but remained in use as a training bus at Reigate until sold by London Country in 1972. For many years, it has been owned by Colin Rivers and is under restoration. It stands at Havers Lane terminus having worked either the 9.55am or 1.55pm Thursday journey from Hertford. This was a wasteful operation since the driver sat here for an hour in the morning or almost an hour and a half in the afternoon before running the return to Hertford. *Colin Rivers collection*

In June 1959, the 386 was extended up to Havers Lane Estate in Bishop's Stortford, but with the winter schedules on 14th October the 386 Thursday duplicate was withdrawn. Whether or not an additional bus was allocated on an occasional basis *'to instructions'* after this date is not known, but as there is no reference in the allocation books, such use would have been very unlikely. In the same schedules, two journeys each morning on the 388 were diverted from Welwyn to Welwyn Garden City to provide a shopping facility. This was a sensible innovation since the limited facilities in Welwyn village were far less attractive than those in Welwyn Garden City.

From 23rd November 1960, the 384 and 386 were diverted into Stevenage bus station to provide a link to the new town shopping centre. They had previously run only via the original town along the old Great North Road, but the diversion was a small if useful added facility for passengers. On the same date, the 386 was diverted through the small hamlet of Ardley between Cottered and Cromer. This diversion involved the use of a single track lane which was so narrow in one place that the field verges left no more than a few inches to spare either side of the bus. It had previously run via a different road through remote countryside with virtually no potential passengers, and the diversion through Ardely may have added small additional revenue. The new routeing paralleled Smith's service from Buntingford to Hitchin which had always run through the village. Although outside the '1933 Special Area', the revised routeing was inside the LPTA where London Transport had rights to run services. To what extent Smith's challenged LT's revision is unknown but having lost an acrimonious dispute in 1948 over the introduction of the 383 to Weston, perhaps they decided not to do so. The addition of 386 journeys through Ardley provided this tiny village with no fewer than six journeys into Hitchin on Tuesdays and eight Saturdays when LT's departure at 6.45pm was followed three minutes later by Smith's journey. Many regular passengers in those days were loyal to the local operator, so how many used the new 386 facility is unknown but the change resulted in an obvious over-provision, continuing little changed except that London Transport's Tuesday service was halved in 1965.

The next changes came with the 1961 summer schedules on 7th June when the 388 was cut back to operate only between Hertford to Welwyn. The separate service to Sawbridgeworth was numbered 380 and the schoolday duplicates were withdrawn. The timetable was adjusted slightly to allow the use of one GS all day, and layovers at Sawbridgeworth gave sufficient time for passengers to complete a small amount of shopping so that they could return on the same bus a little later. With increasing interworking, journeys on the 308 and 308A were scheduled for GSs for the first time, falling passenger numbers allowing the use of the smaller capacity. These schedules introduced much greater interworking across the 308, 308A, 329, 329A, 386 and 388. The 333 Chapmore End journeys remained scheduled for GS, together with some of the Saturday short journeys on the 331 to High Cross.

The GS schedules in the tables below show the complexity of all the interworking. As well as the 308/308A, RFs were allocated to part of the 329 on Saturdays, as well as the 331 High Cross journeys. The 331 remained busy on Saturdays, being one of the few routes scheduled for operation by RT, RF and GS. The 386 Saturday service retained the two RFs. All these changes increased the scheduled GSs to seven on Saturdays and six during the week (plus one Tuesday, Wednesday and Thursday).

GS 44 was transferred from Epping to Hertford on 1st November 1957, initially as a float bus to cover for overhauls. It remained for three years before being delicensed on 1st October 1960 and stored at Romford. After further use as a float bus and staff bus at New Cross, it went to Dorking, and back to Hertford in October 1964 for its last period in service. In September 1959, it has arrived at Prospect Place in Welwyn village on a 388 from Hertford. The terminus at Welwyn involved a clockwise run round the triangular green and was about 100 yards from the main village street which, until by-passed in 1927, had once been part of the Great North Road. The Q plate on the stop states that it is for use only by terminating buses, though why this restriction was deemed necessary is unclear. *Pamlin Prints*

The 388 timetable included a few journeys extended from Welwyn village along the Great North Road to Mardley Hill, which provided commuters with a link to the main line into London from Welwyn North station. GS 29 was allocated to Hertford on 21st June 1961 after its second overhaul and stayed until November 1963. After a few months in storage it was sent to Harlow in May 1964 to start the 389 town service. *Colin Rivers collection*

HERTFORD GS SCHEDULES – SUMMER 1961

MONDAY TO FRIDAY

	TIME DEPART	FROM	TO		TIME DEPART	FROM	TO
		RUNNING NUMBER HG 60		388	6.30 pm	MARDLEY HILL	HERTFORD Bus Stn.
388	6.58 am	FAIRFAX ROAD	MARDLEY HILL	388	7.16 pm	HERTFORD Bus Stn.	WELWYN Prospect Pl.
388	7.49 am	MARDLEY HILL	HERTFORD Bus Stn.	388	8.06 pm	WELWYN Prospect Pl.	HERTFORD Bus Stn.
388	8.39 am	HERTFORD Bus Stn.	WELWYN Prospect Pl.	388	8.53 pm	HERTFORD Bus Stn.	WELWYN Prospect Pl.
388	9.22 am	WELWYN Prospect Pl.	FAIRFAX ROAD	388	9.35 pm	WELWYN Prospect Pl.	FAIRFAX ROAD
388	11.21 am	FAIRFAX ROAD	WELWYN Prospect Pl.			**RUNNING NUMBER HG 63 TUESDAYS ONLY**	
388	12.07 pm	WELWYN Prospect Pl.	FAIRFAX ROAD	LIGHT	9.00am	FAIRFAX ROAD	HERTFORD Bus Stn.
308A	1.10 pm	FAIRFAX ROAD	LT. BERKHAMSTED	329	9.10 am	HERTFORD Bus Stn.	KNEBWORTH Station
308A	1.47 pm	LT. BERKHAMSTED	FAIRFAX ROAD	329A	10.03 am	KNEBWORTH Station	DATCHWORTH
308	2.23 pm	FAIRFAX ROAD	CUFFLEY	329A	10.21 am	DATCHWORTH	HITCHIN
308	3.29 pm	CUFFLEY	FAIRFAX ROAD	386	11.07 am	HITCHIN	BUNTINGFORD Station
308A	4.30pm	FAIRFAX ROAD	LT. BERKHAMSTED	386	12.30 pm	BUNTINGFORD Station	HITCHIN
308A	5.04 pm	LT. BERKHAMSTED	HERTFORD Bus Stn.	386	2.25 pm	HITCHIN	BUNTINGFORD Station
308	5.40 pm	HERTFORD Bus Stn.	CUFFLEY	386	3.49 pm	BUNTINGFORD Station	HITCHIN
308	6.27 pm	CUFFLEY	HERTFORD Bus Stn.	386	5.44 pm	HITCHIN	BUNTINGFORD Station
308A	7.08 pm	HERTFORD Bus Stn.	LT. BERKHAMSTED	386	7.02 pm	BUNTINGFORD Station	HITCHIN
308A	7.38 pm	LT. BERKHAMSTED	FAIRFAX ROAD	386	8.16 pm	HITCHIN	BUNTINGFORD Crown
		RUNNING NUMBER HG 61		331	9.30 pm	BUNTINGFORD Crown	HERTFORD Bus Stn.
LIGHT	7.22 am	FAIRFAX ROAD	HERTFORD Bus Stn.	LIGHT	10.17 pm	HERTFORD Bus Stn.	FAIRFAX ROAD
380	7.28 am	HERTFORD Bus Stn.	SAWBRIDGEWORTH			**RUNNING NUMBER HG 63 WEDNESDAYS ONLY**	
380	8.38 am	SAWBRIDGEWORTH	HERTFORD Bus Stn.	329	12.36 pm	FAIRFAX ROAD	KNEBWORTH Nup End
380	9.34 am	HERTFORD Bus Stn.	SAWBRIDGEWORTH	329	1.25 pm	KNEBWORTH Nup End	FAIRFAX ROAD
380	10.48 am	SAWBRIDGEWORTH	HERTFORD Bus Stn.	329	2.36 pm	FAIRFAX ROAD	KNEBWORTH Nup End
380	12.19 pm	HERTFORD Bus Stn.	SAWBRIDGEWORTH	329	3.25 pm	KNEBWORTH Nup End	FAIRFAX ROAD
380	1.38 pm	SAWBRIDGEWORTH	HERTFORD Bus Stn.	329	4.36 pm	FAIRFAX ROAD	KNEBWORTH Nup End
380	2.34 pm	HERTFORD Bus Stn.	SAWBRIDGEWORTH	329	5.25 pm	KNEBWORTH Nup End	HERTFORD Bus Stn.
380	3.48 pm	SAWBRIDGEWORTH	HERTFORD Bus Stn.	LIGHT	6.18 pm	HERTFORD Bus Stn.	FAIRFAX ROAD
380	4.44 pm	HERTFORD Bus Stn.	SAWBRIDGEWORTH			**RUNNING NUMBER HG 63 – THURSDAYS ONLY**	
380	5.49 pm	SAWBRIDGEWORTH	HERTFORD Bus Stn.	LIGHT	10.58 am	FAIRFAX ROAD	HERTFORD Bus Stn.
380	6.54 pm	HERTFORD Bus Stn.	SAWBRIDGEWORTH	331	11.05 am	HERTFORD Bus Stn.	STANDON Station
380	8.08 pm	SAWBRIDGEWORTH	HERTFORD Bus Stn.	386	11.44 am	STANDON Station	BISHOPS STORTFORD
380	9.04 pm	HERTFORD Bus Stn.	SAWBRIDGEWORTH	386	12.26 pm	BISHOPS STORTFORD	BUNTINGFORD
380	10.18 pm	SAWBRIDGEWORTH	HERTFORD Bus Stn.	386	1.37 pm	BUNTINGFORD	BISHOPS STORTFORD
LIGHT	11.10 pm	HERTFORD Bus Stn.	FAIRFAX ROAD	386	2.46 pm	BISHOPS STORTFORD	BUNTINGFORD
		RUNNING NUMBER HG 62		386	3.57 pm	BUNTINGFORD	BISHOPS STORTFORD
384	7.14 am	Sch FAIRFAX ROAD	DANE END	386	5.06 pm	BISHOPS STORTFORD	STANDON Station
384	7.48 am Sch	DANE END	HERTFORD Bus Stn	386	5.49 pm	STANDON Station	BISHOPS STORTFORD
LIGHT	8.38 am NSch	FAIRFAX ROAD	HERTFORD Bus Stn.	386	7.26 pm	BISHOPS STORTFORD	BUNTINGFORD J Sailors
308	8.45 am	HERTFORD Bus Stn.	CUFFLEY	331	8.30 pm	BUNTINGFORD J Sailors	HERTFORD Bus Stn.
308	9.39 am	CUFFLEY	HERTFORD Bus Stn.			**RUNNING NUMBER HG 64**	
388	10.22 am	HERTFORD Bus Stn.	WELWYN GDN CITY	388	7.36 am	FAIRFAX ROAD	MARDLEY HILL
388	11.07 am	WELWYN GDN CITY	FAIRFAX ROAD	388	8.28 am	MARDLEY HILL	FAIRFAX ROAD
308	11.57 am	FAIRFAX ROAD	CUFFLEY	388	9.19 am	FAIRFAX ROAD	WELWYN GDN CITY
308	12.56 pm	CUFFLEY	FAIRFAX ROAD	388	10.12 am	WELWYN GDN CITY	FAIRFAX ROAD
LIGHT	3.26 pm	FAIRFAX ROAD	HERTFORD Bus Stn.	308A	11.10 am	FAIRFAX ROAD	LT. BERKHAMSTED
333	3.33 pm	HERTFORD Bus Stn.	CHAPMORE END	308A	11.46 am	LT. BERKHAMSTED	FAIRFAX ROAD
333	3.54 pm	CHAPMORE END	HERTFORD Bus Stn.	388	12.21 pm	FAIRFAX ROAD	WELWYN Prospect Pl.
388	4.18 pm	HERTFORD Bus Stn.	WELWYN Prospect Pl.	388	1.07 pm	WELWYN Prospect Pl.	FAIRFAX ROAD
388	5.02 pm	WELWYN Prospect Pl.	HERTFORD Bus Stn.	388	2.21 pm	FAIRFAX ROAD	WELWYN Prospect Pl.
388	5.42 pm	HERTFORD Bus Stn.	MARDLEY HILL	388	3.17 pm	WELWYN Prospect Pl.	FAIRFAX ROAD

RUNNING NUMBER HG 65 MONDAY TO FRIDAY EVERY DAY

388	6.29 am	FAIRFAX ROAD	MARDLEY HILL
388	7.25 pm	MARDLEY HILL	HERTFORD Bus Stn.
333	8.18 am	HERTFORD Bus Stn.	CHAPMORE END
333	8.39 am	CHAPMORE END	HERTFORD Bus Stn.

HG 65 THEN AS FOLLOWS TUESDAY

331	9.00 am	HERTFORD Bus Stn.	BUNTINGFORD Crown
386	9.57 am	BUNTINGFORD Crown	HITCHIN
386	11 18 am	HITCHIN	GREAT WYMONDLEY
386	11.31 am	GREAT WYMONDLEY	HITCHIN
329A	12.30 pm	HITCHIN	DATCHWORTH
329 A	1.21 pm	DATCHWORTH	HITCHIN
386	2.08 pm	HITCHIN	GREAT WYMONDLEY
386	2.21 pm	GREAT WYMONDLEY	HITCHIN
386	4.04 pm	HITCHIN	GREAT WYMONDLEY
386	4.17 pm	GREAT WYMONDLEY	HITCHIN
329A	4.30 pm	HITCHIN	DATCHWORTH
329 A	5.21 pm	DATCHWORTH	KNEBWORTH Nup End
329	5.45 pm	KNEBWORTH Nup End	FAIRFAX ROAD

HG 65 THEN AS FOLLOWS MONDAY, THURSDAY AND FRIDAY

329	9.10 am	HERTFORD Bus Stn.	KNEBWORTH Nup End
329	9.55 am	KNEBWORTH Nup End	FAIRFAX ROAD
329	12.06 pm	FAIRFAX ROAD	KNEBWORTH Nup End
329	12.55 pm	KNEBWORTH Nup End	KNEBWORTH Station
329	1.32 pm	KNEBWORTH Station	FAIRFAX ROAD
329	4.06 pm	FAIRFAX ROAD	KNEBWORTH Nup End
329	4.55 pm	KNEBWORTH Nup End	HERTFORD Bus Stn.

HG 65 THEN AS FOLLOWS WEDNESDAY

329	9.00 am	HERTFORD Bus Stn.	KNEBWORTH Nup End
329	9.45 am	KNEBWORTH Nup End	FAIRFAX ROAD
329	10.51 am	FAIRFAX ROAD	KNEBWORTH Nup End
329	11.40 am	KNEBWORTH Nup End	FAIRFAX ROAD
333	1.18 pm	FAIRFAX ROAD	CHAPMORE END
333	1.49 pm	CHAPMORE END	FAIRFAX ROAD

RUNNING NUMBER HG 66 THURSDAY ONLY

LIGHT	8.45 am	FAIRFAX ROAD	HERTFORD Bus Stn.
331	8.53 am	HERTFORD Bus Stn.	BUNTINGFORD J Sailors
386	9.41 am	BUNTINGFORD J Sailors	BISHOPS STORTFORD
386	11.41 am	BISHOPS STORTFORD	STANDON Station
331	12.21 pm	STANDON Station	HERTFORD Bus Stn.
LIGHT	12.58 pm	HERTFORD Bus Stn.	FAIRFAX ROAD

RUNNING NUMBER HG 66 MONDAY TO FRIDAY EVERY DAY

388	1.16 pm	FAIRFAX ROAD	WELWYN Prospect Pl.
388	2.07 pm	WELWYN Prospect Pl.	FAIRFAX ROAD
388	3.21 pm	FAIRFAX ROAD	WELWYN Prospect Pl.
388	4.07 pm	WELWYN Prospect Pl.	FAIRFAX ROAD
388	6.03 pm	FAIRFAX ROAD	MARDLEY HILL
388	6.55 pm	MARDLEY HILL	WELWYN NORTH STN
388	7.11 pm	WELWYN NORTH STN	WELWYN Prospect Pl.
388	7.23 pm	WELWYN Prospect Pl.	FAIRFAX ROAD

NOTES

HG 63 operates only Tuesday, Wednesday and Thursday

HG 65 operates a different schedule each day after 9.00am

HG 66 operates Thursday am only route 386, then every weekday afternoon

HG 62 morning 384 schools duplicate – to instructions

On 30th September 1962, GS 10 has left Hertford on a 380 to Sawbridgeworth and runs along Townsend Street out of the town. The bus carries the revised blind which has Harlow Bus Station as an intermediate point to indicate the double run into Harlow and back introduced in October 1961. *Peter Mitchell*

HERTFORD GS SCHEDULES – SUMMER 1961
SATURDAY

	TIME DEPART	FROM	TO
		RUNNING NUMBER HG 60	
388	6.33am	FAIRFAX ROAD	MARDLEY HILL
388	7.25am	MARDLEY HILL	HERTFORD Bus Stn.
333	8.18am	HERTFORD Bus Stn.	CHAPMORE END
333	8.39am	CHAPMORE END	HERTFORD Bus Stn.
388	9.00am	HERTFORD Bus Stn.	WELWYN Prospect Pl.
388	9.42am	WELWYN Prospect Pl.	FAIRFAX ROAD
388	11.16am	FAIRFAX ROAD	WELWYN GDN CITY STN
388	12.07pm	WELWYN GDN CITY STN	HERTFORD Bus Stn.
308A	1.16pm	HERTFORD Bus Stn.	LT. BERKHAMSTED
308A	1.50pm	LT. BERKHAMSTED	HERTFORD Bus Stn.
388	2.20pm	HERTFORD Bus Stn.	WELWYN Prospect Pl.
388	3.02pm	WELWYN Prospect Pl.	HERTFORD Bus Stn.
388	4.20pm	HERTFORD Bus Stn.	WELWYN GDN CITY STN
388	5.12pm	WELWYN GDN CITY STN	HERTFORD Bus Stn.
333	6.00pm	HERTFORD Bus Stn.	CHAPMORE END
333	6.21pm	CHAPMORE END	HERTFORD Bus Stn.
388	7.00pm	HERTFORD Bus Stn.	WELWYN Prospect Pl.
388	8.06pm	WELWYN Prospect Pl.	HERTFORD Bus Stn.
388	8.53pm	HERTFORD Bus Stn.	WELWYN Prospect Pl.
388	9.35pm	WELWYN Prospect Pl.	FAIRFAX ROAD
388	10.30pm	FAIRFAX ROAD	TEWIN
388	10.53pm	TEWIN	FAIRFAX ROAD
		RUNNING NUMBER HG 61	
LIGHT	7.22 am	FAIRFAX ROAD	HERTFORD Bus Stn.
380	7.28 am	HERTFORD Bus Stn.	SAWBRIDGEWORTH
380	8.38 am	SAWBRIDGEWORTH	HERTFORD Bus Stn.
380	9.34 am	HERTFORD Bus Stn.	SAWBRIDGEWORTH
380	10.48 am	SAWBRIDGEWORTH	HERTFORD Bus Stn.
380	12.19 pm	HERTFORD Bus Stn.	SAWBRIDGEWORTH
380	1.38 pm	SAWBRIDGEWORTH	HERTFORD Bus Stn.
380	2.34 pm	HERTFORD Bus Stn.	SAWBRIDGEWORTH
380	3.48 pm	SAWBRIDGEWORTH	HERTFORD Bus Stn.
380	4.44 pm	HERTFORD Bus Stn.	SAWBRIDGEWORTH
380	5.49 pm	SAWBRIDGEWORTH	HERTFORD Bus Stn.
380	6.54 pm	HERTFORD Bus Stn.	SAWBRIDGEWORTH
380	8.08 pm	SAWBRIDGEWORTH	HERTFORD Bus Stn.
380	9.04 pm	HERTFORD Bus Stn.	SAWBRIDGEWORTH
380	10.18 pm	SAWBRIDGEWORTH	HERTFORD Bus Stn.
LIGHT	11.10 pm	HERTFORD Bus Stn.	FAIRFAX ROAD
		RUNNING NUMBER HG 62	
388	7.00am	FAIRFAX ROAD	MARDLEY HILL
388	7.52am	MARDLEY HILL	WELWYN NTH. STN.
388	7.52am	WELWYN NTH. STN.	WELWYN Prospect Pl.
388	8.26am	WELWYN Prospect Pl.	WELWYN NTH. STN.
388	8.38am	WELWYN NTH. STN.	MARDLEY HILL
388	8.56am	MARDLEY HILL	FAIRFAX ROAD
388	10.01am	FAIRFAX ROAD	WELWYN Prospect Pl.
388	11.16am	WELWYN Prospect Pl.	HERTFORD Bus Stn.
388	12.25pm	HERTFORD Bus Stn.	WELWYN Prospect Pl.
388	1.07pm	WELWYN Prospect Pl.	HERTFORD Bus Stn.
388	1.53am	HERTFORD Bus Stn.	WELWYN GDN CITY STN
388	2.40pm	WELWYN GDN CITY STN	HERTFORD Bus Stn.
388	3.25pm	HERTFORD Bus Stn.	WELWYN Prospect Pl.
388	4.07pm	WELWYN Prospect Pl.	HERTFORD Bus Stn.
308A	4.47pm	HERTFORD Bus Stn.	LT. BERKHAMSTED
308A	5.19pm	LT. BERKHAMSTED	HERTFORD Bus Stn.
308	6.01pm	HERTFORD Bus Stn.	CUFFLEY
308	6.55pm	CUFFLEY	HERTFORD Bus Stn.
308A	7.36pm	HERTFORD Bus Stn.	LT. BERKHAMSTED
308A	8.10pm	LT. BERKHAMSTED	HFRTFORD Bus Stn.
308A	9.0/pm	HERTFORD Bus Stn.	LT. BERKHAMSTED
308A	9.40pm	LT. BERKHAMSTED	FAIRFAX ROAD
		RUNNING NUMBER HG 63	
329	10.36am	FAIRFAX ROAD	KNEBWORTH Nup End
329	11.25am	KNEBWORTH Nup End	HERTFORD Bus Stn.
329	12.25pm	HERTFORD Bus Stn.	BULLS GREEN
329	12.50pm	BULLS GREEN	HERTFORD Bus Stn.
388	1.15pm	HERTFORD Bus Stn.	WELWYN Prospect Pl.
388	2.00pm	WELWYN Prospect Pl.	HERTFORD Bus Stn.
329	2.40pm	HERTFORD Bus Stn.	KNEBWORTH Nup End
329	3.25pm	KNEBWORTH Nup End	HERTFORD Bus Stn.
333	4.10pm	HERTFORD Bus Stn.	CHAPMORE END
333	4.31pm	CHAPMORE END	HERTFORD Bus Stn.
388	5.25pm	HERTFORD Bus Stn.	WELWYN Prospect Pl.
388	6.07pm	WELWYN Prospect Pl.	WELWYN NTH. STN.
388	6.22pm	WELWYN NTH. STN.	WELWYN Prospect Pl.
388	6.37pm	WELWYN Prospect Pl.	FAIRFAX ROAD
		RUNNING NUMBER HG 64	
329	9.06am	FAIRFAX ROAD	KNEBWORTH Station
329A	10.03 am	KNEBWORTH Station	DATCHWORTH
329A	10.21 am	DATCHWORTH	HITCHIN
386	11.13 am	HITCHIN	GREAT WYMONDLEY
386	11.26 am	GREAT WYMONDLEY	HITCHIN
329A	12.30 pm	HITCHIN	DATCHWORTH
329 A	1.21 pm	DATCHWORTH	HITCHIN
386	2.08 pm	HITCHIN	GREAT WYMONDLEY
386	2.21 pm	GREAT WYMONDLEY	HITCHIN
386	4.04 pm	HITCHIN	GREAT WYMONDLEY
386	4.17 pm	GREAT WYMONDLEY	HITCHIN
329A	4.30 pm	HITCHIN	DATCHWORTH
329 A	5.21 pm	DATCHWORTH	KNEBWORTH Nup End
329	5.45 pm	KNEBWORTH Nup End	HERTFORD Bus Stn.
329	6.40 pm	HERTFORD Bus Stn.	KNEBWORTH Nup End
329	7.25 pm	KNEBWORTH Nup End	HERTFORD Bus Stn.
329	8.40 pm	HERTFORD Bus Stn.	KNEBWORTH Nup End
329	9.25 pm	KNEBWORTH Nup End	HERTFORD Bus Stn.
329	10.10 pm	HERTFORD Bus Stn.	KNEBWORTH Station
329	10.50 pm	KNEBWORTH Station	FAIRFAX ROAD

310 LATE STAFF JOURNEYS IN PUBLIC TIMETABLE

310	11.30pm	FAIRFAX ROAD	WALTHAM CROSS
310	12.18am	WALTHAM CROSS	FAIRFAX ROAD

RUNNING NUMBER HG 65

308A	8.27am	FAIRFAX ROAD	LT. BERHAMSTED
308A	9.01am	LT. BERHAMSTED	HERTFORD Bus Stn.
308	9.31am	HERTFORD Bus Stn.	CUFFLEY
308	10.25am	CUFFLEY	FAIRFAX ROAD
308	11.25am	FAIRFAX ROAD	CUFFLEY
308	12.18pm	CUFFLEY	HERTFORD Bus Stn.
308	12.59pm	HERTFORD Bus Stn.	CUFFLEY
308	1.46pm	CUFFLEY	FAIRFAX ROAD
308	2.27pm	FAIRFAX ROAD	CUFFLEY
308	3.20pm	CUFFLEY	HERTFORD Bus Stn.
308	4.01pm	HERTFORD Bus Stn.	NEWGATE STREET
308	4.32pm	NEWGATE STREET	HERTFORD Bus Stn.
331	5.03pm	HERTFORD Bus Stn.	HIGH CROSS
331	5.30pm	HIGH CROSS	HERTFORD Bus Stn.
331	6.00pm	HERTFORD Bus Stn.	HIGH CROSS
331	6.27pm	HIGH CROSS	FAIRFAX ROAD

RUNNING NUMBER HG 66

388	9.13am	FAIRFAX ROAD	WELWYN GDN CITY STN
388	10.12am	WELWYN GDN CITY STN	HERTFORD Bus Stn.
333	11.12am	HERTFORD Bus Stn.	CHAPMORE END
333	11.39am	CHAPMORE END	FAIRFAX ROAD
329	12.36pm	FAIRFAX ROAD	KNEBWORTH Nup End
329	1.25pm	KNEBWORTH Nup End	HERTFORD Bus Stn.
333	2.10pm	HERTFORD Bus Stn.	CHAPMORE END
333	2.31pm	CHAPMORE END	FAIRFAX ROAD
Light	3.48pm	FAIRFAX ROAD	HERTFORD Bus Stn.
331	3.55pm	HERTFORD Bus Stn.	HIGH CROSS
331	4.22pm	HIGH CROSS	HERTFORD Bus Stn.
329	4.50pm	HERTFORD Bus Stn.	KNEBWORTH Station
329	5.32pm	KNEBWORTH Station	HERTFORD Bus Stn.
388	6.10pm	HERTFORD Bus Stn.	WELWYN Prospect Pl.
388	7.01pm	WELWYN Prospect Pl.	WELWYN NTH. STN.
388	7.13pm	WELWYN NTH. STN.	WELWYN Prospect Pl.
388	7.25pm	WELWYN Prospect Pl.	FAIRFAX ROAD

NOTES

1. Routes 308, 308A and 329 were joint GS / RF operation
2. The 386 was RF operated on Saturday
3. The 331 short journeys to High Cross operated only on Saturday and were joint GS / RF operation
4. The running number for late evening 310 journey to Waltham Cross on HG 64 is not noted on the official allocation and is an assumption
5. The Saturday omo rosters comprised 7GS and 21RF plus 3RF from Epping which swapped with 3RF from Hertford during the day. All GS and RF workings were part of a joint driver roster, many drivers working on both types during the day.
6. A number of journeys during the day worked to and from Fairfax Road to allow a change of drivers. Other duties changed at Hertford Bus Station or en-route at the end of Fairfax Road

On Saturday 4th March 1961, GS 74 has arrived at Datchworth having worked the 4.30pm 329A from Hitchin. The terminus in this small village was very rural, and the bus has reversed in front of the farm building, although the official turn was a few yards further on where the bus reversed into Hollybush Lane. The bus is waiting to work the 5.21pm to Nup End although the driver has set the wrong blind. From Nup End it works the 5.45pm back to Hertford and will later run the three evening journeys on the 329 before completing its day's work.
Peter Mitchell

The 329 timetable had included two short journeys as far as Bulls Green on Saturdays. The 9.16am from Fairfax Road garage arrived at Bulls Green to work the 9.45am back to Hertford, running as duplicate to the 9.25am from Nup End. This catered for the large numbers of passengers who might be picked up through Bramfield. The lunchtime 12.30pm from Fairfax Road was timed to run six minutes ahead of the 12.40pm from the bus station to Nup End. The Bulls Green journey thus carried all the shorter distance passengers so that those travelling to Datchworth Green and beyond would not be left behind. The morning journey was later timed to leave Bulls Green five minutes ahead of the bus from Nup End, but was withdrawn in the summer 1961 schedules as passenger numbers declined. Although the timing of the lunchtime journey was varied slightly, it remained in the timetable until the changes of 16th June 1965.

The 329 / 329A panel timetable dated 22nd May 1963 shows the infrequent service on the two routes. The sole Tuesday 329 morning journey and the 9.06am from Fairfax Road on Saturday were the positioning journeys for the 329A. The 5.21pm 329A from Datchworth on Saturday then ran the 5.45pm 329 from Nup End back to Hertford, the bus then running the three evening journeys. This journey had been withdrawn on Tuesday with the start of this timetable, the bus running light a short distance to Datchworth Green before running pointlessly in service back to Hertford. The more frequent Wednesday and Saturday service on the 329 provided more journeys for Hertford market days. The Saturday 12.25pm short journey to Bulls Green is referred to in the text and the picture on page 138. Peter Aves collection

ROUTE
329 to NUP END   via Datchworth Green and Knebworth

A 6/- ROVER TICKET will take you as far as you like on this and on nearly every other Country Bus route.   Ask the conductor for details.
This service is operated by Pay As You Enter vehicles.
Please have your fare ready as you get on.

Monday, Thursday and Friday

	906	1206	1611
Hertford *Fairfax Road*	906	1206	1611
Hertford *Bus Station*	10T	10T	15T
Hertford *North Station*	16	16	21
Bramfield Church	24	24	29
Bulls Green Horns	30	30	35
Datchworth Green *Plough*	33	33	38
Woolmer Green	38	38	43
Knebworth Station Road	42	42	47
Knebworth Station	43	43	48
Old Knebworth	47	47	52
Nup End	950	1250	1655

Tuesday   Wednesday

				1051	1236	1436	
Hertford *Fairfax Road*			900	55T	40T	40T	1615
Hertford *Bus Station*	910		06	1101	46	46	21
Hertford *North Station*	16		14	09	54	54	29
Bramfield Church	24		20	15	1300	1500	35
Bulls Green Horns	30		23	18	03	03	38
Datchworth Green *Plough*	33		28	23	08	08	43
Woolmer Green	38		32	27	12	12	47
Knebworth Station Road	942		33	28	13	13	48
Knebworth Station			37	32	17	17	52
Old Knebworth			940	1135	1320	1520	1655
Nup End							

Saturday

		906	1036		1224					
Hertford *Fairfax Road*		906	1036		1224					
Hertford *Bus Station*	840	10T	40T	1225	28T	1445	1650	1840	2040	2210
Hertford *North Station*	46	16	46	31	34	51	56	46	46	16
Bramfield Church	54	24	54	39	42	59	1704	54	54	24
Bulls Green Horns	900	30	1100	1245	48	1505	10	1900	2100	30
Datchworth Green *Plough*	03	33	03		51	08	13	03	03	33
Woolmer Green	08	38	08		56	13	18	08	08	38
Knebworth Station Road	12	942	12		1300	17	1722	12	12	2242
Knebworth Station	13		13		01	18		13	13	
Old Knebworth	17		17		05	22		17	17	
Nup End	920		1120		1308	1525		1920	2120	

T—Arrives 1 minute earlier.

329A to Ⓕⓢ HITCHIN   via Knebworth & Langley

Tuesday and Saturday

			SO
Datchworth Church	1015	1321	1721
Knebworth Station Road	24	30	30
Knebworth Station	25	31	31
Old Knebworth	29	35	35
Nup End	32	38	1738
Tower Lodge	35	41	
Langley Chapel	40	46	
St. Ippolytts Cross Roads	50	56	
Hitchin St. Mary's Square	1056	1402	

SO—Saturday only

NOTE—This timetable does not necessarily apply on Bank Holidays.   While every effort will be made to keep to the timetables, London Transport does not undertake that its buses will be operated in accordance with them, or at all.   London Transport will not be responsible for any loss, damage or inconvenience caused by reason of any operating failure or in consequence of any inaccuracies in the timetables.

LONDON TRANSPORT, 55 BROADWAY, S.W.I. ABBey 1234   22.5.63

364/1029F/400 (A)

Four months after the Sawbridgeworth route was renumbered 380, it was diverted on 25th October at Eastwick to operate a double run into Harlow town centre. By 1957, Harlow had grown to become an important centre, while Sawbridgeworth was little changed from pre-war days. The diversion gave a new link from Stanstead Abbotts, Eastwick, Gilston and High Wych into Harlow and was a welcome addition to the network. The double run to Harlow bus station and back added nine minutes to the 380 end to end running time, a time which would simply be unachievable in later years as Harlow's traffic volumes increased rapidly and many roundabouts were built along the road into the town centre. The timings between Hertford and Eastwick were almost unchanged, the former long layover times at Sawbridgeworth being reduced to compensate for an additional nine minutes in each direction.

Hertford was not affected by the widespread replacement of GSs by RFs when the winter 1962 schedules were introduced, the only small change being the loss of one GS on Sundays after the 388 was withdrawn that day. This left just a single GS rostered on Sunday for the 380, relentless cuts in Sunday timetables on the GS routes having reduced the run-out from eight to one in only five years. The 1962 changes are covered in more detail in chapter six. To cover its maximum run out of seven buses, the allocation before the changes consisted of GS 5, 9, 10, 14, 20, 27, 29, 73 and 74 including spares. GS 5, 9, 73, and 74 were all delicensed and sent to Grays, 74 moving on immediately to Romford. They were replaced by GS 3, 34, 50 and 65, GS 50 being quickly replaced by GS 45. GS 33 and 65 came from Amersham, GS 50 from Garston, and GS 34 from store at Grays. GS 50 was relegated to a staff bus in March 1963 and transferred to Abbey Wood.

The Saturday operation on the 331 saw GS, RF and RT all rostered during the day. GSs were rostered to three of the short journeys as far as High Cross on Saturday afternoon, those departing at 3.55pm, 5.02pm and 6.00pm running a few minutes in front of journeys to Buntingford to avoid passengers for Colliers End and beyond being left behind if the Buntingford service was full. GS 45 was the bus fitted with the alternative rear differential referred to in chapter one. It was delicensed at Dorking on 5th February 1963 and spent only a few weeks at Hertford before being relegated for use as a staff bus at Reigate, *Michael Wickham*

From 25th October 1961, the 380 was diverted between Eastwick and Gilston on a double run into Harlow town centre and back to reflect the growing importance of Harlow and take advantage of a new section of Fifth Avenue which had been built to link to the A414. The diversion added nine minutes to the journey time to and from Sawbridgeworth, although the ability to complete this today in the same time would be impossible. GS 10 comes round the roundabout near Harlow Town station where the undeveloped background would be unrecognisable today. *John Hambley collection*

On 22nd May 1963, the opening of the new Harlow garage brought about a major change to routes and schedules at both Harlow and Hertford. The 380 route was withdrawn, the link from Harlow via Gilston to Sawbridgeworth being maintained by extending the 390, although the former 380 Sunday timetable was not replaced. The remainder of the route from Hertford to Harlow was covered by once again extending the 388, although on a slightly reduced timetable on Saturday with the loss of one journey, but the Sunday service was withdrawn. One of Hertford's GSs was replaced with an RF in the joint roster, and some minor timetable cuts reduced the Monday to Friday run out to four (plus one Tuesday and Thursday) and five on Saturday. For the first time, Hertford ran out no GSs on Sundays. The three remaining Sunday journeys on the 388 were included in the RF rosters, but finally withdrawn after 4th November 1964. The GS schedules remained little changed other than minor timetable adjustments until the summer timetables on 16th June 1965, when the 388 timetable was cut back drastically. Journeys to Harlow reduced to just one morning and evening return during the week, the Saturday service being withdrawn completely except for the 8.50am from Harlow which was worked by an RF as a means of running a return journey from an early 390 into Harlow. Eastwick, which would otherwise have been left with no service, had five journeys on the 381 extended from Harlow, but the link to Ware and Hertford was lost other than the two remaining 388 journeys. Between Hertford and Welwyn, the previous 16 journeys were cut to only five Monday to Friday plus a short journey to Tewin mid-morning, and to six Saturday plus two to Tewin in the evening. The two Monday to Friday morning journeys into Welwyn Garden City were withdrawn. These cuts were some of the most drastic on any Country area route at the time, and drew prolonged protests from people and Parish Councils along the route. London Transport did reinstate two journeys during the week, but only on Tuesday and Friday. Given that Hertford market day was Wednesday, this seemed perverse but may have reflected LT's wish for the service not to suceeed. A minor change on 3rd February 1965 resulted in one RF replacing one GS, reducing the requirement to only four.

On 3rd October 1965 the introduction of the winter timetables resulted in widespread cuts across many garages. The 329A into Hitchin on Tuesday and Saturday was abandoned, and the Tuesday 386 timetable from Buntingford to Hitchin was halved from four to two journeys. The scheduling of positioning journeys to and from Buntingford was replaced by the bus working through to and from Hertford. The previous eight journeys from Great Wymondley on Tuesday were reduced to five, the first being run by Stevenage from the additional bus on the 383. Whereas Hertford's 386 drivers had previously taken their break at Hitchin, the revised timetables included working a journey back to Stevenage where the break was taken. The bus then worked back to Hitchin before returning to Hertford, passing the afternoon bus between Braughing and Dassells on its way to Hitchin. The Thursday service to Bishop's Stortford was also scheduled to run direct to and from Hertford, but the road between Buntingford and Standon was not covered in the revisions, thus severing any Thursday service for the few remaining shoppers. A limited Thursday facility, consisting of two journeys, remained however from Braughing and Puckeridge by the local independent B.C.Cannon, a route which outlasted London Transport's GSs on the 386 and was still running in 1972. The Saturday 386 timetable using two RFs remained unchanged other than minor timetable variations, the 331 positioning journeys continuing that day. The 331 timetable was arranged to allow a driver change at Standon in the afternoon.

GS 9 was allocated to Hertford on 23rd May 1956 after its first overhaul. It was due for its second overhaul in April 1959 and was delicensed on 22nd April and taken to Romford to await being called in. For some reason, this was delayed and it returned to service at Hertford on 4th May 1959, remaining until 1st August when it was transferred to Stevenage to release GS 5. This picture was taken during the later period of allocation to Hertford and has worked in to Hitchin on the 329A, which duty ran three short journeys to Great Wymondley during the day. The RF next to it has running number SV26, the main RF duty on the 383. *Alan Cross*

By the time of the extension of the 308 to Goffs Oak in October 1967, the service to Cuffley had been reduced to just four journeys on Monday to Friday and seven Saturday. GS 13 was one of Hertford's last two GSs, and on Saturday 21st September 1968, only a few weeks before Hertford's GSs were finally withdrawn, the bus has arrived at the stop in Robinson Avenue to wait for time before returning to Hertford. *Peter Mitchell*

In order to reduce the overall GS allocation, the Thursday service on the 329 was withdrawn to avoid the need for two buses on that day when the 386 ran. Although the 329A service to Hitchin was withdrawn, the route was altered to run from Nup End via Knebworth and Datchworth village into Hertford on Tuesday and Saturday, thereby introducing a Tuesday service into Hertford since the 329 had not been run that day other than the former positioning journey for the 329A. On Saturdays, two journeys out to Nup End ran via Datchworth, with just one into Hertford after lunch, allowing almost three hours in Hertford before the return. Interworking between routes continued to include the four GSs on 308, 308A, 329, 329A, 333 (Chapmore End), 386 (Tuesday and Thursday). A very minor addition to the 308 timetable was the addition of two Saturday morning short journeys to Horns Mill scheduled for GS operation, but the Wednesday lunchtime Chapmore End journey on the 333 was taken out, leaving just two departures from this tiny hamlet into Hertford at 8.33am and 4.23pm during the week. The four Saturday journeys remained.

Along the narrow lane from Datchworth Green to the Great North Road at Woolmer Green, there were no passengers on the 329, and on 15th May 1966 the service was altered to run via Datchworth village as 329, the 329A route number finally being discontinued. The timetable was reduced to three journeys during the week (but with no service Thursdays) and five Saturdays. Two months later when the summer timetables began on 10th July 1966 , further GS workings were replaced by RF, reducing Hertford's GS run-out to only three Monday to Friday and two Saturday. GS 44 was delicensed on 1st August 1966 and stored at Hatfield, the remaining operational buses being GS 13, 64, and 65.

On 7th October 1967, the 308 was given a short extension to Goffs Oak. This was a curious working since although buses had always terminated at Cuffley Station, they had run light to Goffs Oak in order to run round a loop via Robinson Avenue to return to Cuffley. This extension added four minutes to the journey time and made use of the former dead running. Hertford's remaining GS schedules still included some journeys on 308, 308A, 329, 388 and 386, but from 5th October 1968 the 308A to Little Berkhamsted was abandoned. The four 308 journeys during the week to Goffs Oak remained with seven on Saturday. The 329 had been reduced to only three journeys Tuesday, Friday and Saturday, plus two on Wednesday morning as far as Datchworth. The 386 was reduced to just one return journey to Hitchin on Tuesday, one return to Bishop's Stortford Thursday, with Saturday RF operation continuing unchanged. Although the 388 had the two morning journeys into Welwyn Garden City reinstated, there was no service in the afternoon during the week, and no service to Welwyn village between 8.30am and 5.00pm. With the withdrawal of the 308A, Hertford's last Saturday GS workings were withdrawn, leaving two buses rostered to a few journeys on the 308, 329, 388, and the 386 on Tuesday and Thursday.

GS 64 was delicensed on 13th May 1967 and put into store. It was moved to Stevenage in July, then to Hatfield, Grays and finally Garston before being sold by London Country to Tillingbourne Valley Motors in April 1971. GS 55 was transferred from Garston on the same day as replacement. GS 65 was delicensed in June 1968, and noted in the records for 30th October as 'stored for disposal' at Hertford. It was transferred the following day to Aldenham and noted as 'for scrap'. With the reduction in GS workings from 5th October, GS 55 was delicensed. GS 52 was taken from store at Grays to replace GS 65, but was delicensed on 18th October, GS 55 being relicensed the same day to replace it. Thus Hertford's last two operational GSs were 13 and 55. Their operation quietly withered away until 23rd November when they ran over their old routes for the last time. Both buses were delicensed and withdrawn at the end of service that day, finally bringing to an end London Transport's most complex GS schedules anywhere in the Country area.

The 1965 winter schedules added two short journeys on the 308 to Horns Mill on Saturday morning, presumably to cater for what were still reasonable numbers of passengers travelling into Hertford for shopping. GS 13 has worked one of these and stands in the estate road at Horns Mill to return to Fairfax Road garage.
John Herting

GS 15 and 29 were taken from store at Grays and allocated to Harlow to operate the new 389 town service. The text refers to the gaps in the service which did not help to attract passengers. The panel timetable illustrated on the following page was printed for the start of the route and shows the breaks during the morning and afternoon when many shoppers might have wished to travel. GS 29 loads up in Harlow bus station on a trip to Potter Street during what would be its last period in service. With the early withdrawal of the 389, it was delicensed and sold a few months later. *Alan Cross*

HARLOW

INITIAL ALLOCATION   GS 15 and 29 allocated 1st May 1964

ROUTE OPERATED
389 Potter Street – Harlow town centre – Harlow Town station
Operated 6th May 1964 to 12th January 1965

Were it not for a request by Harlow Town Council early in 1964 for an experimental new bus route, Harlow garage would probably never have operated GSs. The Council, having studied London Transport's route network in Harlow, considered that a service linking Potter Street to the town centre and Harlow Town station would add a new facility for shoppers and commuters. The route was numbered 389 and began on 6th May 1964 for an initial experimental period of six months. At the time, Harlow had a rostered run out of eight RFs, but a decision was taken to operate the route with GSs, presumably because anticipated loadings were not thought to be very high. Harlow did not need any type training on GSs since many of the former Epping drivers who had transferred to the new Harlow garage the previous year would have driven GSs up to October 1962 when Epping's had been replaced.

The route needed two buses to maintain the timetable, and curiously, the duty rosters for the 389 were arranged separately and not integrated with the rest of Harlow's omo rosters. This may have allowed London Transport to agree lower rates of pay for the 389 since there had in past years been an agreement that GS omo work was paid at a lower rate than working on the larger RF. By 1964, those garages still operating GSs had combined duty rosters with RFs with equal pay rates, but by separating the 389 duties, a saving could be made, increased further by the better fuel consumption of the GS over the RF. The route ran from early morning until late evening six days a week with no Sunday service. Four drivers worked on the route, two early turn and two late turn. The savings were all very well, but the timetable had to allow meal reliefs for the drivers, resulting in longer gaps in the service as can be seen from the panel timetable. These breaks had to be taken mid-morning and afternoon leaving an hour gap between departures exactly at times when shoppers might have wanted to travel to and from the town centre.

GS 15 and 29 had been in store at Grays. Both were relicensed and transferred to Harlow on 1st June prior to the start of the route five days later. On the day the 389 began, GS 42 was transferred from Hemel Hempstead, but remained for only one week before being sent back there as a trainer. It may have been the intention to allocate a third bus as engineering spare, but no other GS was drafted in to Harlow during the short period of operation. The 389 did not run on Sundays, so that general maintenance could be carried out then, and a spare GS could be borrowed from Hertford if necessary. Indeed, photos of GS 65 on the route – a Hertford bus at the time – show that this was the case.

The rather inconvenient timetable and occasional irregular running soon detracted from any success the route may have had. London Transport thus proposed to withdraw it with the winter schedules in November 1964, but public protest led to its

ROUTE 389 to POTTER STREET

Monday to Friday

Trains from																	
Bishops Stortford	651	711	751	811	851	911	931	1031	1101	1201	1231	1301	1331	1401	1431	....	1531
London	655	715	755	815	855	915	955	1025	1055	1155	1225	1255	1325	1355	1425	1455	1525
Harlow Town Station	700	728	800	820	900	920	958	1034	1104	1204	1234	1304	1334	1404	1434	1457	1534
Harlow Bus Station	04	32	04	24	04	24	1002	38	08	08	38	08	38	08	38	1501	38
Northbrooks Haydens Road	07	35	07	27	07	27	....	41	11	11	41	11	41	11	41	..	41
Abercrombie Way	12	40	12	32	12	32	...	46	16	16	46	16	46	16	46	..	46
Potter Street Red Lion	20	48	20	40	20	40	...	54	24	24	54	24	54	24	54	..	54
Potter Street Fullers Mead	721	749	821	841	921	941	..	1055	1125	1225	1255	1325	1355	1425	1455	..	1555

Trains from													
Bishops Stortford			1651	1711	1731	1751	1831	1931	2031	2131	2231		
London	1555	1625	1655	1715	1745	1805	1837	1935	2025	2125	2225	..	..
Harlow Town Station	1558	1628	1658	1720	1750	1812	1842	1940	2034	2134	2234		
Harlow Bus Station	1602	32	1702	24	54	16	46	44	08	38	2238		
Northbrooks Haydens Road	05	35	05	27	57	19	49	47	11	41			
Abercrombie Way	10	10	10	32	1802	24	54	52	16	46			
Potter Street Red Lion	18	48	18	40	10	32	1902	2000	54	54			
Potter Street Fullers Mead	1619	1649	1719	1741	1811	1833	1903	2001	2055	2155			

Saturday

Trains from																	
Bishops Stortford	651	711	751	811	851	911	951	1051	1111	1211	1251	1311	1351	1411	1451	1511	
London	655	715	755	815	835	915	955	1055	1115	1155	1215	1257	1315	1355	1415	1455	1515
Harlow Town Station	700	720	800	820	852	920	1000	1100	1120	1200	1220	1300	1320	1400	1420	1500	1520
Harlow Bus Station	04	24	04	24	856	24	04	04	24	04	24	1304	24	04	24	04	24
Northbrooks Haydens Road	07	27	07	27	..	27	07	07	27	07	27	...	27	07	27	07	27
Abercrombie Way	12	32	12	32	..	32	12	12	32	12	32	...	32	12	32	12	32
Potter Street Red Lion	20	40	20	40	..	40	20	20	40	20	40	...	40	20	40	20	40
Potter Street Fullers Mead	721	741	821	841	..	941	1021	1121	1141	1221	1241	..	1341	1421	1441	1521	1541

Trains from													
Bishops Stortford	1551	1611	1651	1711	1751	1811	1851	1911	1951	2011	2051	2111	2151
London	1555	1615	1651	1715	1755	..	1855	1915	1955	2015	2035	2115	2155
Harlow Town Station	1600	1620	1700	1720	1800	1812	1900	1920	2000	2020	2055	2117	2209
Harlow Bus Station	1604	24	04	24	04	1816	04	24	04	24	2059	21	2213
Northbrooks Haydens Road	27	07	27	07	07	..	07	27	07	27		24	
Abercrombie Way	..	32	12	32	12	..	12	32	12	32	..	29	
Potter Street Red Lion	..	40	20	40	20	..	20	40	20	40	..	37	
Potter Street Fullers Mead	..	1641	1721	1741	1821	..	1921	1941	2021	2041	..	2138	

NO SUNDAY SERVICE

NOTE—This timetable does not necessarily apply on Bank Holidays. While every effort will be made to keep to the timetables, London Transport does not undertake that its buses will be operated in accordance with them, or at all. London Transport will not be responsible for any loss, damage or inconvenience caused by reason of any operating failure or in consequence of any inaccuracies in the timetables.

LONDON TRANSPORT, 55 BROADWAY, S.W.1.   ABBey 1234   6.5.64

continuation a little longer. Harlow Council understandably wished it to continue, but despite their objections, it ran for the last time on Tuesday 12th January 1965 having never been worthwhile. Whether this was a further example of London Transport deliberately designing a route 'to fail', as many thought they did in the case of the 479, is pure conjecture, but its driver rosters, timetable and drivers who were resistant to omo were all significant factors in its early withdrawal.

GS 15 was one of the few GSs to be given a third overhaul. It was delicensed immediately following the withdrawal of the 389, returning to Garston on completion where it enjoyed four more years in service. GS 29 was not so fortunate. It was delicensed at the same time and moved to Grays in store until sold.

This panel timetable was produced for the start of the new 389 on 6th May 1964. It shows the longer gaps in the timetable during the day which were necessary for drivers' breaks but which detracted from the convenience of a service which was intended for shoppers.

EPPING

INITIAL ALLOCATION
GS 38, 40, 43 and 44 all allocated 27th November 1953
All licensed for service on 1st December 1953

ROUTES OPERATED
381	1st December 1953 – 9th June 1959
	25th May 1960 – 23rd October 1962
381A	7th June 1961 – 23rd October 1962
393	1st December 1953 – 15th October 1957 (main timetable)
	1st December 1953 – 9th June 1959 (duplicate bus)

MAXIMUM RUN OUT   Three buses plus one for duplicate

Epping's allocation of four Cubs, C 65, 74, 81 and 91, were all replaced on 1st December 1953 by GS 38, 40, 43 and 44. There is no specific record of a training bus being allocated prior to the changeover, but it is probable that a GS from nearby Hertford garage was used. This would have been unusual but probable because of the small size of Epping garage which had no spare capacity. Because of this, the Cubs were delicensed and sent to Romford for storage on the same day that the GS took over operations, which would appear to bear out anecdotal evidence supplied by a former owner of RF 633 that he was present at Toothill on 1st December having travelled out by Leyland Cub when a GS arrived to take over the duty and the Cub was despatched to Romford for storage.

The 381 had been introduced on 30th August 1950 to provide a service for the first time to the small villages of Stewards Green and Toothill east of Epping. It had been planned to begin earlier, but was much delayed because of the poor state of the roads. It was a relatively short route running from Epping Garage to

GS 40 had been in service for only two months when this picture was taken at Toothill terminus on 30th January 1954. The bus has reversed into the lane on the right in the background to turn, and the Green Man pub timing point is opposite on the left. The grab handles below the front windscreens and the paper pay as you enter label have yet to be fitted. *Peter Mitchell*

ROUTES
381 to TOOTHILL
381ᴬ to COOPERSALE COMMON

via Epping

Monday to Friday

	am	am	am	am	am	am	am	am	pm	pm	pm	pm	pm	pm	pm	pm	pm	pm	pm	pm
St Margarets *Station*					758															
Roydon *Temple*					8 8		1015			1215		215			415		614	615		
Tylers Cross *Cross Roads*					817		1024			1224		224			424		623	624		
Broadley Common *Garage*					818		1025			1225		225			425		624	625		
Epping Green *Memorial Hall*			714		826	915	1033			1233	125	233			433	526	632	633	641	
Beaconsfield Estate *Shaftesbury Road*			726		838	927	1045			1245	137	245			445	538	644	645	653	
Epping *Church*			731	810	843	932	1050	1127	1212	1250	142	250	330	4 8	450	543	649	650	658	
Epping *LT Garage*	634	730															651	652		740
Epping *Station Approach*	637	733	733	812	845	934	1052	1129	1214	1252	144	252	332	410	452	545		7 0		743
Stewards Green *Merry Fiddlers*	642	738	738	817	850	939	1057	1134	1219	1257	149	257	337	415	457	550		7 5		
Coopersale Common *Gernon Bushes*	649	745		824		946	11 4	1141		1 4		3 4	344		5 4	557		712		
Mount End *Mount End Road*			743		855				1224		154			420						
Colliers Hatch			749		9 1				1230		2 0			426						
Toothill *Green Man*			754		9 6				1235		2 5			431						

Mon.-Fri.—contd.

	pm	pm	pm	pm	pm	pm
St Margarets *Station*						
Roydon *Temple*	B		B		914	
Tylers Cross *Cross Roads*	736		835		923	B
Broadley Common *Garage*	737		836		924	1142
Epping Green *Memorial Hall*	745	812	844	924	932	1150
Beaconsfield Estate *Shaftesbury Road*	757	824	856	936	944	12 2
Epping *Church*	8 2	829	9 1	941	949	12 7
Epping *LT Garage*	8 4		9 3		951	12 9
Epping *Station Approach*		831		943		
Stewards Green *Merry Fiddlers*		836		948		
Coopersale Common *Gernon Bushes*		843		955		

Saturday

	am	am	am	am	am	am	am	pm	pm	pm	pm	pm	pm	pm
St Margarets *Station*														
Roydon *Temple*						1015			1215				255	
Tylers Cross *Cross Roads*						1024			1224				3 4	
Broadley Common *Garage*						1025			1225				3 5	
Epping Green *Memorial Hall*			730	826	915	1033			1233		125	241	313	
Beaconsfield Estate *Shaftesbury Road*			742	838	927	1045			1245		137	253	325	
Epping *Church*			747	843	932	1050	1127	1212	1250	128	142	258	330	4 8
Epping *LT Garage*	634	730												
Epping *Station Approach*	637	733	749	845	934	1052	1129	1214	1252	130	144	3 0	332	410
Stewards Green *Merry Fiddlers*	642	738	754	850	939	1057	1134	1219	1257	135	149	3 5	337	415
Coopersale Common *Gernon Bushes*	649	745			946	11 4	1141		1 4		156	312	344	
Mount End *Mount End Road*			759	855				1224		140				420
Colliers Hatch			8 5	9 1				1230		146				426
Toothill *Green Man*			810	9 6				1235		151				431

Saturday—contd.

	pm	pm	pm	pm	pm	pm	pm	pm	pm	pm
St Margarets *Station*										
Roydon *Temple*	415		615		815	B			1049	B
Tylers Cross *Cross Roads*	424		624		824	B			1058	B
Broadley Common *Garage*	425		625		825	847			1059	1142
Epping Green *Memorial Hall*	433	526	633	641	833	855	945	1057	11 7	1150
Beaconsfield Estate *Shaftesbury Road*	445	538	645	653	845		957		11 9	12 2
Epping *Church*	450	543	650	658	850	912	10 2	1114	1124	12 7
Epping *LT Garage*						914				
Epping *Station Approach*	452	545	652	7 0	852		10 4			
Stewards Green *Merry Fiddlers*	457	550		7 5	857		10 9			
Coopersale Common *Gernon Bushes*	5 4	557		712	9 4		1016			

Sunday

	am	pm	pm	pm	pm	pm	pm
St Margarets *Station*	1046	1254	3 2	510		845	
Roydon *Temple*	1056	1 4	312	520		855	B
Tylers Cross *Cross Roads*	11 5	113	321	529		9 4	B
Broadley Common *Garage*	11 6	114	322	530		9 5	1047
Epping Green *Memorial Hall*	1114	122	330	538	650	913	1055
Beaconsfield Estate *Shaftesbury Road*	1126	134	342	540	7 7	925	11 7
Epping *Church*	1131	139	347	545	7 7	930	1112
Epping *LT Garage*							1114
Epping *Station Approach*	1133	141	349	547	7 9	932	
Stewards Green *Merry Fiddlers*	1138	146	354	552	714	937	
Coopersale Common *Gernon Bushes*	1145	153	4 1	6 9	721	944	

B—From Routes 393 and 393A.

NOTE—This timetable does not necessarily apply on Bank Holidays. While every effort will be made to keep to the timetables, London Transport does not undertake that its buses will be operated in accordance with them, or at all. London Transport will not be responsible for any loss, damage or inconvenience caused by reason of any operating failure or in consequence of any inaccuracies in the timetables.

LONDON TRANSPORT, 55 BROADWAY, S.W.I. ABBey 1234   7.6.61

361/874W/450 (75)   No.: 857   Kelly & Kelly Ltd., London

The short-lived extension of the 381 to Ongar on Saturday morning was a complete failure. The extension ran for only 14 weeks, and so there were only 28 journeys to and from Ongar. On 11th January 1958, the penultimate Saturday of operation, GS 37 has no passengers as it comes along the lane towards Stanford Rivers, having left Toothill a few minutes earlier. It is very likely it will later return empty from Ongar.
Peter Mitchell

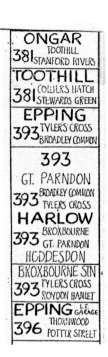

Toothill, a journey of 26 mins with only five journeys per day, and was covered by a single driver as a spreadover duty, the last bus returning to Epping Garage as early as 5.00 pm. When originally planned, an extension of the route to Ongar was included, but had been prevented by the poor state of the road between Toothill and Stanford Rivers where the route would have joined the infrequent journeys on Central area route 175 to Ongar. The road having eventually been improved, the 381 was extended to Ongar on 19th October 1957, although the additional service consisted of two journeys on Saturday mornings to allow time in Ongar for shopping. These two journeys ran through Ongar High Street to turn at Ongar Station the end of the Central Line. Given the small population along the 381 route, the demand for shopping in Ongar on Saturday morning would never have been more than minimal, and the extension was a complete failure. It operated only for 14 Saturdays, the last day being 18th January 1958.

The next change to the 381 was an extension to Roydon on 10th June 1959 which also coincided with the replacement of the GS with an RF which removed GSs from Epping schedules, those on the 393 having been replaced 18 months earlier as described below. The RF allocation was however short lived as one GS was again allocated for the 381 from 25th June 1960 as a duplicate to the regular RF. A further change came with the summer schedules on 7th June 1961 when the 381 was rerouted in Epping to serve the new Beaconsfield Estate. On the same date, the allocation was increased to two buses when a second GS was allocated and journeys were operated over the extended route from Toothill to Roydon. A new route 381A to Coopersale Common was introduced as a direct replacement of the southern part of the 372 which was withdrawn on the same day as part of a major reorganisation of the routes from Epping and Harlow through Hertford to Welwyn Garden City. It is probable that the GS did operate the Coopersale to Epping section of the 372 during 1959 and 1960 although photographic evidence has not been found.

The 393 was another route introduced after the War, starting in June 1949 between Harlow and Hoddesden. It served what were then the small villages of Nettleswell and Great Parndon to give a new link into Broxbourne and Hoddesdon, Harlow itself then being only a small village on the main London to Norwich road, and situated a few miles north of Epping. Two Cubs were allocated, running to an irregular headway with a journey time of just under 50 minutes. Meal breaks were taken in Harlow with the bus taking stand time in Fore Street rather than the normal turning point at the 'Green Man' Public House, and drivers travelled to and from Harlow on the 396 to change over. Increasing passengers resulted in a fourth bus allocated from 1955 when the engineering spare was used as a duplicate bus during the morning peak and on Saturday during main shopping times. As Harlow New Town developed the former villages at Great Parndon and Nettleswell soon disappeared in the rapid expansion, and the 393 became an early conversion to RF operation when the 1957 winter schedules were introduced on 17th October. The GS allocated as duplicate bus remained however until June 1959 when it was also converted to RF. The duplicate operated as EP201 and worked to and from Harlow on the 396, which displays appear on the GS blind schedule. The allocation book also notes approval for one man operation over this

The Ongar destination was added in September 1957. Of interest in this blind is the panel for the 396 workings back from Harlow to Epping Garage. On the following page the blind shows a panel for the 372 on which there were no journeys rostered for GSs The reintroduction of GSs in 1961 resulted in the greatest number of panels covering 381, 381A and 393.

section of the 396 providing another example of GS working journeys on a double deck route. It is also probable that between 1960 and 1962, when GSs returned to Epping, that the 393 had occasional GS workings as the Broxbourne to Epping short workings appear on the blind schedule.

Until the 393 was converted to RF, the allocation to the 381 and 393 required three buses, the fourth being the Engineering spare and duplicate. Epping's original allocation remained unchanged until 1st July 1955 when GS 43 was delicensed for two months. There is no record of a replacement, but photographic evidence shows that GS 71, although allocated to Garston, was used on the 393 and was therefore the bus likely to have been used. There is no record of how long it remained there though. GS 72 was first licensed for service on 8th April 1954 and despatched from storage at Garston to Epping, but remained there for only 12 days before being transferred to Hertford where, with GS 73 and 74, more crew duties were replaced by GSs. GS 73 was transferred from Hertford to Epping on 1st December 1955 returning to Hertford a few weeks later. GS 38 was the first to be sent for overhaul, being delicensed on 1st September 1956 and sent to Works a week later. It was replaced by GS 16 transferred from Amersham. GS 26 arrived fresh from overhaul on 1st December 1956 releasing GS 40 for overhaul, followed two weeks later by GS 41 which was replaced by GS 37 which had been allocated to Chelsham before its overhaul. When GS 43 went for overhaul on 9th January 1957, GS 32 (which became used as a temporary float bus) arrived from overhaul to replace it. GS 41 was reallocated to Epping on 28th January 1957 after overhaul, which released GS 32 to go to Guildford where it remained for only a week before going on to Amersham. When GS 43 returned from overhaul on 4th March, GS 26 was demoted to a second northern area float bus and went to Amersham. GS 44, the last of Epping's original allocation, was sent for overhaul on 21st March 1957 with GS 40 transferring from Chelsham as replacement. GS 44 returned on 8th May, but was not relicensed until 1st June when GS 16 was returned to Amersham.

Following the schedule changes in October 1957, GS 43 was delicensed and withdrawn on 1st November. It proved to be the last day of its service life, having been in use for a little under four years, thus having the dubious record of being the least used GS and the first to be withdrawn. On the same day, GS 44 was transferred to Hertford, but in a complete contrast to GS 43 would see a further nine years' service until withdrawn from Hertford in August 1968. GS 43 languished out of use at Epping until it was taken to Romford on 17th July 1958 where it remained until sale to Corvedale Motors on 24th May 1961.

On 10th December 1958, GS 40 and 41 were withdrawn and despatched to Romford for storage. GS 41 would not see further service, but GS 40 was moved to Garston a week later, and then relicensed for service at Windsor on 1st January 1959. Its use after that however was intermittent, being finally delicensed and withdrawn a year later.

When GSs were reallocated to Epping in May 1960, GS 29 arrived from Dorking and was replaced by GS 44 on 1st April 1961. GS 27 arrived from overhaul as the spare on 26th May. On 1st January 1962 GS 44 was delicensed and was sent to Romford until called in for overhaul two weeks later. GS 27 thus became Epping's last GS until 24th October 1962 when it was transferred to Hertford as part of the major reallocations. The formal allocation book before these changes shows a requirement for two GS on Saturday whereas in practice, an RF would have been used.

GRAYS

INITIAL ALLOCATION
GS 76 Transferred from Garston 8th June 1962
GS 34 Returned from overhaul 21st June 1962 and relicensed on 2nd July

ROUTES OPERATED
372	20th June 1962 – 23rd October 1962
328	20th June 1962 – 23rd October 1962
	Positioning journeys only for 372
399	2nd June 1965 – 12th May 1967

London County Council developed a large new estate at Aveley as part of their 'Overspill Estates' programme after the War. New factories were being built along the Thames at Aveley and Thurrock, and the estate was developed to provide housing for the large new workforce, many of whom urgently needed re-housing from their war-damaged homes in east London. The huge Ford works at Dagenham was also not far away from the new development. By the start of the 1960s Belhus estate, as it had become known, had become largely self-sufficient with its own shops, pubs, churches and social centres, the population having grown to more than 20,000 in ten years.

The 372 was a worthwhile experiment to provide a daytime service within the large Belhus Estate, but proved to be unsuccessful. GS 76 began operation of the route on 18th June 1962, GS 34 arriving two weeks later, after which the two buses were often allocated to the route on alternate weeks. Two weeks before the route was withdrawn, GS 34 has left the shops in Derwent Parade, the concrete estate road and rather stark housing typifying new council housing developments of the period. *Peter Mitchell*

The 372 was designed to provide an off-peak service wholly within the estate and would link the main areas of housing to the centre where shops and other facilities were located. Grays was another garage which had never operated GSs, but given the area within the estate to be served and that passenger numbers were likely to be fairly small, then a GS was the ideal small bus to run the new route. It was intended as an experiment to test the need for such a route, and commenced operation on 18th June 1962. Belhus was a few miles east of Grays so that positioning journeys were run on route 328 to and from the estate's centre at Derwent Parade. The duty required one driver, his lunchtime meal break being taken back at Grays garage which involved running 328 journeys to and from Grays in the middle of the day. The duty began at 9.15am and finished at 5.40pm, the lunch break being taken between 1.00pm and 1.48pm.

There were ten journeys in the morning and eleven in the afternoon, alternate journeys being linked together with a total running time of 24 minutes and a six-minute layover before repeating the sequence. Running round and round the estate all day must have been one of the more tedious duties at the time.

To operate the 372, positioning journeys were operated to and from Grays each morning and afternoon on the 328. GS 34 is on its way from Grays to the Estate, probably on the 1.50pm journey to Belhus. *John Hambley collection*

GS 76 was initially chosen to operate the route and was transferred from Garston on 8th June, ten days before the route began. This presumably gave time for route familiarisation and driver training since none of Grays' drivers had driven GSs. GS 34 went from Garston for its second overhaul on 27th April 1962. On completion it was sent to Grays on 21st June 1962 and would become the route's permanent bus. It was relicensed on 2nd July, GS 76 being delicensed and moved to Romford, but escaped being included in the 21 GSs withdrawn for sale at the year end and was relicensed on 21st September for transfer to Guildford as a temporary 'heater float' bus. Three weeks later it moved to Dunton Green for the same purpose and was delicensed again on 1st November. It had been sent to Dunton Green for the start of the 479, but suffered engine failure and was not used again. GS 34 was transferred to Hertford alongside GS 27 from Epping and GS 33 from Amersham, these three replacing Hertford's GS 5, 9, and 73 which were all delicensed. The 372 was a worthwhile initiative, but passenger numbers were never sufficient to justify its continuation. After just over four months it ran for the last time on 23rd October 1962.

The second period of GS operation at Grays came about after an entirely separate set of circumstances. Although it later became a centre of major traffic congestion, when the Dartford Tunnel opened on 18th November 1963 it represented a great improvement to the local road network and opened up a valuable new link across the Thames. London Transport immediately extended the 722 Green Line route from Hornchurch through Ockenden and the tunnel to Dartford, and at the same time introduced route 300 between Grays and Dartford. Even with the benefit of hindsight, one wonders how such a route might ever have attracted enough traffic to make it profitable. Although the extended 722 route provided a new link between Dartford and Romford, both routes were an immediate failure. The 722 was cut back again to Corbetts Tey and Hornchurch after only one year but the 300, despite weekly losses, continued until the costs of crew operation became too great to continue. On 2nd June 1965, GS operated

route 399 replaced the 300. With a journey time of 25 minutes and five minutes layover at each end, one bus operated a regular hourly headway seven days a week. The Saturday service began one hour later than Monday to Friday, and the Sunday service two hours later still, but otherwise the timetable was the same seven days a week. The 399 ran as a limited stop service.

GS 21 was sent from Crawley in April 1965 for its third overhaul, but did not arrive at Grays until 9th June one week after the 399 began. GS 28 had been unlicensed at Garston, so was transferred to Grays on 2nd June to begin operation of the route. GS 21 was relicensed on 1st July, GS 28 remaining as the spare bus until transfer to High Wycombe on 15th September for the 442. GS 16 was transferred from Reigate to Grays on 9th September 1965 a few days before GS 21 moved away, but noted as remaining delicensed. It is not recorded whether it was temporarily relicensed to cover GS 21 since with a seven day timetable it would have been necessary to have a spare bus allocated. GS 36 was transferred from Dunton Green at the beginning of September, but remained unused until that too was sent for its third overhaul in October. It returned to Grays and was relicensed on 1st December 1965, and with GS 21 became the permanent allocation for the 399. GS 34 was also used for a short period in July 1965, although this is not formally recorded as the bus was allocated to Garston as a trainer during the operation of the 399. Presumably it was temporarily transferred to cover some maintenance issue with either GS 21 or 28 not long after the 399 began.

On 5th April 1967, five weeks before the 399 was eventually abandoned, GS 21 was exchanged with GS 54 from St Albans. This is noteworthy since GS 54 was the bus fitted with 'Loadmeter' equipment which recorded passenger numbers. No doubt it had been used to record numbers on the 382, which carried few people, and its allocation to Grays was undoubtedly to confirm the obviously poor loadings to support the withdrawal of the 399 on 12th May.

Immediately following the last day of the 399, GS 36 and 54 both went to Northfleet where GS 53, 58 and 66 had been delicensed on the same day.

GS 34 had been allocated to Grays for the 372 in 1962, but in February 1965 was allocated to Garston as a training bus. Although not recorded as spending time at Grays, it was transferred there for a short period in July 1965 and on 11th July it runs down the southern approach road towards Dartford Tunnel on the journey back to Grays. This location is unrecognisable today as is the almost complete lack of traffic. *Peter Mitchell*

6   The Beginning of the End

1962 was a year of major changes to the whole of London Transport's bus and coach fleet, enormous numbers of buses being moved around the fleet on a daily basis. In the Central area, the last two phases of the trolleybus conversion scheme were completed in January and May, large numbers of new Routemasters were delivered throughout the year, and even greater numbers of redundant RTs and RTLs were delicensed and either stored or sold off together with all the trolleybuses made redundant from the final conversions.

In the Country area, there were few changes in the first part of the year, but the winter schedules which came into force on 24th October, although not resulting in significant service cuts, involved major operational changes and widespread reallocations of the single deck fleet across many Country area garages. The schedules included the large scale replacement of GSs by RFs, and were in effect 'the beginning of the end' for the GS fleet.

Although large numbers of GSs were withdrawn in 1962, they were not the first, ten already having been sold in 1961, GS 24, 32, 37, 40, 41, 43, 49, 61, 63, and 70 all being disposed of that year. 74 GSs therefore remained in stock at the beginning of 1962. Of those, GS 78 had been delicensed at Dunton Green in May 1961 before being demoted to a training bus and sent the following month to Harrow Weald central area garage. Its transfer from Dunton Green proved to be the end of its revenue earning life. Its use as a staff bus is referred to in chapter seven, and it remained at Harrow Weald until February 1963, then to Garston for two further months as a trainer before being finally delicensed. It remained in store at Garston until being sold in January 1964. More details of the ten buses sold in 1961 noted above are included in chapter eight.

During the first eight months of 1962, many GSs were sent for their second overhaul, GS 50 being the first to go to Chiswick on 24th January from Amersham. It was returned there on 26th March but remained out of use until transferred to Garston on 25th April and licensed for further service. The second was GS 47 on 29th January. For the previous two years it had been stored unlicensed out of use at Reigate and was returned there unlicensed on 11th April. It then spent a short period at Harrow Weald, presumably to cover for some work needed on GS 78, although no records of this have been found. On 7th May it went to East Grinstead to replace GS 58 which went for overhaul. By the end of August 1962, ten GSs had been overhauled, although few were immediately returned to service. GS 34 for example was delicensed at Garston on 27th April, but once completed, went into store at Grays on 21st June where it remained until reallocated as part of the major changes in October. After GS 48 went from Northfleet to Chiswick on 29th August, only one other bus – GS 65 – was overhauled before the changes of 24th October, being sent from Garston on 10th October.

There had been a number of routes not approved for RF operation where narrow, sometimes single track, roads were covered, but the restrictions were not consistent. There were several locations on routes approved for RF operation which were equally narrow so that many of the restrictions limiting operation to GSs in 1954/55 had, by 1962, been gradually lifted. This applied to routes 333,

Sixteen Green Line RFs were delicensed following the entry into service of the new RMCs at the end of August 1962, all being converted to one man buses to replace GSs, mostly at Chelsham and Amersham. RF 305 was one of five transferred to Amersham and licensed for service on 24th October 1962. On 22nd August 1964, it waits at Chesham Broadway on a 348A journey from Tring to Pond Park Estate, the 397 to Tring having been replaced by an extension of the 348 and 348A in the changes. *Gerald Mead*

333B, 348, 348A, 381, 393 and 481, routes 386A, 479 and 492 having been withdrawn as referred to in previous chapters. The 387 operated by Tring, the 464, 465 485 operated by Chelsham, and the 397 and 398 operated by Amersham had always been approved for RF operation. The lifting of the restrictions on the routes above therefore allowed the complete replacement of GSs at Amersham and Epping, those at Chelsham and Tring not having been restricted anyway. The arrival of the RMCs was effectively the beginning of the large scale reallocations which followed.

Throughout 1962, a programme of fitting heaters across the whole fleet was under way, 182 Country area RTs being completed in three batches during the year. On the same day that the RMCs went into service on the 715/715A, a memo from the *'Rolling Stock Engineer (Road Services) – Chiswick'* relating to the fitting of heaters to GSs went to all the divisional engineers. The list contained 37 GSs to be collected between 11th September and 25th October from 13 different garages, and listed a further nine whose heaters would be fitted at normal overhaul, plus GS 28 which had been fitted first as the pilot. Following the 24th October changes therefore, almost all GSs remaining licensed for service would have heaters fitted. Two GSs were used as a heater float.

The Winter 1962 schedules precipitated the delicensing of no fewer than 23 GSs on 24th October, comprising the entire allocation at Chelsham, and Hemel Hempstead, as well as others from Amersham, Hertford, Windsor, Stevenage, St Albans and Garston. Epping's GS 27, although replaced with an RF, was transferred to Hertford for further service. Of Chelsham's allocation, GS 1, 3, and 4 went to Reigate, and GS 7, 8, 11 and 81 to Northfleet. Only GS 6 from Chelsham saw a further brief spell of service at Dorking, but was relegated to training duties early in 1963 before withdrawal and sale. Hertford's GS 5, 9, and 73 went to Garston as did GS 68, 80, and 83 from Hemel Hempstead and GS 72 from St Albans. Having been delicensed at Windsor, GS 77 remained there until being transferred to store at Reigate on 21st November. Of Amersham's allocation, GS 30, 31, 69, and 75 were delicensed and transferred to Garston, but the remainder were all transferred for service elsewhere to replace some of those delicensed. GS 42, 51, and 55 went to Hemel Hempstead, GS 52 to St Albans, GS 56 to

Stevenage, and GS 33 to Hertford. GS 34, noted above, had been in store at Grays since 21st June, and was now licensed and transferred to Hertford. On 1st November four more GSs which had been temporarily out of use at other garages were licensed and sent to Dorking (GS 6), Tring (GS 75 as a training bus), Northfleet (GS 66) and Stevenage (GS 64), while GS 48 went to St. Albans on its return from overhaul at Chiswick.

The reduction in the maximum run out at the four garages whose GSs were replaced were not significant:

GARAGE	1st JULY	24th OCTOBER
TRING	1 GS	1 RF
AMERSHAM	4 RF / 9 GS	12 RF
EPPING	5 RF / 1 GS	6 RF
CHELSHAM	6 GS	5 RF

- Tring's GS 33 was transferred to Amersham on 2nd July, to be replaced by an RF for route 387 before the October changes. Tring also had RF 589, rostered as a crew bus for use on route 352 on Saturdays and a few peak hour journeys on the 387 as a means of balancing crew rosters on the 301/302.
- Epping only had GS 27 allocated, but the allocation book notes two GS on Saturday. This may have been borrowed from Hertford, or a spare RF would have been used.
- Amersham's run out was reduced by one bus each day.
- Chelsham's run out was reduced by one bus each day, but a further bus was withdrawn during off peak each day as a result of timetable cuts. The larger capacity of the RF also allowed a reduction from four to two buses each morning and afternoon for the school journeys to Merle Common School at Holland.
- Northfleet's weekday run out of 5 RF and 6 GS was unchanged, but on Sundays was reduced from 3 RF and 2 GS to 2 RF and 1 GS.
- Hertford's weekday run out was also unchanged but 2 GS on Sunday was reduced to one.

Overall, the scheduled GS requirement across the fleet was reduced to 34 Monday and Wednesday, 35, Tuesday, Thursday and Friday, 32 Saturday and five Sunday. The comparative figures at 1st July were 53, 46, and 16 respectively, one additional bus being added at Hertford on Tuesday and Thursday. With the addition of engineering spares at Chiswick and across the 13 remaining operating garages, the total requirement was between 50 and 55 buses. With 74 remaining in stock, there were therefore approximately 20 which could be held for disposal.

The complex reallocations had released all those with either with the lowest or highest stock numbers, the remainder having been fitted with heaters for continuing service. After 24th October, GS 45 was the first to go for overhaul on 31st from Dorking, also being one of those allocated for the fitting of heaters at the same time. GS 20 and 62 had been used as 'Heater Floats' whilst others were away. GS 62 was removed from the float programme and sent to Tring for staff transport on 9th October. It was delicensed on 1st November when replaced by GS 75, and sent for overhaul and fitting of heaters on 15th November. GS 54 returned from overhaul on 24th November and was temporarily stored at Garston.

In a further complex movement, it was relicensed on 1st December to allow GS 50 to go to Hertford, releasing GS 74 which was delicensed and sent to Romford for store.

The daily movement record for 19th December 1962 lists these GSs in store:

Garston	GS 67, 68, 69, 71, 72, and 80
Romford	GS 74
Grays	GS 2, 5, 9, and 73
Northfleet	GS 7, 8, 11, 79, and 81
Reigate	GS 1, 3, 4, and 77

GS 57 was also in store at Reigate having been returned from overhaul on 7th December. It went to Crawley in January 1963 to replace GS 84 which was withdrawn and sold two months later among those purchased by Tillingbourne Valley. Having been stored from delivery until its first allocation at Leatherhead in January 1956, GS 84 had seen only six years' service, but it would run for slightly longer with Tillingbourne before they sold it in July 1970.

None of the 20 GSs above would see further revenue earning service with London Transport and were all sold, the majority going during 1963. It will be noted that GS 10, 75, 82, and 83 are not mentioned above despite being among the low and high numbered buses. GS 10 was one of those fitted with heaters and survived into London Country ownership. The other three did not have heaters fitted and were all withdrawn from service during 1963 along with GS 6 mentioned above. GS 76, similarly without heaters, was withdrawn at Dunton Green early in 1963 and sold in 1964. As 1962 came to a close therefore, the fate of the GS fleet had been set in motion. Their numbers dwindled steadily as further timetable cuts eroded their numbers. Routes such as the 308A, 433, and 852 were gradually withdrawn, whilst operation of the 316, 448, and 448A were handed over to the independent operators who ran a share of them jointly with London Transport. Timetable cuts on many other rural RF routes allowed spare RFs to replace GSs, and at Dunton Green, the 471 was converted entirely at the end of 1966, the restriction to GS operation between Knockholt through Cudham to Green Street Green having been relaxed. Over the next seven years before the Country area was transferred to London Country, all except two last GSs were withdrawn from revenue earning service.

To conclude this chapter we will mention the GS that was repainted red, believed to have been GS 50. According to a conversation Alan Charman had with Colin Curtis, this was for possible use on a service during the rebuilding of Elmers End railway bridge in the 1960s. Colin Curtis also mentioned that having some GSs in red had been considered in the 1950s for the 264, on which the then weak Walton Bridge had required the extended use of elderly 1T1s.

On 22nd September 1962, GS 81 passes Rushetts on the road from Crockham Hill to Edenbridge on a 465. From Edenbridge it will work the next 485 to Westerham and from there a 464 back to Holland. It has only four more weeks in service before being replaced with an RF. It was withdrawn and stored at Northfleet before being sold in 1963. *Peter Mitchell*

7   Overhaul, Maintenance and Staff Buses

In accordance with standard London Transport practice the GSs were overhauled as a small class every three to four years. Because of this and because they were 'non-standard' in the sense that they were mechanically different from the rest of the fleet, their overhauls were dealt with at the Chiswick Tram Shed together with the RLH, TD, RFW and T (15T13) classes. Mechanical units were handled at Chiswick Works. The Tram Shed survives today remaining in use as Stamford Brook garage. The GS bodies were not separated from the chassis, the body and chassis number combination therefore remaining together throughout their lives. Final checks and Certificate of Fitness approval were carried out generally at Aldenham, with small numbers being dealt with at Garston.

There were very few changes to the bodywork during their lives. An early addition was the fitment of two external grab rails at the front above the bonnet below the windscreens, fitted in order to facilitate cleaning of the windscreen. They were the same type fitted to the front nearside of the RT below the canopy. As with all London Transport parts, they were allotted a specific part number, RT001D17. Service advice reference BD277 of May 1954 confirming the addition of these was added to the GS Garage Spares (Body) schedule revised on 16th February 1955. GS 79 – one of those stored at Reigate – was selected as the first to be so fitted, following which instructions were sent to the operating garages for them to be fitted there. In June 1954, all buses in the fleet were fitted with rear reflectors, and once again were given their own unique part number SK3463C. These had become a legal requirement, and the instruction stated that they should be fitted *'as a priority'* at garages. It had originally been intended to fit lamps to the nearside rear of the body, but it was decided they were no longer required. Instead they were fitted as step lamps

Experiments on fitting flashing direction indicators were carried out on a number of RTs in 1956, but it was 1959 before the final versions began to be fitted across the whole fleet. Experience in service however found that the indicator switch unit was prone to premature failure. In 1959, this led to C.A.V. Ltd, the manufacturers, redesigning them and supplying replacements at their own expense. Buses which had been fitted with the originals had them replaced, while the redesigned units were fitted to those buses which had not been treated. The GS fleet began to receive the later version at their second overhaul. A number of GSs whose second overhaul was not programmed until 1960 or 1961 were called back into works for the indicator units to be fitted. No doubt the flashing indicators were a welcome improvement and obviated the need for the driver to give hand signals through the small sliding offside cab window, which could be draughty and at times stiff to operate.

Chapter six refers to the fitting of heaters to 47 buses in September and October 1962. Apart from the need to improve passenger comfort in cold weather, there had also been a request from the Union for the fitment of a heater for the driver. Ten had already been sold by the end of 1961, but all others with a planned overhaul date after January 1960 were selected. GS 28 was the first to be dealt with as the 'pilot', and GS 45, 48, 52, 54, 56, 57, 64, and 65 were fitted

with heaters during their normal overhaul. The remaining 37 buses selected were called back into Chiswick Tram Shed for two days for the heaters to be fitted, the first being GS 50 on 11th September, the last GS 38 on 19th October. These 37 buses comprised GS 10, 12–23, 25-27, 29-31,33-36,38, 39, 42, 44, 46, 47, 50, 51, 53, 55, 58, 59, 60, and 66. GS 62 was completed out of sequence in May 1963, having been the northern area 'heater float' bus whilst others were away from their garages. GS 62 spent time at Amersham, Garston and Hertford to cover various buses during these absences, also spending time as a training bus at Tring, the detailed dates of which are referred to in chapter six.

The main overhaul process took approximately ten working days. GS 2 and 3 were the first to be sent to Chiswick on 2nd January 1956 from Hertford and Chelsham respectively, returning to service on 14th and 29th March. GS 2 was reallocated to Hitchin, GS 3 returning to Chelsham. GS 4 followed from Amersham on 4th January, returning to Chelsham on 15th March. These were followed by GS 1 (Chelsham), 5 (Leatherhead), 11 (Reigate), 8 (Hitchin), 6 and 7 (Chelsham), in that order before the end of March 1956. GS 11 had first been allocated to Chelsham but was sent to Chiswick for a few days in December 1954 before going to Dorking until the end of May 1955. It was then delicensed and stored at Reigate before its first overhaul, following which it was re-allocated to Chelsham on 1st May 1956. Having been so little used, overhauling GS 11 at this early stage seemed unnecessary, but it remained in service at Chelsham until October 1962 having received its second overhaul in October 1959. It was however one of those delicensed in the 1962 changes and did not see further service.

GS 33 was sent from Tring for its second overhaul on 12th October 1961. In the workshop at Aldenham, it is undergoing an exhaust test, its overhaul and repaint having been completed. It was relicensed and returned to service at Amersham on 1st January 1962. *Vectis Transport Publications*

Buses were called in at the rate of generally three per month so that at any one time, two were at the Tram Shed being overhauled, the other being at Chiswick Works. Buses then went to the main overhaul works at Aldenham for final checks before being relicensed for service, although many were transferred to their operating garages unlicensed. The first batch of buses had seen little more than two years' service by the time of their first overhaul, but given the total time taken for the first complete cycle, those buses at the end of the period had been in service for over four years. Indeed, the rate slowed towards the end of 1957 until the first cycle was completed when GS 79 went from Northfleet on 11th February 1959, GS 84 from Leatherhead on 23rd March and finally GS 82 from Dorking on 15th April. The cycle was completely halted for six weeks during the 1958 strike. GS 73 and 74 had been sent in from Hertford on 24th March and 21st April respectively, but it was 3rd July and 1st September before they were returned to Hertford. The longest delay was to GS 67 which went in from Garston on 5th May a few days before the strike, and not returned there for service until 1st October almost five months later. Overhauls across the whole fleet ceased completely during the six week strike, and there was a long period before the backlog could be reduced. The GS fleet was a low priority, and it was 1st September before the next bus GS 74 was called in.

A review of the first overhauls shows that GS 84, the final vehicle remaining in store, was transferred to Leatherhead on 1st January 1956 to allow GS 5 to be sent for overhaul as noted above. The schedule shows that very few of the early numbered vehicles returned to their original garage as a process of 'one in / one out' was adopted, freshly overhauled buses probably being returned by the same ferry driver. It was not until 16th July 1956 however that Amersham received a replacement for GS 4, GS 16 then being allocated after overhaul having been at Hertford from new. After overhaul on 9th January 1957, GS 32 became a float vehicle visiting Epping, Guildford, Amersham, East Grinstead and Dorking for short periods before finally settling down at Swanley on 1st November 1957 to replace GS 40.

The later reduction in overhaul rate to two buses per month resulted in the majority of buses returning to their origin garage. Two buses became out of sequence with their planned overhaul dates. GS 34 was delayed in its original delivery, going to Amersham instead of the original intention of Guildford, and had its overhaul delayed by three months, going to Chiswick on 5th March 1957 and returning to Amersham on 1st May.

The second cycle began almost immediately after the completion of the first with GS 2 being called in from Stevenage on 6th May 1959 and continued with the low numbered buses. Only 57 GSs were overhauled up to GS 66, nine buses from this batch (24, 32, 37, 40, 41, 43, 49, 61 and 63) having been sold during 1961 together with GS 71. This second cycle was a very slow process and was to extend into 1963, only one bus being overhauled in most months. The remainder in the batch GS 67 to GS 84 were to only ever receive one overhaul, almost all of these having been stored when new and having covered less mileage than the rest of the fleet.

When buses were due to be called in to Chiswick at a certain pre-determined date, they were generally delicensed on the last day of the preceding month and stored awaiting transfer. Equally, on their return, unless the date was on the first or last day of the month, buses would remain unlicensed until the first of the following month. This saved the cost of a full month's road licence fee where a bus might otherwise only be available for service for part of that month. Grays, and more frequently Romford (London Road), were used as holding garages for buses mostly from Stevenage, Hertford and Epping awaiting overhaul, and were returned there on completion. There are many instances of GSs being returned to Hertford from Romford for example having been temporarily stored there after being overhauled. They were exchanged for another which was then driven back to Romford that day to await being called in for overhaul. Presumably, Romford was able to supply ferry drivers to complete this both to and from garages and Chiswick Works. A similar arrangement existed in the north west area where Garston was used in a similar way, and at Reigate in the south.

At the end of October 1954, GS 45 suffered a serious front end accident on the Northfleet routes and was delicensed on 1st November to be sent to Chiswick for major repairs. At the same time, the opportunity was taken to change the rear differential ratio before being returned to service (noted in LT Archive LT315/4278 Experiment S7597). The work was done to test the revised ratios on hilly routes and, once repairs were completed, it was sent to Dorking on 4th March 1955. The 433 was perhaps the hilliest route operated by GSs, with long steep climbs up to both Ranmore and Coldharbour. In a full day on the route, a GS would make no fewer than 16 ascents of these hills and were a good test of the different ratios to see how the bus performed on such steep climbs. On 9th March, it returned to Chiswick for a few days before going back to Dorking, and a month later on 13th April it was transferred to Chelsham for a period on the 464, 465, and 485. These routes were not as consistently hilly as the 433, but the ascent of Crockham Hill from Edenbridge was both long and in parts quite steep. On return to Chelsham garage each day, buses also had to make the long ascent of the 1:6 Titsey Hill up to Botley Hill high on the North Downs. On 25th April, GS 45 went to Dunton Green for the 471. This route had some hilly sections which were longer but generally not steep, the exception being the climb up Star Hill to Knockholt Pound from Dunton Green which, although long and steep, was covered only on positioning journeys from the garage. Finally on 11th May, GS 45 returned to Northfleet. Three weeks later on 1st June it went back to Chiswick, presumably for an assessment of its performance, being returned to Northfleet where it remained for several months. It was allocated again to Dorking on 1st February 1956 where it remained until delicensed and transferred to Reigate on 1st August 1957. On 21st August it was called in to Chiswick for its first overhaul. It temporarily returned to Reigate on 2nd October, before being relicensed for service at Dorking on 1st November where it remained for the next five years. After its second overhaul in December 1962, it returned again to Dorking until going to Hertford for two years in March 1963. This proved to be its last revenue earning service, ending its days as a staff bus based at Reigate, surviving into ownership by London Country. No record of GS 45's hill climbing performance or resultant fuel consumption has been found, but since no other GSs appear to have received the alternative differential, then presumably a decision was made that it was not worthwhile making a general change. It is also worth mentioning that some skill is required to calibrate the fuel injectors on the GS Perkins engine. On hilly routes, performance could very easily be impaired with badly set injectors, especially with a good load of passengers. No doubt the fitters at these garages gained some valuable experience with GS 45 and other buses in their charge.

A lucky few received their third and final overhauls during 1964 and 1965. These were GS 10, 12, 13, 14, 15, 17, 21, 33, 36, 42 and 55, GS 42 being the very

GS 36 was one of the ten GSs that passed into London Country ownership. It ended its revenue earning career when it was delicensed at Northfleet on 4th October 1969, but remained there in store until April 1970, when it was allocated to St Albans as a training bus. It was finally withdrawn at the end of October 1972 and stored at Garston before sale to a scout group in March 1973. It is now one of the many GSs in preservation. On 17th June 1972 it appears to have been abandoned, parked in the rear corner of Luton garage. It has no L Plate displayed, so it may be that its use as a trainer came to an end before its final withdrawal. *Peter Aves*

last of all, being overhauled in December 1965 and completed at Aldenham in January 1966. GS 42 not only was one of the last two in normal service but was also the last GS to leave the Chiswick Tram Shed before it was handed over to the B.E.A fleet of Routemasters.

In his book *40 Years with London Transport* the late Colin Curtis mentions that '*the GS was not kind to its engine oil, having a tendency to turn to a thick black treacle in a short time*'. When started from cold, the Perkins engine took time to warm the oil and thin it down. If the bus was driven too hard before the oil became sufficiently thinned out, instances of damage and even engine failure occurred. This was a particular problem at Chelsham as mentioned in chapter two. Although on the edge of London suburbs, it was sited in an exposed position and was the highest garage in the Country area. Its location also meant that it experienced lower temperatures much of the time, particularly in winter, and on the morning run out buses had a 20-minute journey to Oxted before starting service. The climb from the garage to the cross roads at Botley Hill about two miles away was not steep but rather a steady climb. Although this could be accomplished generally in top gear, it did require the bus to be driven hard 'foot down' from a cold start, resulting in a number of engine failures.

After a year in service, a report was prepared by the Office of the Engineering Superintendent (Road Service) Chiswick. Dated 4th March 1955, it was entitled 'Service Experience with GS type Single Deck Vehicle – One Man Operated', and was a review of all aspects of the GSs performance since their introduction. The first line refers to 83 GSs in service which was of course correct at the time. Such was the surplus of GSs once deliveries had been completed that GS 84 stood idle until it was finally licensed on 1st January 1956 and sent from store at Reigate for service at Leatherhead.

There was little serious complaint from drivers on the GS's general performance, items noted being condensation on the front screens and rear window, the front fog lamp being obscured by mud, a lack of illumination for the ticket machine, and some reflection on the windscreen at night from the internal lights. The position of the nearside mirror – partly obscured by the top of the doors – was also mentioned. The report covered a great many mechanical and electrical aspects, but few were noted as being of any great concern, the majority being little more than 'teething problems' associated with any new bus type. The mounting for the horn was moved, since its original position bolted to offside front wing structure had resulted in a number of fractures due to the excessive vibration. At a meeting of the Road Services sub-committee on 27th August 1954, a decision was taken to fit a deflector shield to the front nearside saloon lamp to eliminate reflection in the front windscreen at night, and on 1st October a lengthy discussion took place about the problem of mud splashing up onto the rear of the GSs which led to the fitting of longer mud flaps and a splash guard fitted between the rear wheels and mud flaps. Drawings for this addition were prepared in November 1954, and the work carried out at garages.

When delivered, the GS and RF fleets were not fitted with the London Transport 'Bullseye' at the rear. In December 1954 it was noted that at the Chairman's request to *further the identification of vehicles*, this was to be fitted to the back of all single deck passenger vehicles with the exception of codes RF1/2 and RF3. The RF1/2 buses were the Private Hire fleet which already had them, the RF3 buses being the Private Hire RFW class, which at the time did not have them but were later also added to the programme.

Although the GSs were operated as one-man buses, they did not display any notices to this effect other than a small paper label in the top of the nearside windscreen which was barely visible from any distance. In December 1954 it was felt necessary to add transfers to the front nearside quarter light window. Special transfer Part Number BP12576 ('Pay as you enter' and 'Tender exact fare') was added to the LTE drawing, the transfers then being fitted at garages.

The problems with engine failure due to thick engine oil when cold have been referred to. These had resulted in a total of 19 instances of seized engines, 13 of which were in the South area. No doubt, a number of these had been at Chelsham although specific garages are not mentioned. There had been 30 substitutions due to clutch failure in various forms resulting in jammed gears, although this may have been partly due to drivers becoming familiar with the crash gearbox, the operation of which could be slightly different on each bus. The reverse gate with first and second gear being to the right of third and fourth (as opposed to the left as was the convention) may also have been a factor.

GS 32 was part of Dunton Green's initial allocation, and stands at Orpington station with an STL on the stop in front. This official London Transport photograph is interesting since it illustrates the rear of the GSs as they were when delivered. The rear reflectors which became a legal requirement early in 1954 have yet to be fitted, and there is no London Transport 'Bullseye' transfer in the centre of the lower rear panel beneath the emergency door. The full width mud flap between the rear wheels has also not yet been fitted. These minor changes were made during the latter part of 1954. *London Transport Museum*

Before the GSs went into service, fuel consumption had been expected to be around 20mpg, but it soon became apparent that this was not achievable in normal service. The report included detailed month by month fuel and oil consumption figures for both north and south areas for the whole of 1954. In the Northern Division, each garage was reported separately. These are reproduced below and show that fuel consumption was just over 15 mpg taken overall, Hertford's GSs returning the highest figure of 16.2 mpg. Oil consumption was a little over 2000 mpg, Hertford's GSs again returning the best performance, while that at Hitchin – with operation only on the 383 – appears to have been particularly poor. Despite these consumption figures being less good than expected, the GS was nevertheless economic to operate. Their unladen weight of only four tons was an important factor, especially when compared to the RF bus which, though larger, had an unladen weight of seven tons 10cwt – almost twice that of the GS.

Northern Division
Average over six monthly period ending 2.11.54

Garage	Service miles operated	Fuel oil gallons	Miles per gallon	Lub. oil gallons	Miles per gallon
Hertford	146,091	9,015	16.2	51	2,864
Hitchin	26,874	1,830	14.6	19	1,414
Garston	63,454	4,372	14.5	26	2,440
Tring	15,149	1,050	14.4	8	1,894
Amersham	154,553	10,455	14.7	85	1,818
Epping	53,635	3,420	15.6	21	2,554
Division total	459,756	30,142		210	
Division average			15.25		2,189

Southern Division
Monthly summary 1954

Four weeks ending	Service miles operated	Misc. mileage	Private hire mileage	Fuel (gallons) service	Lub. oil (gallons) total
26th January	101243	1879	46	6832	37.5
23rd February	101673	2591	34	6973	56.5
23rd March	101949	1694	66	6794	66
20th April	99335	1288		6448	57.5
18th May	101911	1095	22	6538	36
15th June	102386	2218	58	6738	42.5
13th July	103925	1764	90	6726	55.5
10th August	107292	2255	138	5815	45.5
7th September	107467	2280	160	6819	50.5
5th October	108437	1906	114	7049	57.5
2nd November	105733	1289		6857	51.5
Division total	1141316	20529	728	74589	556.5
Division average				15.30 MPG	2052.72 MPG

Opposite The small engine compartment and lift-up bonnet made access slightly difficult when compared to the underfloor engines on the RF. To carry out routine maintenance it was mostly necessary to stand on the front bumper and lean in under the bonnet over the large radiator clearly visible in this view of GS 9. If the bus had been running for any length of time, then the radiator could be extremely hot, making the job somewhat uncomfortable. The GS was so reliable however so that, other than checking water and oil levels, little routine work was necessary. The front nearside panel which housed the fare chart could be quickly be removed completely to give easy access from the inside. *London Transport*

The report concludes by stating that *'it is felt that although a fairly large list of defects has been encountered, these are more or less inevitable with a new vehicle and when these matters are dealt with and rectified, the vehicle will be far more satisfactory than would appear from the observations made in this report. It is considered to offer a better road performance than the Cub vehicles which it replaces, and takes no more time to service'*. In service over ensuing years, failures of GSs on the road would be few and far between. They proved extremely robust and reliable on rough country roads and were all capable of a full service life, which few of them eventually enjoyed. London Transport's vehicle policy changed and economy of operation with a standardised fleet became more important.

Routine maintenance carried out at garages was reasonably straightforward. The hydraulic brakes had vacuum assistance, and could feel 'soft' at times. If the driver needed to brake hard for any reason, there could sometimes be a fraction of a second delay before the brakes came on, and the brake pressure needing to be applied could vary from bus to bus. The braking performance on a GS bore no comparison to the RF, whose air brakes provided consistently smooth progressive braking. A red indicator light next to the speedometer in the cab showed that the vacuum tank was operational when the engine was running. The brake fluid

reservoir was under the cab floor, a hinged flap next to the gear lever giving easy access to the filler. With hydraulic brakes however, it was a two man job to bleed when necessary. The whole front panel below the nearside windscreen where the fare chart case was located was easily removable to gain access to the rear of the engine, but other maintenance was somewhat awkward necessitating the fitter to stand on the front bumper while leaning over the radiator underneath the lift up bonnet.

Fitting blinds in a GS was very simple. The front blind box was accessed by a large lift up panel above the windscreens. It was fitted with a folding stay to hold it in place when lifted and only required a T key to open one catch of a type standard on the whole fleet. The blinds could be slotted into position very simply and were held in place top and bottom by two spring loaded rods holding the blind close behind the glass. A second small flap, above the offside windscreen, gave access for the driver to see the blind as he turned it to set the correct display. The rear blind had to be changed from a ladder from the outside and was identical to those fitted to the RF, an easy operation nevertheless.

STAFF BUSES

London Transport had always provided staff buses from its very early days, and ran a considerable network of them to and from its works at Aldenham and Chiswick. Once the post-war fleet renewal programme had been completed, most of the staff buses then in use were replaced by pre-war RT2s, which in turn were largely replaced by RTLs from the late 1950s as large numbers of them started to become redundant from successive service cuts. Some staff bus services however used single deckers, and 10T10 and 15T13 Regals had periods of use before the GSs were made available after October 1962. The 26-seat GS was to prove a reliable and able workhorse.

Reigate

Reigate had been a major repair centre in early London Transport days, and had a large number of Chiswick employees. It operated staff buses to both Aldenham and Chiswick with pick up points from Woodhatch and Redhill. The use of GSs as staff buses from Reigate began in 1963 soon after the major withdrawals from passenger service in October of the previous year. The daily journey was onerous with a morning trip to Chiswick, then on to Aldenham. At the end of the shift, the bus returned via Chiswick in the afternoon and then home to Reigate each day. If the fuel pump and injectors on a GS were suitably adjusted, they were capable of high speed. In the early years of Alan Charman's ownership of GS 62 he heard anecdotal stories from former Reigate engineering staff of 50mph being achieved at Roehampton and on the newly dualled section of the A217! During Alan's ownership of the bus, the biggest issue has always been the fuel pump settings, which had obviously been adjusted to allow such higher speeds on staff bus runs.

RTL 454 was one of Reigate's long term staff buses, but was delicensed and stored in April 1963. RT 2585 took over in May, and was supplemented by one of the GSs made redundant from the October 1962 changes. RT 2585 was transferred to Alperton as a trainer in June 1965.

GS 26 replaced RT 2585 and stayed until it was withdrawn and delicensed in February 1967. GS 62 replaced it, and was the longest serving Reigate staff bus until finally withdrawn in February 1973. GS 48 was allocated in April 1963, but remained for only two months, followed by GS 52 for a further two months. GS 56 arrived in August 1963 and remained for a year. It was delicensed on 21st August 1964 and officially noted as stored. GS 21 was transferred from Guildford on 21st August and remained until February 1963 to be replaced by GS 45, which remained until April 1969. GS 52 returned for a second time to replace GS 45 and stayed until August 1970, when it swapped places with GS 28 from Abbey Wood as noted below. GS 28 then remained until February 1973. A third GS was added in February 1966 when GS 12 arrived, having been out of use at Crawley since the 852 had been withdrawn the previous October. It remained until October 1969, when GS 10 replaced it. GS 10 would prove to be the last, surviving until October 1973.

All known Reigate staff buses are shown in the table on page 185. Those still allocated in December 1969 were taken into Central area stock, and retained by London Transport as shown in the table. Oddly however, they acquired London Country 'Private' blinds, with a message to contact any London Country Garage to 'hire a bus'.

Tring

With a substantial number of redundant GSs following the October 1962 changes, one was allocated to Tring as a dedicated staff bus, running each day to and from Aldenham. GS 62 arrived from Amersham on 9th October 1962 having spent short periods as the northern area 'heater float' bus. It stayed until it went for overhaul a year later. GS 75 replaced it until September 1963 when it was withdrawn and sold two months later. GS 62 was then reallocated having been in store since its overhaul, and remained for fifteen months until replaced by RT 1103 in November 1964. It was then transferred to Dunton Green where it ran until the last day of the 471. The allocation summary was: GS62, 9th October 1962 – delicensed 1st November; then to Garston 15th November 1962. GS75, 1st November 1962 – September 1963. GS62, September 1963 – December 1964 then to Dunton Green

Harrow Weald railway staff bus

A more unusual use took place between 1960 and 1963 where a GS was allocated to Harrow Weald during the period when the Metropolitan Line was being quad-rupled and upgraded. In this case, the GS was used to ferry staff to various working points along the line as the works progressed. RTL 435, had been the Harrow Weald staff bus until January 1960, but was replaced by GS 21. GS 78 arrived from Dunton Green to take over in June 1961, when GS 21 went for its overhaul. GS 78 remained (with assistance from GS 47 noted below) until February 1963, when it was transferred to Garston as a trainer. The allocation summary was: Long-term: GS 21, January 1960 until August 1961 and sent for overhaul on 14th June. GS 78, 26th May 1961 – February 1963. Short-term: GS 26, 15th February 1960 (from store) Reigate – 22nd February 1960 to Hemel Hempstead. GS 47, 12th April 1961 (from overhaul) – 7th May 1961 to East Grinstead

GS 62 spent long periods as a staff bus, culminating in a final six year period at Reigate where it made the daily journey to Chiswick and Aldenham. It was one of the staff buses retained by London Transport but maintained at Reigate by London Country. Despite the ownership, note the London Country 'Private' blind referred to in the text. It stands in the space in Reigate garage where the staff buses were always parked alongside another, which is probably GS 10. Both buses have had their fleetnames painted over, so this picture was probably taken shortly before both buses were sold in April 1973. Alan Charman has now owned GS 62 for longer than London Transport. *PM Photography*

Abbey Wood and Plumstead

The south side of the Thames was an area from which a considerable number of staff travelled to Aldenham, having been previously based at the former tram works at Charlton. Staff buses operated from Abbey Wood or Plumstead, a GS being used for several periods. One bus travelled up to New Cross Gate, then via the Old Kent Road and Elephant and Castle, before heading north over Blackfriars Bridge, up to Kings Cross, Archway and on to Aldenham. The unusual sight of a GS in the heart of the City, twice a day, wearing London Transport green livery lasted well into the 1970s.

GS 44 was used at New Cross for a short period at the beginning of 1961, but was transferred back to the Country area at Northfleet on 8th March 1961. GS 50 took over more permanently at Abbey Wood in April 1963, and stayed there until March 1967. GS 18 was allocated to Plumstead from August 1965 and operated in parallel with GS 50 from August 1965 until February 1966, followed by GS 35 for a year and then GS 56. GS 10 and 66 followed these, with GS 66 returning in January 1968. GS 13 replaced GS 10 in March 1969 and moved its base of operations back to Abbey Wood in July 1969. At that time GS 28 replaced GS 66 at Plumstead, only to move to again Abbey Wood in August. GS 13 and GS 28 maintained the service from Abbey Wood into 1970, with one at least available. London Transport had officially transferred them from the Country to the Central area in December 1969, although they retained green livery and London Transport fleetnames to reflect their ownership after London Country took over. In August 1970 GS 28 was exchanged with GS 52 from the Reigate to Chiswick service. GS 13 retired in April 1973 and, after a short spell with RF 317, GS 52 continued until April 1974, after which RT 4168 took over. These two garages had the largest number of GS staff buses over a long period, as shown in the table opposite.

GS 35 was withdrawn at Windsor at the beginning of 1966 and transferred to Plumstead for staff bus duties. It remained there for a year before being stored at nearby Abbey Wood garage for almost a further year before sale to a private buyer. It made the long journey to Chiswick and Aldenham every day and looks to be almost full as it passes through the City. Note the AM garage code and Plumstead board in the side holder which carried the later pay as you enter sign.
Alan Cross

The use of the GS meant that London Transport was to retain five vehicles when London Country was formed on 1st January 1970. GS 10 and 62 were stationed at Reigate and maintained by London Country staff. GS 28 was subsequently transferred to Reigate and GS 10 transferred back to Chiswick at some point in 1971 but the exact date is unknown. It was later transferred to Reigate until October 1973, when it was sold. GS 13 remained at Abbey Wood, being covered by GS 28 during maintenance and periods when it was unlicensed. The year 1973 was to be the final one for the GS staff buses when the all-conquering RF took over at Reigate.

SCHEDULE OF GS STAFF BUSES

GS	Kept by LT	Went to LCBS	Sold before 31.12.69	Dates Allocated From	To	GARAGE	GS	Kept by LT	Went to LCBS	Sold before 31.12.69	Dates Allocated From	To	GARAGE
							44			X	Feb 61	Mar 61	New Cross and Abbey Wood
10	X			Dec 67	Apr 69	Plumstead							
				Oct 69	Apr 73	Reigate	45		X		Feb 65	Apr 69	Reigate
12		X		Feb 66	Oct 69	Reigare	47			X	12.4.61	7.5.61	Harrow Weald[1]
13	X			Mar 69	Jul 69	Plumstead	48			X	Apr 63	Jun 63	Reigate
				Jul 69	Apr 73	Abbey Wood (short periods unlicensed)	50			X	Apr 63	Mar 67	Abbey Wood
18			X	Aug 65	Feb 66	Plumstead	51			X	1.11.60	8.3.61	New Cross
21			X	Jan 60	Jan 60	Amersham	52			X	Apr 63	Jul 63	Dunton Green
				Feb 60	Aug 61	Harrow Weald then overhaul					Jul 63	Aug 63	Reigate
				21.8.64	Mar 65	Reigate					Aug 70	Aug 72	Abbey Wood
											May 73	Apr 74	Abbey Wood
26			X	15.2.60	22.2.60	Harrow Weald	56	X			Aug 63	Aug 64	Reigate
				Jun 65	Feb 67	Reigate (replaced by GS 62)					Feb 67	Jul 67	Plumstead
28	X			Jul 69	Aug 69	Plumstead	62	X			9.10.62	1.11.62	Tring
				Aug 69	Aug 70	Abbey Wood (cover for GS 13 unlicensed)					Sep 63	Dec 64	Tring
											Feb 67	Feb 73	Reigate
				Aug 70	Feb 73	Reigate	66		X		Jul 67	Jul 69	Plumstead
35			X	Feb 66	Feb 67	Plumstead					Aug 69		Garston – trainer[2]
							75			X	1.11.62	Sept 63	Tring
							78			X	26.5.61	Feb 63	Harrow Weald[3]

[1] Used as staff bus for one month after overhaul.
[2] End date not known.
[3] Transferred from DG after withdrawal of 413B.

Where possible, precise dates of transfer have been included, but the daily records do not accurately show all movements for staff buses and trainers. The month of transfer has therefore been used.

When London Country Bus Services commenced operations on 1st January 1970, a total of 15 GSs remained in stock. Ten were transferred to the new company and five retained by London Transport. Of the ten transferred to London Country, GS 36, 42 and 55 were in use as trainers, GS 17 and 33 remained in service at Garston for the 336A (one for service and one spare), and the others GS 12, 14, 45, 64 and 66 were in withdrawn condition and did not run for London Country, being placed upon the disposal list. GS 42 which was a trainer at Garston was subsequently re-instated to passenger service for 336A after GS 17 suffered engine failure, and was in use on the last day of operation there as described in the Garston section in chapter four.

8 Sale and Afterlife

The GS was a rugged and reliable small bus. Its relatively light unladen weight of four tonnes contributed to an economic fuel consumption of around 15 miles per gallon, or higher still on flatter routes with few hills, and was better than many equivalent buses at the time. Their relatively low service mileage referred to earlier therefore made them an attractive and economic second hand bus for small operators.

At any one time since their introduction, a minimum of around 20 GSs remained idle in their garages either delicensed, as engineering spares, or in store. Once timetables started to be cut back as a reaction to falling passenger numbers, the proportion of those not required for service increased. A total of 37 GSs would eventually be sold to small bus and coach operators, a few of which saw service with more than one such company. Many also remained with their second owner for longer than they had with London Transport, some remaining in service into the early 1970s.

After the drastic service cuts which followed the 1958 strike, it became obvious that there was no point in retaining all of the original fleet of 84. Great Yarmouth Corporation Transport, whose routes were entirely crew operated, had made a decision to experiment with one man operation on two of their less important routes. Rather than invest in new buses, it looked at the possibility of hiring some suitable small buses for the trial, and secured the long term loan of five GSs from London Transport. The first to go were GS 63 and 70 which were despatched respectively from Hitchin on 7th September and from Garston on 12th September. GS 72 was delicensed at Hertford on 15th September 1958, arriving at Great Yarmouth two days later. GS 68 was taken out of service at Tring a week later and the last of the five, GS 61, followed a week later still from Amersham. After a period of driver training, they entered service on route 6 to Cobholm and 8 to Gorleston-on-Sea a little way south of Yarmouth itself. No doubt London Transport were hoping that Great Yarmouth would purchase them on completion of their trial, but it was not to be. All were returned on 5th August 1959 and put into store at Gillingham Street garage in Victoria, and one month later all moved to Grays where they remained out of use.

GS 68 was relicensed on 1st April 1960 and returned to service at Tring as temporary cover for GS 33 which was withdrawn for a month presumably for some repair. GS 68 was delicensed again on 1st May,

GS 61 was delicensed at Amersham on 22nd September 1958 and was the last of the five GSs hired by Great Yarmouth Corporation. It rests in the garage between trips on route 6 in front of a Leyland PD and Guy Arab. The bus was returned to London Transport on 5th August 1959 and stored at Gillingham Street garage. It did not see further use and languished out of use until sold to Corvedale Motors in 1961.
Michael Dryhurst

then two months later sent to Hemel Hempstead, again as temporary cover while GS 19 went for overhaul. It remained at Hemel Hempstead until the October 1962 changes when it was finally withdrawn for sale. GS 72 was relicensed on 1st November 1959 and sent to St Albans where it remained until October 1962 when it was withdrawn and stored at Garston. The remaining three buses returned from Yarmouth did not see further service and were therefore the first GSs to have been withdrawn from service after less than five years on Country area routes.

The daily movement records for 5th August 1959 – the date when the Great Yarmouth buses were returned, include a list of ten GSs noted as *'withdrawn and stored for disposal'.* The list comprised GS 24 at Dunton Green, GS 32 at Swanley,

GS 61 was one of the five GSs hired by Great Yarmouth Corporation in 1959. On its return to London Transport it did not see service again and was one of five GSs purchased by Corvedale Motors of Ludlow in 1961. It was withdrawn in May 1965. It is seen here having been smartly repainted into Corvedale livery.
Peter Aves collection

GS 49 at Northfleet, GS 40 at Windsor, GS 37, 41, and 43 at Romford, and three of the Yarmouth buses – GS 61, 63, and 70. GS 24, 32, and 49 were moved to Romford on 10th February 1961, having remained at their respective garages for the previous 18 months. GS 41 was the next bus withdrawn after the three GSs which went to Yarmouth and not returned to service again. It was delicensed at Epping on 10th December 1958, having completed a few days more than five years' service, having been licensed at Dorking on 1st December 1953.

Other than GS 41, 61, 63, and 70, the remaining six had been in service less than six years before withdrawal. On 11th January 1961, GS 40 and 41 were the first of their class to be sold when they went to West Bromwich Corporation. Six days later GS 61 was the first of several purchased by Corvedale Motors at Ludlow. They were the first small bus company to purchase second hand GSs, and GS 43, 49, and 63 followed in May, and finally GS 37 going to Corvedale on 13th June. Corvedale would later purchase GS 68 and 72 which they collected from Garston on 4th March 1963. GS 70 was sold to West Ham Borough Council in April, and GS 24 to the London Fire Brigade social section at the beginning of June. They ran GS 24 for almost three years before selling it to a dealer, who in the end sold it to Tillingbourne Valley.

Of these first 10 sold, GS 32 was the only one to go to a dealer when it went to Birds at Stratford-upon-Avon on 12th June, but was quickly sold on to Barry's Coaches at Moreton-in-Marsh who two months later sold it on to Corvedale Motors. Corvedale Motors were therefore the first small independent to take advantage of GSs, and having acquired six in 1961, purchased two more in 1963. No further GSs were sold in 1961, nor any in 1962, but their wholesale replacement by RFs in October 1962 referred to in detail already led to a further 20 being sold in 1963 for a variety of uses.

The attraction of the GS for small independent operators led to a total of 37 being purchased for further service. The majority of these were purchased direct from London Transport, but a small number were acquired later from their original purchaser. Of the total of 37, no fewer than 27 were acquired by only three operators, Tillingbourne Valley building up the largest fleet of 13 although not all saw revenue earning service. The other two were Corvedale Motors of Ludlow who acquired eight, and Southern Motorways six.

The joint operation with London Transport of the 448 route from Guildford to Ewhurst had a long history and is described in chapter three. When Tillingbourne purchased the first batch of five GSs in 1963, it led to the unique instance of GSs from both operators being used on the same route. Tillingbourne put 1, 3 and 4 into service at the end of March 1963, GS 67 and 69 following two months later. Apart from the 448, they ran a short town service in Guildford to Warren Road, and a rural route to Farley Green. This route paralleled London Transport's 425 as far as Albury where, by the gates to Albury Park, the route turned right and climbed up some narrow roads to the small village of Farley Green. It ran to an hourly headway, and buses worked alternate journeys to Farley Green and Warren Road on a two hourly cycle, thus maintaining the hourly headway very efficiently with two buses. The route passed Tillingbourne's garage in Chilworth which thus provided a convenient point for changing drivers during the day. The hourly headway on both routes ran all day until the last departure to Farley Green at 9.34pm, 10.03pm to Warren Road, and the last journey from Guildford to Chilworth at 10.30pm. On Sundays, one bus operated a two hourly headway on both routes with the last departure to Farley Green an hour earlier at 8.34pm. One bus was allocated all day to the 448, running every 90 minutes between Guildford and Peaslake until Tillingbourne's last departure at 8.58pm. This bus then worked the 9.41pm from Peaslake to Chilworth to complete the day's work. Other than commencing later on Sunday, the operation was the same seven days a week.

GS 82 has stopped outside Tillingbourne's garage at Chilworth to change drivers on a Sunday sometime in the summer of 1970. The Farley Green route still ran four journeys on Sunday afternoon, but would soon be withdrawn that day. The bus had been purchased in January 1970 from London Transport who had transferred it to their service fleet in 1963. It was the last GS in service with Tillingbourne when sold in March 1972
Alan Edwards

In 1970, GS 84 is in Tillingbourne's yard at Chilworth in front of GS 24 (fleet number 5), and GS 69 (fleet number 2) which had been scrapped in September 1965 following an accident. Obtaining spares for their GSs became more of a problem from the late 1960s, and in 1969 Peter Aves travelled on former GS 76 from Guildford to Peaslake. The bus seemed to perform poorly, and when asked, the Tillingbourne driver lamented the deteriorating state of the GSs. Cannibalisation of some was the only way to keep the others on the road.
Peter Larkham

The shortlived joint operation came to an end on 11th August 1964 when London Transport withdrew from the route in the face of decreasing passenger numbers. Tillingbourne was prepared to take over operation of the whole timetable but – wisely as it transpired – refused to pay anything to London Transport to acquire the route.

The 448A to Pewley Way was also taken over, and Tillingbourne continued to operate the former timetable in its entirety, three buses being required. It was a period when the decline in passengers was accelerating, and by the autumn of 1965 Tillingbourne were unable to continue the timetable as it was. On 29th November, the section beyond Peaslake to Ewhurst was abandoned as was the whole of the former 448A to Pewley Way. The panel timetable below shows the reductions on all of Tillingbourne's routes.

TILLINGBOURNE VALLEY SERVICES LTD

GUILDFORD — PEASLAKE   Commencing 29th NOVEMBER, 1965

Guildford (Onslow Street)	...			7.28	7.58	8.28	9.43	10.28	11.13	11.58	12.43	1.28	2.13	2.58	3.43	4.28	5.13
Merrow Church	...	...		7.41	8.11	8.41	9.56	10.41	11.26	12.11	12.56	1.41	2.26	3.11	3.56	4.41	5.26
Newlands Corner	...	...		7.45	8.15	8.45	10.00	10.45	11.30	12.15	1.00	1.45	2.30	3.15	4.00	4.45	5.30
Shere (Tel. Exch.)	...	6.53	7.23	7.53	8.23	8.53	10.08	10.53	11.38	12.23	1.08	1.53	2.38	3.23	4.08	4.53	5.38
Gomshall (Compasses)	...	6.56	7.26	7.56	8.26	8.56	10.11	10.56	11.41	12.26	1.11	1.56	2.41	3.26	4.11	4.56	5.41
Peaslake (War Memorial)	...	7.08	7.38	8.08	8.38	9.08	10.23	11.08	11.53	12.38	1.23	2.08	2.53	3.38	4.23	5.08	5.53

*

Guildford (Onslow Street)	...	5.31	5.58	6.43	7.31	8.31	9.31
Merrow Church	...	5.44	6.11	6.56	7.44	8.44	9.44
Newlands Corner	...	5.48	6.15	7.00	7.48	8.48	9.48
Shere (Tel. Exch.)	...	5.56	6.23	7.08	7.56	8.56	9.56
Gomshall (Compasses)	...	5.59	6.26	7.11	7.59	8.59	9.59
Peaslake (War Memorial)	...	6.11	6.38	7.23	8.11	9.11	10.11

* Not Saturday

Peaslake (War Memorial)	...	7.11	7.41	8.11	8.41	9.11	10.26	11.11	11.56	12.41	1.26	2.11	2.56	3.41	4.26	5.11	5.56
Gomshall (Compasses)	...	7.23	7.53	8.23	8.53	9.23	10.38	11.23	12.08	12.53	1.38	2.23	3.08	3.53	4.38	5.23	6.08
Shere (Tel. Exch.)	...	7.26	7.56	8.26	8.56	9.26	10.41	11.26	12.11	12.56	1.41	2.26	3.11	3.56	4.41	5.26	6.11
Newlands Corner	...	7.34	8.04	8.34	9.04	9.34	10.49	11.34	12.19	1.04	1.49	2.34	3.19	4.04	4.49	5.34	6.19
Merrow Church	...	7.38	8.08	8.38	9.08	9.38	10.53	11.38	12.23	1.08	1.53	2.38	3.23	4.08	4.53	5.38	6.23
Guildford (Onslow Street)	...	7.51	8.21	8.51	9.21	9.51	11.06	11.51	12.36	1.21	2.06	2.51	3.36	4.21	5.06	5.51	6.36

Peaslake (War Memorial)	...	6.41	7.26	8.14	9.14	10.14
Gomshall	...	6.53	7.38	8.26	9.26	10.26
Shere (Tel. Exch.)	...	6.56	7.41	8.29	9.29	10.29
Newlands Corner	...	7.04	7.49	8.37	9.37	
Merrow Church	...	7.08	7.53	8.41	9.41	
Guildford (Onslow Street)	...	7.21	8.06	8.54	9.54	

SUNDAYS ONLY

Guildford (Onslow Street)	...	12.43	2.13	3.43	5.13	6.43		Peaslake (War Memorial)	...	1.26	2.56	4.26	5.56	7.26
Merrow Church	...	12.56	2.26	3.56	5.26	6.56		Gomshall (Compasses)	...	1.38	3.08	4.38	6.08	7.38
Newlands Corner	...	1.00	2.30	4.00	5.30	7.00		Shere (Tel. Exch.)	...	1.41	3.11	4.41	6.11	7.41
Shere (Tel. Exch.)	...	1.08	2.38	4.08	5.38	7.08		Newlands Corner	...	1.49	3.19	4.49	6.19	7.49
Gomshall (Compasses)	...	1.11	2.41	4.11	5.41	7.11		Merrow Church	...	1.53	3.23	4.53	6.23	7.53
Peaslake (War Memorial)	...	1.23	2.53	4.23	5.53	7.23		Guildford (Onslow Street)	...	2.06	3.36	5.06	6.36	8.06

GUILDFORD—KINGSFIELD (FARLEY GREEN)

Guildford (Bus Station)	...		8.00	8.34	10.34	12.34	2.34	4.34	5.34	6.34	7.34	8.34	10.00
Shalford (Station)	...		8.07	8.41	10.41	12.41	2.41	4.41	5.41	6.41	7.41	8.41	10.07
Chilworth (New Road)	...	6.54	7.47	8.13	8.47	10.47	12.47	2.47	4.47	5.47	6.47	7.47	8.47	10.13
Chilworth (Station)	...	6.56	7.49	8.15	8.49	10.49	12.49	2.49	4.49	5.49	6.49	7.49	8.49	
Albury (Drummond Arms)	...	7.01	7.55		8.55	10.55	12.55	2.55	4.55	5.55	6.55		8.55	
Albury (Park Gates)	...	7.03	7.57		8.57	10.57	12.57	2.57	4.57	5.57	6.57		8.57	
William IV	...	7.11	8.05		9.05	11.05	1.05	3.05	5.05	6.05	7.05		9.05	
Kingsfield (Farley Green)	...	7.19	8.13		9.13	11.13	1.13	3.13	5.13	6.13	7.13		9.13	

Kingsfield (Farley Green)	...	7.20	8.20	9.20	11.20	1.20	3.20		5.20	6.20	7.20	9.20
William IV	...	7.28	8.28	9 28	11.28	1.28	3.28		5.28	6.28	7.28	9.28
Albury (Park Gates)	...	7.36	8.36	9.36	11.36	1.36	3.36		5.36	6.36	7.36	9.36
Albury (Drummond Arms)	...	7.39	8.39	9.39	11.39	1.39	3.39		5.39	6.39	7.39	9.39
Chilworth (Station)	...	7.44	8.44	9.44	11.44	1.44	3.44		5.44	6.44	7.44	9.44
Chilworth (New Road)	...	7.46	8.46	9.46	11.46	1.46	3.46	4.46	5.46	6.46	7.46	9.46
Shalford (Station)	...	7.52	8.52	9.52	11.52	1.52	3.52	4.52	5.52	6.52	7 52	
Guildford (Bus Station)	...	7.59	8.59	9.59	11.59	1.59	3.59	4.59	5.59	6.59	7.59	

SUNDAYS ONLY

Guildford (Bus Station)	...		2.34	4.34	6.34	8.34		Kingsfield (Farley Green)	...	1.20	3.20	5.20	7.20
Shalford (Station)	...		2.41	4 41	6.41	8.41		William IV	...	1.28	3.28	5.28	7.28
Chilworth (New Road)	...	12.47	2.47	4.47	6.47	8.47		Albury (Park Gates)	...	1.36	3.36	5.36	7.36
Chilworth (Station)	...	12.49	2.49	4.49	6.49			Albury (Drummond Arms)	...	1.39	3.39	5.39	7.39
Albury (Drummond Arms)	...	12.55	2.55	4.55	6 55			Chilworth (Station)	...	1.44	3.44	5.44	7.44
Albury (Park Gates)	...	12.57	2.57	4.57	6.57			Chilworth (New Road)	...	1.46	3.46	5.46	7.46
William IV	...	1.05	3.05	5.05	7.05			Shalford (Station)	...	1.52	3.52	5 52	7.52
Kingsfield (Farley Green)	...	1.13	3.13	5.13	7.13			Guildford (Bus Station)	...	1.59	3.59	5.59	7.59

GUILDFORD—WARREN ROAD

		NS	NS	NS			NS		
Guildford (Farnham Road)	...	9.03	10.03	12.03	2.03	4.03	5.03	6.03	7.03	8.03
London Road (Station)	...	9.10	10.10	12.10	2.10	4.10	5.10	6.10	7.10	8.10
Sanford Arms	...	9.12	10.12	12.12	2.12	4.12	5.12	6.12	7.12	8.12
One Tree Corner	...	9.16	10.16	12.16	2.16	4.16	5.16	6.16	7.16	8.16
Warren Road (Longdown Rd.)	...	9.18	10.18	12.18	2.18	4.18	5.18	6.18	7.18	8.18

		NS	NS	NS			NS		
Warren Road (Longdown Rd.)	...	9.20	10.20	12.20	2.20	4.20	5.20	6.20	7.20	8.20
One Tree Corner	...	9.22	10.22	12.22	2.22	4.22	5.22	6.22	7.22	8.22
Sanford Arms	...	9.25	10.25	12.25	2.25	4.25	5.25	6.25	7.25	8.25
London Road (Station)	...	9.27	10.27	12.27	2.27	4.27	5.27	6.27	7.27	8.27
Guildford (Farnham Road)	...	9.32	10.32	12.32	2.32	4.32	5.32	6.32	7.32	8.32

NS — Not Sunday.

This Tillingbourne panel timetable was printed following the significant cuts to their routes in November 1965 which were the result of a significant drop in passengers and a long term shortage of drivers. The former London Transport services to Ewhurst and Pewley Way were withdrawn completely, and the Warren Road and Farley Green routes were cut from hourly to two hourly to enable operation by one bus. The 45 minute headway to Peaslake also saved one bus, thus halving the daily run out to three buses.
Peter Aves collection

The GSs continued to give Tillingbourne valuable service, and more than justified their purchase. By 1970 however, the GSs were in need of replacement. They were 17 years old and spares were less easy to acquire. A variety of second hand replacements were purchased but it was not easy to find small buses that could operate along the narrow roads and at the same time perform well on the steep hills – particularly the long climb up to Newlands Corner on the Peaslake route. GS 69 was scrapped for spares after an accident in 1965, but the remainder were gradually withdrawn in 1969 and 1970. GS 76 remained in service until April 1971, but GS 64 and 82 which had been acquired later than the others were used on a route based in Horsham and remained until 1972. GS 4 and 24 had been progressively stripped for spares and the remains were sold for scrap in May 1971.

Southern Motorways used their GSs on routes around the Petersfield and Alton area in Hampshire. They purchased five in June 1963, and a sixth (GS 22) two years later. Although GS 9 was not used in service, the others all enjoyed a long service life, GS 11 survived until July 1971, but GS 2 and 7 remained in service for longer than they had with London Transport, not being withdrawn until May 1972 (GS 7) and October 1972 (GS 2). Of Southern Motorways, six GSs, GS 2 was the only one to pass into preservation. After a number of owners, it was acquired by John Huxford in 1994, and remains in his ownership. It was still in Southern Motorways attractive red livery but was eventually returned to London Transport green by Colin Rivers and Peter Aves, who repainted it in 2003. It has been a regular performer on Country Bus Rallies running days for many years.

GS 2 was purchased by Southern Motorways at the same time as GS 7 and on 15th April 1965 waits at Lodsworth village before returning to Midhurst. It was sold for preservation in November 1972. Many years later John Huxford acquired the bus and following some further restoration it was used by Country Bus Rallies on their running days. *Graham Holleymann*

Southern Motorways purchased five GSs from London Transport in 1963 which came from the large number withdrawn in the 1962 replacement programme. They were repainted in Southern Motorways attractive maroon, red and cream livery with large fleetnames clearly influenced by London Transport. It is at the terminus in Emsworth on a journey on route 7 to Thorney Island a few miles west of Chichester. Southern Motorways withdrew the bus in May 1972, selling it later that year with GS 2. GS 7 was intended to provide spares for GS 2, but instead went to a school before being finally scrapped *Peter Mitchell*

The two GSs acquired by Bickers in September 1969 enjoyed a period of revenue earning service on some former routes of Eastern Counties. Bickers was a small operator who ran a limited service from its home village of Coddenham into Ipswich in Suffolk. The main rural routes north of Ipswich were run by Eastern Counties who had a small outstation in the large village of Debenham some 10 miles from Ipswich. Five buses were based there and were used on three separate but infrequent routes into Ipswich, one of which had occasional journeys via Coddenham. Debenham outstation also ran a very limited service to the small town of Eye a few miles north of Debenham, two weekly market day routes to Norwich and a school service to the town of Stowmarket. In the widespread withdrawals among all the National Bus Company operators on the early 1970s, Eastern Counties closed the Debenham outstation. Bickers took the opportunity to take over the former Eastern Counties routes and grew the business considerably over the following years. Although the GSs proved too small for some journeys, they were used frequently on the routes between Debenham and Ipswich, lasting in service until early 1976 by which time they were more than 22 years old. GS 60 was preserved and after varied ownership is currently owned by Roger Wright and used regularly in service on one of the routes operated in conjunction with the Epping-Ongar railway.

The expansion of Bickers' bus operations is referred to in text. In September 1969, they purchased GS 56 and 60, both buses having been withdrawn from service by London Transport more than two years earlier. They were repainted in their light green livery but have yet to have the Bickers fleetname applied. They are in the company's yard in the village of Coddenham near Ipswich with a locally registered 1968 Bedford 8 seater Dormobile and a Harrington Cavalier bodied coach. Both GSs were later sold for preservation, GS 60 briefly appearing at Country Bus Rallies running days. *E W M Abbott*

GS 67 was purchased by Roy Gould from Tillingbourne in 1969 and has been in his ownership ever since. In the early years of his ownership, he painted it red with black mudguards. In the early 1990s, Surrey County Council subsidised a successful network of routes on summer Sundays and Bank Holidays linking popular places in the Surrey Hills. GS 67 was used by Nostalgiabus on route 416 between Redhill and Polesden Lacey where it connected with route 433 run by London and Country using GS 13. GS 67 waits at Redhill bus station for one of those journeys.

After its period with Tillingbourne Valley, GS 67 went to Roy Gould for preservation, and for a few years was used in service on the 'Surrey Hills' leisure bus routes which linked Guildford, Dorking and Reigate with Leith Hill and Polesden Lacey. It was joined by GS 13, which was acquired by London Country to operate the long circular route from Guildford which ran via Polesden Lacey, Burford Bridge (near Boxhill), Dorking, Coldharbour, Forest Green and Newlands Corner. GS 13 was the penultimate bus to be sold by London Transport and went straight into preservation. After a period at Greenwich Transport Museum and Sussex, it went to London Country in April 1992. London Country numbered the route 433 to reflect the original route from Dorking to Coldharbour, and for a few years in the 1990s, a GS once again served Coldharbour. GS 67 operated the route numbered 416 between Redhill and Polesden Lacey, and both GSs were timed to meet there at certain times of the day. After being sold on again by London Country, GS 13 was acquired by Memory Lane Transport based in Dorking and used on their Sunday operation of the route between Dorking and Guildford. The route number 32 was used since by then Tillingbourne had taken over what was once London Transport's 425 route, Tillingbourne renumbering routes into their own series. GS 13 was part of a small fleet consisting of RF 26 and 315, BL 95 and a former Royal Blue MW coach, all of which saw use on the 32. Both the authors enjoyed many Sundays driving these buses over the former 425 route, although GS 13 later saw less use than the RFs and BL.

The 47 GSs which did not see further passenger service passed through many owners and saw a wide variety of uses. Many were used for transport for social groups and workers, a small number ending their days with building contractors. Some were converted as mobile homes and caravans, finally being dumped in a field where they gradually deteriorated into wrecks. One of the more bizarre uses was of GS 28 purchased by Ronnie Lane of the Small Faces rock band. It was used to transport the group and its back-up crew for about a year until sold in August 1974 to be converted to a mobile caravan.

This book has concentrated on the operational lifetime of GSs and their original purpose of carrying passengers on bus routes. It is not the intention here to include endless details about the final usage and fate of every GS for to do so would fill another book on its own. It would be an exaggeration to say that the GS has become the most popular bus of all time among enthusiasts, but it is certainly true that London Transport enthusiasts regard them with enduring interest and affection. Despite the relatively short life many of them had with London Transport, enthusiasts 'of a certain age' (including the authors) have fond memories of travelling on them in service along the country lanes of the Home Counties more than half a century after most of them had disappeared. Interest in them is perhaps captured in the oft repeated assertion that 84 were built and 85 preserved! Alan Charman has now owned GS 62 for longer than London Transport and still runs over some of the original routes. Around ten or a dozen have regularly appeared on running days over the last 20 years and the authors have been very lucky to have driven several over old routes. But spares and servicing has become more difficult in recent years, and their appearance is becoming less and less common. The nostalgia for these little buses however seems undiminished and will last for a few more years.

London Transport sold GS 38 to British Rail Western Region in May 1965. It was used by them in South Wales for many years, and is seen here in Porthcawl on 16th July 1965 shortly after purchase. *Alan Cross*

GS 47 was withdrawn from Northfleet in February 1966 and stored at Reigate, where it remained until sold to the London Transport St John Ambulance Corps in 1967, the conversion being carried out at Aldenham. It was transferred to the Devon section of St John Ambulance in 1979, and later passed to the West of England Transport Collection at Winkleigh. It was later acquired by a private owner in Surrey, but scrapped in the early 1990s. The bottom picture shows it with the rear doors open and acting as a Mobile First Aid Post at an event in central London. Preserved Cravens RT 1431 is visible behind the GS.
E W M Abbott

GS 2 was withdrawn at Stevenage on 24th October 1962 and sent to Grays for storage where it remained until purchased by Southern Motorways on 21st June 1963. This picture was perhaps taken within a few days of that since Southern Motorways have pressed the bus into service, simply painting out the London Transport fleetname, but leaving the GS 2 fleetnumber in place. It was soon repainted into their smart maroon and cream livery, in which condition it was acquired by John Huxford many years later for preservation. Over the last 20 years, Peter Aves has driven the bus on many occasions over its old routes. It is picking up passengers in Petersfield for a journey to Midhurst with a Duple bodied AEC Reliance belonging to Liss and District behind.
Roy Marshall

GS 71 spent its entire LT working life at Garston, being delicensed in the October 1962 changes and then stored until June 1965 when it was sold to Stevensons at Uttoxeter as their No.27. Here it stands awaiting a turn to the village of Bramshall about three miles out of the town. It was subsequently sold to Wombwell Diesels in October 1972 for scrap.
Roy Marshall

This is probably GS 50 in a derelict state prior to the body being refitted to a Ford chassis. After sale in 1968, it ended up on the Isle of Barra in the Outer Hebrides where this picture was probably taken. It had been allocated to Amersham for almost nine years until second overhaul in March 1962, after which it became a staff bus. GS 50 is thought to have been the one repainted red by London Transport for potential use during the rebuilding of the Elmers End railway bridge. The remains of a London Transport fleetname are just evident on the very worn red paintwork. *Roy Marshall*

VEHICLES TRANSFERRED TO LCBS 1st JANUARY 1970

DATE SOLD BY LCBS	GS NUMBER	DATE WITHDRAWN BY LT	LAST GARAGE IN SERVICE	DATE WITHDRAWN BY LCBS	LAST GARAGE	SOLD TO	BUS NOW PRESERVED
April 71	12	1.10.69	RG (t)	(b)	RG	Winstones Ltd, Harefield	YES
April 71	14	1.12.67	LH	(b)	GR	Tillingbourne Valley Motor Services, Chilworth	YES
March 73	17	(a)	GR	April 71	GR	Sampsons Coaches, Cheshunt, Herts.	YES
June 72	33	(a)		31.3.72	GR	Mr G. Burgess, London W4 (For preservation)	
March 73	36	4.10.69	NF	30.10.72	SA (t)	Four Hills Venture Scout Group, Dorking	YES
June 72	42	(a)	GR	31.3.72	GR	Bearn, Epsom (Dealer)	YES
April 71	45	Apr 69		(b)	RG	Dr Moore, Farnborough, Hants	YES
Dec 72	55	4.10.69	NF	30.8.72	RG (t)	Tentrak Expeditions Ltd, Chislehurst, Kent	YES
April 71	64	30.5.67	HG	(b)	GR	Tillingbourne Valley Motor Services, Chilworth	YES
April 71	66	30.10.69	GR (t)	(b)	GR	Winstones Ltd, Harefield	

(a) - GS 17, 33 and 42 were not withdrawn by London Transport. They were still licensed for service at Garston on 31st December 1969, being transferred to London Country the following day

(b) - GS 12, 14, 45, 64 and 66 were not used by London Country having previously withdrawn by London Transport

1. GS 12 was used as a trainer at Reigate until the end of October 1969.

2. GS 14 was withdrawn from Leatherhead at the end of GS operation there. It remained at Leatherhead until London Country moved it to Reigate (presumably) on 1st January 1970 although this is not recorded.

3. GS 45 was based at Reigate as a staff bus until being delicensed and stored there in April 1969

4. GS 64 was withdrawn from Hertford, and subsequently stored at Stevenage, Hatfield and Grays for various periods. It was transferred to Garston (presumably) on 1st January 1970, although this is not recorded.

5. GS 66 was withdrawn from Northfleet on 30th May 1967, and then used intermittently as a staff bus at Plumstead until August 1969 when it was transferred to Garston for a short period as a trainer. It was finally delicensed at the end of October 1969.

SCHEDULE OF LONDON TRANSPORT'S GS DISPOSALS BY DATE

DATE SOLD	GS NUMBER	DATE WITHDRAWN BY LT	LAST GARAGE IN SERVICE	STORED BEFORE SALE AT	SOLD TO	BUS NOW PRESERVED
16.1.61	40	29.1.60	WR	WR	West Bromwich Corporation Sports Dept.	YES
16.1.61	41	10.12.58	EP	RE	West Bromwich Corporation Sports Dept.	
17.4.61	61	29.9.58	MA	GY	Corvedale Motor Co. Ludlow	
26.4.61	70	12.9.58	GR	GY	West Ham Borough Council	
8.5.61	63	7.9.58	HN	GY	Corvedale Motor Co. Ludlow	YES
24.5.61	43	17.7.58	EP	RE	Corvedale Motor Co. Ludlow	YES
24.5.61	49	1.11.58	NF	RE	Corvedale Motor Co. Ludlow	
8.6.61	24	5.8.60	DG	RE	London Fire Brigade	
10.6.61	32	1.11.58	SJ	RE	Bird's Commercial (Dealer) Stratford Upon Avon	YES
13.6.61	37	1.6.60	HG	RE	Corvedale Motor Co. Ludlow	
1.3.63	1	24.10.62	CM	RG	Tillingbourne Valley Services Ltd, Chilworth	YES
4.3.63	68	24.10.62	HH	GR	Corvedale Motor Co. Ludlow	
4.3.63	72	24.10.62	SA	GR	Corvedale Motor Co. Ludlow	
11.3.63	3	24.10.62	CM	RG	Tillingbourne Valley Services Ltd, Chilworth	
15.3.63	4	24.10.62	CM	RG	Tillingbourne Valley Services Ltd, Chilworth	
2.5.63	8	24.10.62	CM	NF	Gravesend Old Peoples' Welfare Centre	
15.5.63	67	24.10.62	GR	GR	Tillingbourne Valley Services Ltd, Chilworth	YES
15.5.63	69	24.10.62	MA	GR	Tillingbourne Valley Services Ltd, Chilworth	
12.6.63	9	24.10.62	HG	GY	Southern Motorways Ltd, Emsworth	
13.6.63	11	24.10.62	CM	NF	Southern Motorways Ltd, Emsworth	
13.6.63	79	1.11.62	NF	NF	Southern Motorways Ltd, Emsworth	
21.6.63	2	24.10.62	SV	GY	Southern Motorways Ltd, Emsworth	YES
26.6.63	7	24.10.62	CM	NF	Southern Motorways Ltd, Emsworth	
26.7.63	6	1.6.63	GR (t)	GR	The Rank Organisation, London	
6.9.63	5	24.10.62	CM	GY	Hippersons Supplies Ltd, Essex	
6.9.63	74	1.12.62	HG	RE	Passenger Vehicle Sales Ltd (Dealer) Ilford	
4.10.63	80	24.10.62	HH	GR	Chemical Building Products Ltd, Hemel Hempstead	
25.11.63	75	24.10.62	MA	GR	Knightswood Coaches Ltd, Watford	
4.12.63	48	19.6.63	RG (t)	Works	Mr A Shurey, Cranford, Middlesex	
4.12.63	83	24.10.62	HH	GR	British Railways Board	
3.1.64	78	5.4.63	GR (t)	GR	Ronsway Coaches, Hemel Hempstead	
19.2.64	82	19.2.63	DS	DS	Transferred to LT Service Fleet as 1311 CD.	
18.3.64	84	19.6.63	RG (t)	RG	Tillingbourne Valley Services Ltd, Chilworth	YES
8.5.64	77	24.10.62	WR	RG	Cambarra (Aircraft Spares) Ltd, Clandon, Guildford	
20.5.64	76	1.11.62	DG	DG	Tillingbourne Valley Services Ltd, Chilworth	YES
16.10.64	81	24.10.62	CM	NF	Mr D J Mayhew, Bromley	
26.10.64	25	13.8.64	GF	GF	Tillingbourne Valley Services Ltd, Chilworth	
18.12.64	19	1.8.64	DG		Mr I W Mayo, Chaldon, Caterham	YES
18.12.64	27	1.9.64	HG	GY	Ozalid Ltd, Loughton, Essex	
5.1.65	23	1.12.64	DG	DG	Thames Weald Ltd, Sevenoaks, Kent	
8.1.65	30	1.9.64	GR		Ozalid Ltd, Loughton, Essex	
10.2.65	20	1.9.64	WR		Norman Hay Ltd, Hounslow	
11.3.65	31	1.9.64	GR	GR	Mr. D. Abel, Worthington House, London, EC1	
17.3.65	71	24.10.62	GR		John Stevenson Ltd, Uttoxeter, Staffs	
27.4.65	29	22.1.65	HA	RE	Negron Construction Ltd, Victoria Street, SW1	
13.5.65	38	Feb. 65	DG	DG	British Railways Board	

20.5.65	22	Feb. 65	DG	DG	Southern Motorways Ltd, Emsworth	
19.1.66	16	30.11.64	DG	GY	J W Ward & Son, Bourne End, Hemel Hempstead	
11.3.66	18	Feb. 66	AM (S)	AM	Prowting Holdings Ltd, Ruislip, Middlesex	
1.9.66	73	24.10.62	HG	HF	Multiple Sclerosis Society, Bromley, Kent	
23.6.67	47	11.2.66	NF	RG	St John Ambulance Brigade	
10.1.68	35	Feb. 67	AM (S)	AW (?)	H. Lotery & Co. Newport, Monmouth	
12.1.68	26	Feb. 67	RG (S)	RG	Mr Cave, Teddington Parent Teachers Assoc.	YES
26.1.68	51	4.10.65	HH	GR	H. Goldman Ltd, Cricklewood	
25.3.68	44	1.8.66	HG	HF	Stanley Hugh Leach Ltd, Hayes, Middlesex	
26.3.68	46	Jan. 66	NF	??	Stanley Hugh Leach Ltd, Hayes, Middlesex	
5.6.68	39	2.1.67	DS	RG	Mayflower Family Centre, Canning Town, E1	
19.8.68	50	Mar. 67	AW (S)	NF	Burinson Walshe Ltd, London, W12	YES
27.8.68	53	13.5.67	NF	NF	Mr Denham, Chesham, Bucks	
24.9.68	58	13.5.67	NF	NF	National Trust, Lapworth, Staffs.	
17.12.68	21	18.2 68	HE	GR	Stanley Hugh Leach Ltd, Hayes, Middlesex	
20.3.69	15	15.2.69	GR	GR	Stanley Hugh Leach Ltd, Hayes, Middlesex	YES
2.5.69	57	Jan. 68	NF	CM	Upper Avon Navigation Trust, Lapworth, Staffs	
15.7.69	65	30.6.68	HG	Wks	For Scrap - Wombwell Diesels Ltd, Wombwell, Yorks.	
5.9.69	56	2.1.67	DG	CM	G. Bicker Ltd, Coddenham, Suffolk	
19.9.69	60	1.2.67	GR	GR	G. Bicker Ltd, Coddenham, Suffolk	YES
4.11.69	54	4.10.69	NF	NF	Midland Poultry, Craven Arms, Shropshire	YES
4.11.69	34	30.10.65	GR	GR	M.I.R.A. Warwickshire	
23.12.69	59	2.1.67	DG	GY	Tillingbourne Valley Services Ltd, Chilworth	
18.10.73	10	1.10.73	RG (S)	Wks	G M Records & Tapes, Wardour Street, London W1	YES
26.10.73	62	Oct. 73	RG (S)	RG	Mr G. H. Turnbull, Harpenden, Herts	YES
21.3.74	28	Feb. 73	RG (S)	RG	Ronnie Lane Enterprises, Chiswick, London, W4	YES
9.5.74	13	Unknown	AW (S)	AW	Aylmer Motor Works, Highgate, London, N2	YES
16.8.74	52	Unknown	AW (S)	AW	Mr G. Smith, Headcorn, Kent	YES

1. The withdrawal dates for GS 61, 63 and 70 are those when they were delicensed and sent to Great Yarmouth. They returned on 5.8.59 but did not see further service with London Transport.

2. A number of those noted as preserved are not in running condition and have not been seen for some time. Some may not still exist. In addition to those noted, there may be others in a dereclict state which were not known at the time of writing

3. GS 65 was delicensed at Hertford on 30th June 1965 following a serious accident. It was moved to Aldenham on 31st October 1968 until sold in July 1969. It was the only GS sold for scrap and was probably dismantled for spares, although this is not recorded.

4. GS 10 was delicensed as a staff bus on 1st October 1973 and is recorded as being transferred to Aldenham on 18th October, the day on which it was sold.

GS 32 was one of the batch of the first ten GSs sold in 1961, but was a remarkable survivor. It passed through six owners before ending up as a builder's store shed. In 1992, it was discovered by John Clarke in this condition. He purchased it, completely restoring it over many years, subsequently appearing at many rallies and running days.
John Clarke

APPENDIX GS Overhaul Dates

	1956	1957	1958	1959	1960	1961	1962	1963	1964	1965	1966
1	April			September							
2	March			June							
3	March			September							
4	March			August							
5	April			October							
6	May			December							
7	May			December							
8	May			October							
9	May			November							
10	June				May		Heater			March	
11	April			October							
12	June				January		Heater		October		
13	June				May		Heater			February	
14	June				February		Heater		November		
15	June				March		Heater			January	
16	July				July		Heater				
17	July				June		Heater			April	
18	July				August		Heater				
19	August				August		Heater				
20	August				September		Heater			February	
21	September					August	Heater			June	
22	October				December		Heater			May	
23	October				October		Heater			January	
24	October										
25	October				January		Heater				
26	December					October	Heater				
27	November					May	Heater				
28	December					September	Heater			August	
29	November					May	Heater				
30	November					June	Heater				
31	November					July	Heater				
32		January									
33		January				December	Heater			October	
34		April					Jun Heater				
35		February					Jun Heater				
36	December					November	Heater			November	
37	December										
38	October					February	Heater				
39		March					Feb Heater				
40		January									
41		January									
42		February				December	Heater				January
43		March									
44		May					Apr Heater				

	1956	1957	1958	1959	1960	1961	1962	1963	1964	1965	1966
45		October					Dec Heater				
46		June					Jun Heater				
47		March					Apr Heater				
48		August					Oct Heater				
49		April									
50		May					Mar Heater				
51		May					May Heater				
52		August						Feb Heater			
53		June					Aug Heater				
54		August					Nov Heater				
55		March				Sept	Heater			August	
56		September						Jan Heater			
57		September					Dec Heater				
58		June					July Heater				
59		June					Sept Heater				
60		April					Mar Heater				
61			January	YARMOUTH							
62		October						May Heater			
63			February	YARMOUTH							
64		July					Oct Heater				
65		November					Dec Heater				
66		June					Sept Heater				
67			September								
68			April	YARMOUTH							
69			October								
70		December		YARMOUTH							
71			October								
72			April	YARMOUTH							
73			June								
74			August								
75			November								
76			December								
77				January							
78				February							
79				March							
80				February							
81				April							
82				April				to 1311CD			
83				May							
84				March							

The five buses sent to Yarmouth received an overhaul during the six months prior to despatch as LT were hoping they would be purchased after the trial period in Great Yarmouth. However no sale took place and the buses were returned and went into store at Gillingham Street garage.

Where 'Heater' is shown the GS had this fitted between overhaul. Where a month is also given the heater was fitted during overhaul.